The
Philadelphia
Riots
of 1844

RECENT TITLES IN
CONTRIBUTIONS IN AMERICAN HISTORY

Series Editor: Jon L. Wakelyn

Roots of Maryland Democracy, 1753-1776
David Curtis Skaggs

Party and Faction in American Politics: The House of Representatives,
1789-1801
Rudolph M. Bell

Roscoe Pound: Philosopher of Law
David Wigdor

Efficiency and Expansion: Foreign Trade Organization in the Wilson
Administration, 1913-1921
Burton I. Kaufman

Space, Time, and Freedom: The Quest for Nationality and the
Irrepressible Conflict, 1815-1861
Major L. Wilson

The New Deal in Georgia: An Administrative History
Michael S. Holmes

The Gun in America: The Origins of a National Dilemma
Lee Kennett and *James LaVerne Anderson*

Confederate Women
Bell Irvin Wiley

Rights of Union Members and the Government
Philip Taft

THE PHILADELPHIA RIOTS OF 1844

A Study of Ethnic Conflict

MICHAEL FELDBERG

Contributions in American History
Number 43

Greenwood Press
Westport, Connecticut
London, England

Library of Congress Cataloging in Publication Data

Feldberg, Michael.
  The Philadelphia riots of 1844.

  (Contributions in American history ; no. 43)
  Based on the author's thesis, University of Rochester.
  Bibliography: p.
  Includes index.
  1. Philadelphia—Riots, 1844-   I. Title.
F158.44.F44   974.8'11'03   75-65
ISBN 0-8371-7876-2

Library of Congress Catalog Card Number: 75-65
ISBN: 0-8371-7876-2

First published in 1975

Greenwood Press, a division of Williamhouse-Regency Inc.
51 Riverside Avenue, Westport, Connecticut 06880

Printed in the United States of America

Contents

List of Maps   vii

Preface   ix

1   Jacksonian Philadelphia as a Setting for Violence   3

2   The Irish   19

3   The Nativists   41

4   Patterns of Conflict   78

5   The Kensington Riots   99

6   Interlude   120

7   The Southwark Riots   143

8   Aftermath   162

9   Conclusion   178

Bibliography   195

Index   201

List of Maps

Philadelphia in 1844, showing "The City,"
Southwark, Moyamensing, Passyunk, southern portions of
Kensington, Northern Liberties, Spring Garden, and portions
of Port Richmond and Penn Township   11

Third Ward, Kensington, in 1844   101

Third Ward, Southwark, in 1844   146

Preface

The Philadelphia Native American riots of 1844, which took the lives of at least twenty persons and injured more than one hundred others, were the bloodiest in the city's history. They occurred in two phases: the first in early May, when several thousand angry Protestant nativists invaded the immigrant Irish Catholic neighborhood around the Nanny Goat Market in Third Ward, Kensington, an industrial suburb in what is now North Philadelphia. The crowd battled with the Irish residents for two days, burning dozens of their homes and two Catholic churches. The second phase of rioting erupted on July 5 and 6, when another large group of aroused nativists in Southwark, currently a part of South Philadelphia, exchanged cannon fire with a regiment of Pennsylvania state militia that had been assigned to guard a Catholic church. The nativists' ire was provoked by reports that the church had been armed by local Catholic residents. A crowd gathered, troops were sent to disperse them, the nativists resented the soldiers' presence, and the shooting began.

Most accounts of the bloody summer of 1844 have attributed the conflict between the Irish and nativist communities primarily to religious differences. In particular, they focus on the fight between the Catholic clergy and evangelical Protestants over whether Catholic children would be permitted to use the authorized Catholic version of the Bible as an official text during reading exercises in the public schools. (This issue and its consequences are examined in Chapter 4.) But this study seeks also to place the struggle between the nativists and Catholics that culminated in the 1844 riots in a wider context, viewing it as an ethnic, rather than simply a religious, conflict.

By ethnic, I mean a complex of cultural, class, occupational, social, and political (as well as religious) differences that isolated the immigrant Catholic Irish in Philadelphia from their native-born, Protestant neighbors.

Chapters 2 and 3 trace the divergent social experiences and institutional developments in the two communities. These chapters weigh the importance of the differences between the Irish and native occupational roles, political party loyalties, ideological beliefs, voluntary associations, and religious faiths in generating frictions and misunderstandings between them. The chapters also explore the tendency of both groups to use violent protest and collective disorder frequently as a means of solving their problems or expressing their grievances. Chapter 1 sets the stage for this discussion by examining the city itself as an environment that encouraged a resort to collective violence in cases of intergroup or intercommunity conflict. The uses of collective violence in Jacksonian Philadelphia also provide the focus for Chapters 5 and 7, which narrate the events of the Kensington and Southwark riots, respectively. Many readers will recognize here the influence of George Rudé and Charles Tilly on my work, and they are referred to the bibliography for reference to my article, "The Crowd in Philadelphia History: A Comparative Approach," for further elaboration on this subject. Finally, Chapters 6, 8, and 9 trace the growth of the demand for a better policed and tightly governed Philadelphia in the aftermath of the Native American riots. These chapters explore the development of a professional police force for the city, the consolidation of its political boundaries and administration, and the institutionalization of ethnic rivalries through ethnic politics. Chapter 8 in particular discusses these and other reasons for the decline in conflict and fighting between the native Protestants and Irish Catholics after 1844.

This work first came to life as a dissertation, completed six years ago at the University of Rochester under the direction of Herbert G. Gutman, presently at the City College of New York. His patient guidance then is still deeply appreciated. David Montgomery of the University of Pittsburgh first suggested this topic to me. My debt to him, and to his able student Bruce Laurie, can be ascertained from the notes to the various chapters. Since then, many friends and colleagues have read various portions of the manuscript or articles drawn from it and graciously suggested improvements: Francis Broderick, Thomas N. Brown, Paul Faler, Carter Jefferson, Pauline Maier, and Eric Robinson of the University of Massachusetts at Boston; Milton Cantor of the University of Massachusetts at Amherst; Allen F. Davis and Mark H. Haller of Temple University; and Stanley Dry of Boston. What errors remain must certainly be charged to my account.

Stella Feldberg and Miriam Margolies generously and cheerfully typed
the many drafts of the manuscript. My wife Laura helped with the early
research and has also contributed with her patient encouragement
throughout these past six years.

The completion of a first book is an emotional as well as a professional
landmark, and the author is tempted to thank everyone who helped him
start on his career, or propped up his ego when the going got rough, or
supported him in any of the numerous ways so essential to the completion
of a dissertation and its conversion into a publishable manuscript. In my
case, the list would take pages, and it would be impossible now to recall
all who made contributions. But if I may be permitted a small indulgence,
I would like to extend special thanks to Laura, my parents, and my friends
outside the halls of academia, whose interest in my work enabled me to
believe in its wider importance. Finally, two men, Edward W. Fox of
Cornell University and R. James Kaufman of the University of Texas at
Austin, offered special encouragement at critical moments in my education.
I hope this present work will in part at least justify their confidence in me.

The
Philadelphia
Riots
of 1844

1
Jacksonian Philadelphia as a Setting for Violence

The ghetto riots of the 1960s and the resurgent ethnic consciousness of the 1970s have kindled a renewed interest in the history of racial and ethnic confrontations in nineteenth-century America. Historians have been reexamining the role that group conflict and collective violence have played in the American past,[1] and the direction in which their findings point has become clear: the various majorities and minorities making up nineteenth-century American society were in constant competition for improved positions in the social hierarchy. As a result, the ethnic and racial history of the nineteenth century was marked by a steady stream of conflicts that all too frequently spilled over into bloody confrontations and violence. In fact, for some groups, such as free blacks in antebellum northern cities or the immigrant Irish in the 1840s and 1850s, violence appears to have played an integral role in the process of accommodation and adjustment by which these groups reached a modus vivendi with the native-born white majority.[2]

Yet by no means did all ethnic and immigrant minorities have an equally difficult time gaining acceptance in American society. Clashes between native citizens and newly arrived immigrants, such as the Philadelphia riots of 1844, grew out of specific circumstances peculiar to certain settings rather than from any built-in flaws in the American character or the inherent barbarity of particular immigrant groups. Slights that provoked the Irish, for example, were passed over by the German immigrants, and conversely some patterns of behavior by the Irish newcomers which inflamed the native-born majority in the 1840s had been tolerated among the Germans in the 1820s and 1830s. It seems fair to say, in fact, that during the 1840s Philadelphia's Irish Catholics became the target of evangelical Protestant hostility while the city's German Catholics were practically ignored. What was it about the Irish in particular that provoked Protestant

3

nativists to resent their presence in Jacksonian Philadelphia? Why was it that skilled artisans were disproportionately represented in the anti-immigrant, anti-Catholic nativist movement during the 1840s, while middle- and upper-class native Protestants were much less so? To what degree did economic factors determine the social composition of the nativist movement, and to what degree were cultural distinctions at the heart of Irish-native conflict? Finally, why did this particular ethnic rivalry escalate into a series of violent confrontations whose bloody destructiveness startled even the most hardened observers of other violent outbreaks in Philadelphia in the decade before 1844? The remaining pages of this work will supply at least tentative answers to these questions. To begin at the beginning, however, the story must be placed in its proper setting, in both time and space.

The Jacksonian era in Philadelphia was easily the most unsettled and violent in the city's history. Just how turbulent the city had become in those years can be illustrated by a list of the dozen or so most important collective outbursts in the 1830s and 1840s. The sequence actually began in 1828, when immigrant Irish weavers and native Americans battled in suburban Kensington. A race riot disturbed the black ghetto in Southwark in August 1834 and again in July 1835. The summer of 1835 was notable also for a disruptive general strike led by the city's dockworkers, while in that same year a respectable crowd of Philadelphia's middle- and upper-class whites, led by the mayor of Philadelphia himself, dumped a crate of abolitionist literature into the Delaware River. This action foreshadowed the burning three years later of abolitionist-built Pennsylvania Hall, a large assembly building erected in downtown Philadelphia to serve as a forum for the national abolition movement. On the same night that the hall was destroyed, a crowd attacked the Friend's Shelter for Colored Orphans. Two years later, in June 1840, residents of Front Street, Kensington, in what is now North Philadelphia, rioted to prevent the construction of a railroad through their neighborhood; they continued their attacks on railroad construction workers for two years until the project was finally abandoned. The summer of 1842 brought an Irish attack on a group of black temperance marchers in Moyamensing, while the fall brought a protracted and often violently destructive handloom weavers' strike. The weavers were bold enough to attack a posse and severely manhandle the sheriff. This flood of violence peaked in the great Native American riots of 1844, which, in their two phases, first in early May and then in early July, killed at least twenty and injured well over a hundred. A five-year

lull ensued after the bloody summer of 1844, in which only relatively minor firemen's fights and gang wars disturbed the city's peace. In 1849, however, a postelection riot at a pub called the California House turned into a full-scale race war in which several blacks and whites were killed.[3]

Not all the rioting in Jacksonian Philadelphia had significant social content; many drunken brawls, firemen's fights, and election riots simply provided outlets for excessive physical energy or filled the recreational needs of the young men who worked long hours in the city's workshops with no provision for their leisure-time needs.[4] Most of the important riots, however—those with lasting significance—reflected in some way the dislocations emerging in American society in the 1830s and 1840s. It is no longer fashionable for historians to speak of the "spirit of an age," but clearly Philadelphia in the 1840s was gripped by a strong sense of economic, social, and moral decline. This uneasiness and loss of confidence became manifest not only through outbursts of collective violence but through a variety of popular movements and numerous voluntary associations. For the most part, these developments have been interpreted by historians and sociologists as reflections of deep-seated insecurities and anxieties prevalent throughout Jacksonian America, and there is much in the behavior of the times to support their contention. In the year 1844 alone, aside from the Native American riots, the prophet of Mormonism, Joseph Smith, and his brother were assassinated by hysterical vigilantes in Nauvoo, Illinois. In Philadelphia, an evangelical minister named William Miller predicted that the apocalypse would occur on July 12, and hundreds of his followers, taking him at his word, abandoned all their worldly possessions to lighten their burden on the ascent to heaven. Some Millerites even climbed trees to be nearer to Christ as he descended. Throughout the late 1830s and early 1840s, waves of Protestant revivalism swept through Philadelphia, and evangelists found willing listeners among the rich and poor, educated and uneducated. Even the usually rowdy firemen organized their own series of lectures on the virtues of fundamentalism and the evils of hard language and hard liquor. Public crusades were mounted to close the city's bars, halt the Sunday delivery of mail, and stop the running of the excursion trains to the countryside on the Sabbath. Colportage societies attempted to put a free Bible in the hand of every citizen. These wide-ranging efforts, from the anti-Mormonism of the West to the Sabbatarianism of the East, were remarkable not so much for their fundamentalist faith, which has been a constant in American society, but rather

for the intensity of the commitment of those who embraced them.[5]
What were the changing conditions that so profoundly disturbed the
equilibrium of Jacksonian America, and Jacksonian Philadelphia in
particular? One of the most important changes came in the physical
character of the city itself.[6] In the decade of the 1840s, Philadelphia's
population increased from about 250,000 persons to about 360,000.
Because Philadelphia was already an older, established city by the 1840s,
much of this new population did not spread itself into the newer, peripheral
areas but rather tried to crowd into the center city and abutting industrial
districts in search of work in the warehouses, workshops, and factories
that had been constructed long before their arrival. Already crowded,
Philadelphia could offer neither adequate housing nor sufficient employment to all of the new arrivals, even if it fared somewhat better than its
sister cities New York and Boston. The mere numbers of new citizens
were only part of Philadelphia's problems in the 1840s. Many of the
newcomers were impoverished European immigrants, runaway slaves
and free blacks, and rural migrants from the back-country areas of
Pennsylvania and the Middle Atlantic states. These groups brought with
them cultural values incompatible with those of a city whose dominant
values were chauvinistically white native Protestant, just as they brought
rural skills to an economy based primarily on specialized craft manufacturing done by highly trained, skilled artisans. The combination of rapid
growth, incompatible populations, and overburdened social and economic
institutions proved extremely volatile when combined with the violent
traditions of the city and the nation. The interplay of social and economic
developments, the inadequacy of Philadelphia's institutions, and the
persistence of its violent traditions will be examined in the next several
chapters.

The condition of Philadelphia's law enforcement system is an obvious
place to begin when considering the city as a setting for social violence.
Measured against the rapidly increasing population and the escalating inci-
dence of collective disorder, Jacksonian Philadelphia's institutions of social
control were vastly overmatched. A small band of constables and part-time
watchmen policed the city. As elected officials or appointees with political
connections, the constabulary and watch took pains to avoid actions that
might hurt them physically or their party politically. It was not until the
1850s that the city fathers created a full-time, paid, professional police
force, and even that body took years to develop a relatively nonpartisan

outlook. Before then, many Philadelphians resisted the idea of a professional police force, and for a variety of reasons. Many endorsed the libertarian maxim that proclaimed, "That government governs best which governs least." Opponents of a professional police force drew as well on the traditional American mistrust of standing armies inherited from the Revolutionary era. While the original target of this hostility had been British lobsterbacks and mercenaries, as opposed to a home-grown and legally authorized police force, the antipathy to a uniformed corps of law enforcers continued well into the Jacksonian era. When advocates of a professional police finally won out in Philadelphia, Boston, and New York City in the 1840s and 1850s, some spokesmen continued to rail against "administrative tyranny" and the "abridgement of the people's liberties" that professional police forces represented. In Jacksonian Philadelphia, philosophical principles proved to be only one source of opposition to police professionalization, however. Some citizens feared that a full-time force would necessitate an increase in the tax rate. Others, especially the elected constables, fought against losing their jobs. Political leaders found great convenience in having a supply of jobs on the night watch available for distribution to their loyal followers.

However crass, this patronage system was not insufferable to most Philadelphians, who in fact expected the administration of law and justice to be highly responsive to the popular will. Even the invariable wholesale turnover in personnel that followed the defeat of an incumbent party, or the tendency of politically connected night watchmen to sleep at their posts, was tolerable in peaceable times. The Jacksonian years in Philadelphia were hardly tranquil, however, and the inefficiency of the city's peacekeeping system led to serious problems. Even with the best of intentions, unreliable night watchmen and elected constables were merely part-time officials whose first concern was for their full-time occupations or political careers, even though the policing of disorder had clearly developed into a full-time preoccupation by the turbulent 1840s. But the intentions of the constabulary and watch were not always the best. When blacks, abolitionists, and other unpopular minorities were attacked and their property destroyed, these same elected officials predictably dragged their feet in coming to aid the victims. After all, it was the voting majority, not the outcast minority, that kept the constabulary in office. Constables were probably influenced as well by the fact that they earned their pay not for the time they spent keeping the peace but rather for delivering

warrants, serving papers, and collecting debts. They were paid a small per diem stipend for each day on official riot duty plus expenses, but this incentive was clearly unequal to the risks. The reward system for constables, with its stress on process serving rather than peacekeeping, indicates that few Philadelphians truly expected their elected officials to risk very much in order to maintain a rigorous public order. Party loyalty rather than daring and initiative was probably a much more important prerequisite for office.[7]

The combination of antistatist traditions, democratic election of officials, and public tightfistedness guaranteed that peacekeeping in Philadelphia was never "preventive" (as those who advocated police professionalization liked to call it) but rather reactive. The watch patrolled only at night, and even that task was performed irregularly. During the daylight hours, no law officers patrolled the streets. If a constable was needed, he had to be called from his office or workbench, and he almost always arrived too late to prevent crime or disorder. If a riot had already started and the fighting gotten out of hand, the constable had to notify the county sheriff—if he could be found—who would then convene an unarmed volunteer posse. It usually took several hours to rouse posse members from their homes, shops, and offices in order to convene them at a central point. If, after all this preparation, the posse proved inadequate, as it did on several occasions in the 1840s, the sheriff turned to the local commander of the state militia. This gentleman in turn gathered *his* volunteers at a central point and marched them to the scene of the disorder, a process that took several additional hours. In the Native American riots of 1844, the time-consuming series of delays proved disastrous. It was not until the second day of killing and burning in Kensington, during the May phase of the rioting, that militia General George Cadwalader was able to ready his men and convince them to risk their lives in defense of an Irish Catholic neighborhood.

Political considerations, social prejudices, and ideological premises aside, the administrative subdivision of the county into no fewer than twenty-nine autonomous municipalities and districts doomed peacekeeping in greater Philadelphia to impotence. The county map looked like a crazy quilt, with suburban patches sewn on representing expansion in the decades preceding the 1840s. None of the administrative units in the county was joined to the others, except for the purposes of building roads and electing a county sheriff. Philadelphia in the Jacksonian period was limited to a two-mile square between the Delaware and Schuylkill

rivers from Vine to South streets, which forms the current center city
district (see map 1). The remainder of the county was composed of the
districts, contiguous industrial areas such as Kensington, Northern
Liberties, Southwark, and Moyamensing, which shared their borders
with the city, and more remote rural sections, such as Kingseesing and
Byberry, which were sparsely populated and remote from the bustling
downtown. Even within the built-up city and districts, administrative
balkanization was the rule. Each of the city's twelve wards had its own
elected alderman, tax assessor, and local judge, along with its own
politically appointed night watch, while each ward in the districts elected
its constables, assessors, and judges. The city was overseen by a mayor, a
select council, and a common council, while each of the districts elected
its own board of commissioners. Few of these local officials tried to
coordinate their efforts with those in other districts. The fact that city
officials were usually Whigs and district officials Democrats did little to
promote cooperation. The only public servants with jurisdiction throughout the entire county were the county commissioners, who maintained
the roads and public works, and the sheriff, who served as chief magistrate
for the county.[8]

For at least two decades before the 1840s, some civic leaders pleaded
with the state legislature to consolidate these many jurisdictions under
one set of officials, but a majority of the city's ruling elite joined with
district political bosses to block consolidation. City taxpayers refused to
pay for the municipal improvements so badly needed in the burgeoning
suburbs. Furthermore, union with the tax-poor districts would have
lowered the value of the city's municipal bonds, a direct concern of the
wealthy ruling elite. Had the city and districts combined, politically
connected jobs in both places would have been eliminated as senseless
duplication was reduced, and so leaders in both parties resisted consolidation. Finally, because population in outlying districts outnumbered that
of Philadelphia proper by two to one, city Whigs feared that combination
with the Democratic suburbs would end their control over their political
fiefdom. Although many of Philadelphia's social problems and destructive
outbreaks stemmed from the rapid, uncoordinated growth of the entire
metropolitan area, a coalition of wealthy Whig city bondholders and
Democratic district party bosses successfully resisted political or administrative consolidation until 1854, when the state legislature finally over-
rode their objections.[9]

Philadelphia's archaic political subdivisions seriously hindered law en-

forcement and spawned glaring injustices. A thief in the city needed only
to cross South Street into Moyamensing to escape arrest by city watchmen.
The county sheriff was the only person empowered to pursue criminals
from one jurisdiction to another. When riots erupted in Southwark
or Kensington, the mayor of Philadelphia proper would assemble his
watchmen at South or Vine streets to keep crowds from wandering
across district boundaries, but he could do nothing to disperse them so
long as they remained in the districts themselves.[10]

With no adequate police force to depend on, advocates of order
depended on the city's tradition of voluntarism to keep the peace and
protect private property. Looking back at a bygone era, older Philadelphia
gentlemen reminisced in the 1840s about the days when a citizen would
raise the cry "Assist the sheriff!" or "Assist the mayor!" and several up-
standing citizens would gladly step forward to help apprehend a criminal,
throttle some rowdy drunks, or disperse a disorderly crowd. While these
recollections might have been somewhat colored by the passage of time,
they do demonstrate the degree to which Philadelphia depended on the
willingness of its own respectable citizenry to keep the peace and the
power of deference to keep the lower classes in their place. On several
occasions, including the aftermath of the Native American riots, respectable citizens organized their own ward patrols to keep order. Even members
of the elegant Philadelphia Bar Association abandoned their desks to
guard St. Mary's Roman Catholic Church during the nativist unrest, and
the staid gentlemen seem to have had a grand time marching with muskets
and camping out of doors. Those who argued against a paid, full-time
police force for Philadelphia claimed that professionalization would rob
the city of its traditional democratic, public participation in peacekeeping.

Voluntarism produced a degree of humaneness in riot control that our
current age of police professionalization has lost. Since posses were composed of amateurs who refused to carry guns, or in some cases even to
wear badges, serious injuries or deaths rarely occurred when authorities
collided with crowds. At the same time, it must be conceded that modern,
professional police forces, so long as their discipline remains good, do
control crowds and protect property far more effectively than did
Jacksonian posses. Equally important, the volunteers, much like the
elected officials who led them, all too frequently failed to protect the
rights of unpopular minorities. During the second phase of the Native
American riots, only a handful of the six hundred or so persons sum-

moned by Sheriff Morton McMichael turned out for the defense of
St. Philip's Catholic Church in Southwark. Only two persons volunteered
to help Sheriff John Watmough prevent the burning of abolitionist-owned
Pennsylvania Hall. Even in instances when public opinion backed the
posse, its nerve was known to fail. During a weavers' strike in 1842, when
the sheriff's men arrived in Kensington to disperse a strikers' rally, all
but three friends in the posse abandoned Sheriff William Porter at the
first sign of resistance by the weavers.[11]

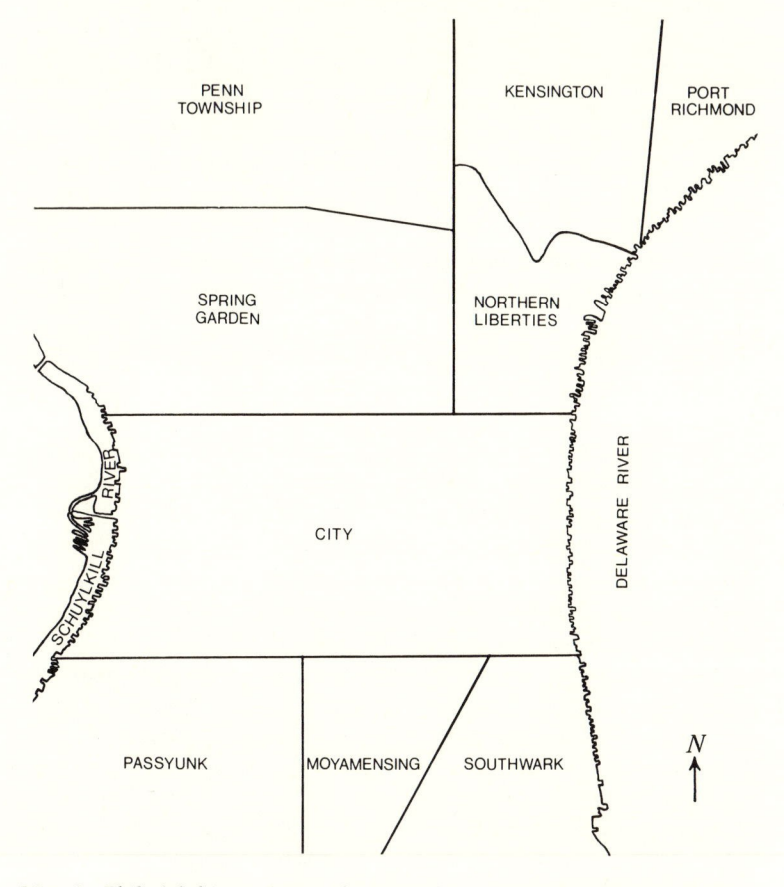

Map 1 Philadelphia in 1844, showing the center city, Southwark, Passyunk, Northern Liberties, Southern Kensington, and Spring Garden.

Occasionally, the price of a posse's failure proved quite high, for then the militia had to be brought in to restore order. Like the posse, these soldiers were volunteers—but with a difference. Armed with lethal weapons and accustomed to discipline and commands, militia companies were more likely to crush uprisings and disorders with bloodshed and even loss of life. During some riots in the 1830s and 1840s, militia units were brought in from communities outside the city so that the soldiers would not feel the constraint of facing neighbors at the end of their rifle sights. The militiamen who fired on civilians in suburban Southwark at the height of the second phase of the Native American riots came from Germantown, a suburb several miles from Philadelphia and even farther from Southwark. Before 1844, Philadelphia's public officials hesitated to call on the militia precisely because of this possibility of escalating bloodshed. Yet the absence of a "preventive" civilian force that might nip incipient disorder before it blossomed into a riot left the sheriff with few alternatives short of summoning the troops. Despite the unavailability of alternatives, the step was never a popular one. During the Native American riots, nativist crowds greeted the soldiers with hoots and jeers and accused them of disloyalty to American ideals. In the aftermath of the battle between troops and nativists in Southwark, many citizens held the military completely responsible for the deaths on both sides.

Fragmentation and subdivision characterized the social relationships as well as the political geography of Jacksonian Philadelphia. The ever-quickening pace of industrialization and urbanization and the influx of many disparate groups tended to disrupt or obliterate established class lines, neighborhood boundaries, ethnic patterns, and political alignments. Most historians agree that in the rapid expansion of the 1830s and 1840s, citizens of the American city lost social knowledge and physical contact with one another for the first time. As a result, individuals found their sense of solidarity with the wider community diminished. In an effort to compensate, they reinvested their loyalties in smaller, more manageable units confined to members of their own ethnic or religious groups or co-workers in their own occupations. By 1844, one contemporary observer noted that Philadelphia was broken up into "divitial interests" and "cliques" that revolved "in orbits separate, and far from being concentric," while the city's most recent historian, Sam Bass Warner, Jr., has summed up the 1830s and 1840s in a less abstract vein by calling them "*par excellence* the era of the urban parish church, the athletic club, the fire company, and the gang."[12]

It may be too much to say that Philadelphians suddenly lost their sense of community[13] in the Jacksonian years; on the contrary, some recent work has shown that the city had been long divided by chasms between the rich and the poor, the native-born and the immigrant. One historian, John K. Alexander, has called Philadelphia in the 1790s the "city of brotherly fear."[14] Yet, in the Jacksonian period it seems that Philadelphia was more seriously splintered than ever before into a myriad of class, racial, ethnic, religious, and occupational communities. Then as now, ethnicity, race, and religion tended to assign different groups and classes to different ranks in society: native white Protestants perched at the top of the social and economic pyramid; native skilled artisans, small businessmen, and clerks held the middle; and blacks, Irish and German immigrants, and native-born laborers filled out the broader bottom. An investigation into occupational and economic mobility in Philadelphia during the 1840s by Stuart Blumin tends to suggest that the upward mobility for individuals once believed to have characterized the Jacksonian era was beginning to narrow for the city's working people and that economic and social disabilities in general were becoming harder to overcome.[15] Perhaps the increasing occupational competition among the various religious and ethnic cliques in those years helps explain the tendency of working-class Philadelphians, many of them recent immigrants, to find themselves locked into their places in the lower orders.

Whatever the entanglements and subtleties of class, ethnic, cultural, or racial distinctions, one observation about the 1840s pushes its way to the fore and particularly intrudes into the story of the Native American riots: while all individuals belonged simultaneously to a particular class, racial or ethnic group, religious denomination, and occupation, most persons usually chose one of these identifications as primary at any given moment and subordinated the others to it. Thus in the late 1820s and the 1830s, both native-born skilled artisans and semiskilled immigrant Irish handloom weavers saw themselves as members of a united working class or, in the parlance of the day, mutual occupants of the "lower orders." They joined together to form a citywide trades' union, which won several hundred strikes for higher wages or shorter hours in the years before the depression of 1837. By the 1840s, the onset of economic hard times combined with the cultural differences between native Protestants and Irish Catholics to throw the two groups into competition with each other and destroy their class solidarity.[16] Almost every one of the new groups and subcommunities that emerged in the Jacksonian era was organized

according to some strict principle of exclusiveness, and by the 1840s ethnicity and religion became the dominating criteria. Unions, clubs, fire companies, gangs, neighborhoods, schools, orphanages, hospitals, benefit societies—the network of social institutions that permitted the city to function—were restricted in membership wherever possible to those who shared a common form of worship or a similar view on the benefits or evils of rum or the accident of birth on American soil.

Philadelphia's weak peacekeeping machinery encouraged competing or hostile ethnocultural subcommunities to use physical force in resolving their disputes and power struggles. Although working-class groups were more likely than their middle- and upper-class counterparts to resort to open street warfare, groups from every part of the social spectrum used violence at one time or another in their dealings with other groups. While wage earners destroyed property and physically intimidated their employers in order to win wage-and-hour struggles, well-dressed gentlemen from the opposite end of the income scale were burning Pennsylvania Hall. Similarly, when the working-class residents of Front Street in Kensington rioted against the Philadelphia and Trenton railroad, the neighborhood's prosperous landlords (including a local alderman) joined them to prevent the unwanted intrusion. At times, Philadelphia crowds proved quite democratic in their entrance requirements as well as effective in presenting their arguments.[17]

In the rapidly changing social and economic climate of Jacksonian Philadelphia, violence and intimidation proved to be tools used effectively by various groups to gain an advantage in their search for power and stability vis-à-vis their competitors. In this sense, much of the collective disorder of the 1830s and 1840s was "political," that is, it was part of the social bargaining process among groups seeking to preserve or advance their respective rankings in society.[18] In the case of the violent strikes of the era, economic leverage and the safeguarding of employment were at stake for the strikers, while control over the conditions of employment and costs impelled employers to resort to strikebreaking techniques. The antiabolition riots of 1835 and 1838 also reflected both economic and social tensions: working whites feared that emancipation would loose a flood of free black laborers into northern manufacturing centers, just as they feared that black freedom would raise the social status of a previously degraded race. At the same time, these whites found allies in the middle and upper classes who normally condemned violence because these more

privileged groups also perceived a social threat in the abolitionist movement. As Leonard L. Richards has pointed out, northern "gentlemen of property and standing" feared that the wealth, social pretensions, and increasing political influence of abolition leaders, especially those drawn from the ranks of the new industrialists, posed a threat to the prestige and influence of the old-wealth elite, and so they joined with their social inferiors to terrorize the abolitionists and destroy their property.[19] A combination of political influence and economic gain provided the stakes in the Kensington antirailroad riots: the railroad corporation had used its influence to persuade the legislature to grant a right-of-way through the streets of Kensington, so local residents used their physical power as an "equalizer" until such time as their own political strength and lobbying abilities could be brought to bear at Harrisburg in defense of their property values and peace of mind. While violence was certainly not a fine-honed political tool, often enough it served to gain ends that the tedious process of electoral give-and-take could not accomplish.

For all its effectiveness, collective violence was not used with equal frequency by all groups in Jacksonian Philadelphia. Its two leading employers, by no coincidence, were the adversaries in the Native American riots of 1844: laboring Irish Catholic immigrants and skilled, native-born Protestant artisans. These groups above all bore the brunt of the economic and social disruption that marked the Jacksonian years in Philadelphia. These were the groups that competed most directly for jobs, housing, places in the school system, and the glories of victory in the firemens' fights and gang wars. The native craftsmen in particular were the ones most afflicted by the introduction of technological changes in industry, especially the emergence of the factory system of production. It was the immigrants and their children who were most likely to accept employment in the hated factories or hire themselves out to the merchants and masters who retained unskilled outworkers at the expense of the traditional skilled artisans.

Still, we must beware of "reducing" Philadelphia nativism simply to economic causes or to a class consciousness turned sour in a long depression.[20] The specific cultural and religious issues that divided the Irish from the nativists possessed a vitality of their own and would very likely have generated some hostility even in prosperous times. That the conflict turned violent can be explained in part by the weakness of peace-keeping forces in the Jacksonian city. But the violence would never have

begun if not for the tendency of native-born artisans to appeal to collective violence and their own version of "popular sovereignty" whenever they felt their rights were threatened. This tendency to collective violence by the city's skilled artisans will be explored further in Chapter 3. But the Irish Catholic immigrant community must also receive some of the blame for provoking the major confrontation in May 1844, or at least for not trying hard enough to avoid it. Like the skilled Philadelphia artisan, the Irish Catholic immigrant had his own violent traditions, his own set of pressing economic needs, and his own exclusionist social, cultural, and religious organizations.

NOTES

1. The literature discussing the history of racial, ethnic, and immigrant group conflict with the native white majority has been greatly expanded in recent years. The literature specifically relevant to Philadelphia will be cited throughout this work. For general treatments of immigrant, ethnic, and racial conflict and violence in American history, see Hugh Davis Graham and Ted Robert Gurr, eds., *Violence in America: Historical and Comparative Perspectives* (Washington, D.C.: U.S. Government Printing Office, 1969), especially chaps. 2 and 3, and Richard Hofstadter and Michael Wallace, eds., *American Violence: A Documentary History* (New York: Alfred Knopf, 1970).

2. For examples of "contention" and resistance as responses to ethnic and racial subordination, see Minako Kurokawa, ed., *Minority Responses* (New York: Random House, 1970), chap. 5.

3. For brief accounts of most of these incidents, see Sam Bass Warner, Jr., *The Private City: Philadelphia in Three Periods of Its Growth* (Philadelphia: University of Pennsylvania Press, 1968), chap. 7.

4. Fire fights involved members of the city's volunteer fire companies, most of whom were young men in their twenties who came from working-class backgrounds. The volunteer companies competed with each other for the honor of having been first to reach the scene of a fire, and frequently companies would battle on the way to the fire or at the hydrant for the glory of putting out the fire. In the 1840s, when the companies took on a pronounced ethnic character and competition among them increased accordingly, the fighting became more destructive and bloody. For a fuller discussion of fire fights, see Bruce G. Laurie, "Fire Companies and Gangs

in Southwark: the 1840s," *The Peoples of Philadelphia: A History of Ethnic Groups and Lower-Class Life, 1790-1940,* ed. Allen F. Davis and Mark H. Haller (Philadelphia: Temple University Press, 1973), 71-87.

5. For a brief discussion of the psychological aspects of the reform and nativist movements of the 1840s, see David Brion Davis, "Some Themes of Counter-Subversion: An Analysis of Anti-Masonic, Anti-Catholic, and Anti-Mormon Literature," *Mississippi Valley Historical Review* 47 (September 1960):205-224.

6. For Jacksonian Philadelphia as a setting for violence, see Elizabeth M. Geffen, "Violence in Philadelphia in the 1840s and 1850s," *Pennsylvania History* 36 (October 1969): 381-410.

7. For the slowness of public officials to respond to riots against unpopular minorities, see Warner, *Private City,* 134-135. For the fee structure of law-enforcement officials in Jacksonian Philadelphia, see William R. Dickerson, *The Letters of Junius, Exposing to the Public, for Their Benefit, the Mal-Practices in the Administration of the Law, the Corruption in the Offices in the State House Row, in the County of Philadelphia, the Extortions Practised by the Public Officers, etc.* (Philadelphia: W. R. Dickerson, 1850).

8. For the administration of the city and districts, see Warner, *Private City,* chap. 6.

9. On consolidation, see Warner, *Private City,* 152-157, and Eli Kirk Price, *The History of Consolidation in the City of Philadelphia* (Philadelphia: Lippincott, 1873).

11. For the St. Philip's incident, see chap. 7. For Pennsylvania Hall, see Pennsylvania Hall Association, *A History of Pennsylvania Hall* (Philadelphia: Pennsylvania Hall Association, 1838). For the weavers' riot, see chap. 2.

12. Russell Jarvis to *Public Ledger,* July 26, 1844; Warner, *Private City,* 61.

13. There is no single satisfactory definition of "community" that is widely accepted throughout the humanities and social sciences. Warner argues in chap. 1 of *Private City* that Philadelphia was a community in the second half of the eighteenth century, by which he means that all its residents had a social knowledge of one another, shared basic values, and were able to cooperate in necessary civic undertakings. Yet, when discussing the impact of the Revolutionary War on the city, Warner concedes that serious class and economic divisions split the population. In fact, conflict and violence had been part of the Philadelphia environment well before the Revolutionary era. For some good examples of this, see John K. Alexander, "Poverty, Fear, and Continuity: An Analysis of the Poor in Late Eighteenth-Century Philadelphia," in *Peoples of Philadelphia,* 13-35.

14. John K. Alexander, "The City of Brotherly Fear: The Poor in Late Eighteenth-Century Philadelphia," in *Cities in American History,* ed. Kenneth T. Jackson and Stanley K. Schultz (New York: Knopf, 1972), 79-97.

15. Stuart Blumin, "Mobility in a Nineteenth-century City: Philadelphia, 1820-1860" (Ph.D. diss., University of Pennsylvania, 1968), 155.

16. David Montgomery, in his article, "The Shuttle and the Cross: Weavers and Artisans in the Kensington Riots of 1844," *Journal of Social History* 5 (Summer 1972): 411-446, presents the clearest case for the assertion that nativism represented the direct decline of class consciousness among Philadelphia's working people in the 1840s and the growth, in its stead, of a consciousness of cultural differences among the Irish and native groups comprising the working class.

17. For an excellent discussion of the social mixing that characterized certain kinds of popular crowds, see Leonard Richards, *"Gentlemen of Property and Standing": Anti-Abolition Mobs in Jacksonian America* (New York: Oxford University Press, 1970). For the antirailroad riots in Kensington, see Michael Feldberg, "Urbanization as a Cause of Violence: Philadelphia as a Test Case," in *Peoples of Philadelphia,* 58-63.

18. For a discussion of the role of violence in the distribution of social rewards, see Herbert L. Neiburg, *Political Violence* (New York: St. Martin's Press, 1969), chap. 1.

19. Richards, *"Gentlemen of Property and Standing,"* chap. 5.

20. For the dangers of economic "reductionism" in the analysis of cultural conflict, see Joseph R. Gusfield, *Symbolic Crusade: Status Politics and the American Temperance Movement* (Urbana: University of Illinois Press, 1966), 57ff.

2
The Irish

illegibly resentment

False

In April 1844, the Philadelphia *Public Ledger* retold a probably apocryphal anecdote about a "poor Irishman, in Brooklyn" who, while digging a foundation, "was buried, all but his head, by the earth sliding." The *Ledger* went on: "Pat took the affair very quietly, and cracked jokes with those who were digging him out. He thought he was as good a native American as the best, since he had been dug out of Yankee soil."[1]

Less than a month after this anecdote enlivened the *Ledger*'s otherwise dour pages, anti-Irish rioting and bloodshed exploded in Philadelphia. Little lightness indeed leavened the acrimonious conflict between Philadelphia's Catholic Irish and Protestant native Americans. Yet even this humorous reference encapsules the main elements in the conflict: archetypal Pat was a menial laborer and of course poor; like thousands of his fellow countrymen, he labored in a large East Coast city; and his quip shows that, again like his compatriots, he knew that his presence on American soil generated nativist animosity. Characteristically, this knowledge did not prevent him from having a laugh at his hosts' expense. While Catholic Irish immigrants were sensitive to hatred and resistance from native Americans, they were never daunted by it for long. Nativist attacks only reinforced the sense of cohesion and isolation within the Irish Catholic community. Conversely, the Irish sense of unity and separateness reconfirmed many native Americans in their resentment of these supposedly unassimilated and unacculturated immigrants.

Most of the historical literature on the conflict between the Irish and native Americans in the 1840s has been sympathetic to the Irish, and deservedly so.[2] The discrimination that native Americans of all classes practiced against the Irish typifies the kind of dominant group oppression of immigrant and racial minorities that has recurred throughout American history.[3] But the Irish who came here in the 1830s and 1840s were singled

out for special attention. The nativist movement of the 1840s was aimed
not so much at immigrant minorities in general as the Irish in particular.
Protestant Philadelphians paid little attention to other groups of Catholic
immigrants, such as the French or Germans. Protestant immigrants, notably the English, suffered little open discrimination, at least according to
the surviving evidence. Unlike the others, the Irish consistently managed
to provoke nativist hostility. While native Americans cannot be excused
for their discrimination against the Irish, we must still ask what it was
about the Irish Catholic immigrant minority in Philadelphia that set it on
a collision course with the Protestant majority.[4]

The great potato famine of the mid-1840s drove unprecedented numbers
of Irish peasants to the United States. By the time of the American Civil
War, the Irish constituted more than a quarter of New York City's population and close to a fifth of Philadelphia's. While most of this immigrant
mass was made up of post-1845 arrivals, smaller numbers of Irish immigrants had been landing in America's East Coast ports for the previous
thirty years, propelled by the dozen or so smaller crop failures that had
plagued Ireland. The prefamine Irish of the 1820s and 1830s concentrated
in a few cities, such as Philadelphia, Boston, and New York, and thereby
made themselves highly visible. In the 1830s, the yearly number of new
Irish settlers in the United States reached an average of twenty thousand,
double what it had been in the 1820s. The years 1840 and 1841 saw a
quickening of the pace, with thirty-six thousand Irish registering in 1841
alone. (Doubtless many others entered from Canada without registering.)
A year later, the figure ballooned to just under fifty thousand. Several
thousand of these new arrivals landed in or wandered to Philadelphia each
year. By most estimates, Philadelphia was at least 10 percent Irish in 1844,
the year of the Native American riots. Not since the eighteenth century,
when the Palatinate Germans had formed a noticeable portion of the city's
population, had Philadelphians been forced to concern themselves with the
problems of assimilating and acculturating a sizable foreign minority.[5]

In numbers alone, the Irish influx alarmed urban native Americans.
When combined with the migrants off the nation's own rural farms, the
immigrants placed a severe strain on the already inadequate housing supplies and civic services of Jacksonian cities. Furthermore, the Irish arriving
in the 1830s and 1840s presented their hosts with a long list of cultural and
social peculiarities and problems that set the immigrants and the American
natives on separate paths of development. The typical south Irish immigrant

had been a peasant; he brought with him a large family, a dislike for cities, and few industrial skills. His cultural values were grounded in a rural life of hardship and untimely death. His religion, Roman Catholicism, declared English Protestantism its mortal enemy, and it was to Anglicized versions of Protestantism, after all, that the vast majority of American citizens adhered.[6] The Irish were starting in Jacksonian Philadelphia with serious handicaps.

In a perceptive insight, William V. Shannon has observed that "the history of the Irish in America is founded on a paradox. The Irish were a rural people in Ireland and became a city people in the United States."[7] Few people came less well equipped for the transition. In the Old Country, cities had traditionally served as strongholds for the Anglo-Irish Protestant ruling class; the majority of Catholic Irishmen identified instead with their rural villages. Life as tenant farmers in the Irish countryside had taught the immigrants few useful skills with which to earn a decent living in an American city. The small number of Irish laboring people who escaped the rigors of digging and carrying when they came to the United States were those who applied their previous experience in the cottage industry of Ireland—a fairly common winter pastime—to the weaving, tailoring, and shoemaking industries in America's seaboard cities. Yet, in their pay and hours these indoor workers fared no better than those who dug canals or struggled under hods. A small number of the newly arrived found work in factories as unskilled hands at wages that most native-born operatives would not consider. The absence of a significant group of middle-class businessmen in their own ranks doomed at least the first generation of south Irish immigrants to hard lives and low incomes in the bottom portion of America's working classes. The mark of poverty, always a stigma in American civilization, clung to the immigrant Irish Catholics until well after the Civil War.

Their poverty in America was nothing new to the immigrant Irish; for some, their lives might well have seemed filled with luxury. Deprivation had shaped the Irish Catholic consciousness for centuries. The Catholic peasantry in particular had been an exploited and oppressed majority in their own homeland for at least two hundred years before the Great Hunger. In 1690, the victory of William of Orange over the Celtic Catholic warlords at the battle of the Boyne confirmed the ascendancy of the English crown in Irish affairs. William's victory also assured the domination in Ireland itself of the Anglo-Irish Protestant landlords who depended

on London to uphold their power. These landholders owned three-fourths
of the land of Ireland and controlled two-thirds of its commerce and
trade. In addition to suffering the economic oppression imposed by these
landlords' exorbitant "rackrents," the Catholic populace labored under
the burdens of a draconian penal code enacted by the Protestant-controlled
Irish Parliament. Catholics were deprived of the vote and the rights to
enter universities, to teach, to carry a gun, and to practice law. Restrictions
on inheritance and land tenure meant that only by converting to Protestantism could a native Irishman accumulate significant landholdings. While
the various provisions of the penal code were only erratically enforced
and some were lifted by the beginning of the nineteenth century, their
continuance on the statute book—and their occasional invocation in times
of political repression—served as a constant reminder to the Catholic majority of its subordination to a foreign-supported Protestant minority
on its native soil.[8]

Left but the meagrest subsistence after their rents were paid, native
Irish Catholics learned to live on a sparse diet, to labor long, to lose many
of their children at birth, to suffer disease, to bear up under a harsh life
until an early death brought blessed escape, and yet to keep alive a burning
hatred of the English and their Irish Protestant retainers and fiercely
resist them to whatever degree possible through revolts and terrorism in
the rural countryside. The Whiteboys, the Hearts of Steel Boys, the Molly
Maguires, and other terrorist bands who protested landlord inequities had
made the Irish who migrated to America in the antebellum years familiar
with the political uses of collective violence.[9] For many, violent protest
seemed the only possible means of political expression in a system whose
channels were closed to the great mass of nonlandowners.

Understandably, the insecurity and bleakness of their miserable lives
instilled the Irish peasantry with a widespread fatalism, a pessimism to
which Irish Catholicism gave perfect expression. The church stressed the
unknowable power of God, the sinful imperfection of man, the transience
of life in this world, and the rewards of divine transcendence in the next.
The fact that so much of the discrimination against them was based on
their religious beliefs simply reconfirmed the Catholic masses of Ireland
in their devotion to the church. Anti-English and antilandlord hostility were
inseparably bound up with professions of faith in Catholicism. Irish nationalism and the desire for home rule, aborted by the Act of Union of
1801, which dissolved the Irish Parliament and provided Irish seats in the

English Parliament at Westminster, became ineluctably intertwined with the aspirations of the Catholic Church, which hoped for the lifting of restrictions on its actions and the abolition of tithes to support the Irish Anglican establishment through a restored (and Catholic-controlled) Irish parliament at Dublin.[10]

When hunger drove the Irish from their homeland to the shores of Jacksonian America, the immigrants brought their history of oppression and hatred along with their meagre baggage. Escaping from Anglo-Irish exploitation, they entered a land dominated by yet another group of ascendant Protestants. This time, however, the Catholic Irish would form but a small minority in a larger population. Their fatalistic view of reality was discordant with the optimistic spirit of the enterprising Jacksonian population, and definitely opposed to the reform spirit of the age of which even the nativist movement considered itself a part. Catholic spokesmen were politically and temperamentally conservative. They attacked abolitionists, prison reformers, public school enthusiasts, and prohibitionists alike, classifying the lot as "sickly sentimentalists" who would tamper with God's divinely ordained order in this world and who would deny the essential sinfulness and unworthiness that characterized mankind since the fall of Adam.[11]

While the immigrants were skeptical about reform of mankind as a general undertaking, it is no coincidence that many of the reforms rejected by the Irish and their leaders (notably universal public education, temperance, and abolition), threatened the structure of their community's social organization, economic status, or customary patterns of behavior. Public education, for example, in a politically controlled system dominated by Protestant educators, seemed to threaten the hold of the Catholic church on its young. In the late 1830s and 1840s especially, the public schools in urban America were clearly guilty of evangelizing for Protestantism through a campaign to smear "popery," as the schoolbooks were fond of calling it. Abolition, on the other hand, might well have seemed an economic threat to the Irish since emancipation of the slaves implied that the North would be flooded with unskilled blacks eager to compete with the immigrants for lower-class jobs. The Irish were already tasting the bitter fruit of job competition with newly arrived blacks because Philadelphia was close to the upper South and received many runaways and free Negroes escaping oppression below the Mason-Dixon line. On another level, any movement proposing to elevate blacks could not help

but diminish the status of those very whites, the immigrant Irish, who stood just above the black population in the social pecking order. Finally, temperance, a reform movement closely associated with the evangelical Protestant churches, struck at the heart of Irish group sociability. In poor immigrant neighborhoods, the local pub provided one of the few congenial settings for an evening's entertainment among friends and compatriots. The antiliquor agitation, which seemed ready to convert the voluntary temperance cause into a crusade to legally prohibit the sale of intoxicants, threatened to deprive the Irish of this consolation and comfort. It even posed a potential danger to Irish Catholic religious observances. Wine was part of the sacraments of the church, and the Irish feared that at least some of the more fanatical in the Protestant antiliquor movement would ban the use of alcohol in religious services. While there was an Irish Catholic temperance movement in Philadelphia, named after the revered Father Matthew, who had done so much for the cause in Ireland, leaders of the Irish community feared the rise of an organized political movement developed around the liquor issue. Like public education, control over the sale of alcohol was vested in the hands of public officials through their licensing powers, and thus the reformers, should they choose to follow the path of prohibition, would be in a position to force their views on the Irish Catholic minority through the electoral process. As a vulnerable minority, the leaders of the Catholic community feared unbridled majority rule on issues of culture or religion.

The church, the tavern, the firehouse, and the outdoor market provided the setting for Irish community life in Philadelphia. Uprooted from their rural villages, the Irish established these new neighborhood institutions to replace those left behind. In Philadelphia, more than most other East Coast Irish communities in the Jacksonian era, it took some special effort to maintain community isolation and solidarity—that is, to keep apart from the native Protestant majority and out of contact with its institutions. The task proved difficult because of Philadelphia's characteristic housing pattern, which did not fully ghettoize the arriving immigrants. Low-density row housing predominated in the city, and when the influx of population stimulated the housing market in the 1830s, private developers simply extended the row pattern into the suburbs, spreading the newcomers in every direction. At the same time, owners of the older houses in the center city, although they were already living cheek to jowl with one another along the narrow cobbled streets, packed their

neighborhoods even more by throwing up shanties in the backyards and narrow alleyways behind their tidy homes. Thus, where new blocks of suburban row housing were made available, as in the manufacturing districts of Moyamensing or in Third Ward, Kensington, the Irish found enough space to cluster together in sizable numbers. But at the same time, Irish families were spread out rather evenly through the backyards and alleyways of every ward in the city proper. To provide leadership for this dispersed following, Irish clergymen and politicians had to work doubly hard at creating organizations and institutions that would reach into these downtown Irish neighborhoods.

Such an effort proved costly and time-consuming. A shortage of money and trained priests delayed completion of a network of parish churches until the 1860s. The first parochial schools were built in the early 1850s in response to Catholic objections to the Protestant nature of the public schools and with memories of the 1844 riots still fresh. Before then, only two girls' schools served Philadelphia's Catholic youth. Built at great expense to many who could least afford it, the parochial schools of Philadelphia became (and continue today) the strongest urban Catholic school system in the United States. Aside from the activities of the church itself, the lay community also created institutions designed to serve its members' needs. Most sizable Irish neighborhoods developed their own volunteer fire companies, street gangs, benefit and burial societies, and, in the 1850s, building and loan associations. These latter enabled members to accumulate capital and acquire real estate without going hat in hand to Protestant-controlled banks. In addition, the Irish spawned several Democratic clubs and nationalist societies. Two students of Philadelphia's Irish, John K. Kane and Dennis Clark, have both concluded that, wherever possible, Irish Catholics in Jacksonian Philadelphia created separate social, political, religious, and economic institutions run by Irish Catholics to serve Irish Catholics and to profit Irish Catholics.[12]

By the 1840s, self-imposed Irish isolation furnished Philadelphia's nativists with what they considered to be solid evidence that the new immigrants were ungrateful guests who refused to assimilate into the institutions of their new homeland. In turn, the Irish argued that nativist hostility had forced separatism on them. Deprived of good opportunities in the job market, shunted off into the city's poorest housing, ridiculed in the public schools for their religious beliefs, excluded from conducting religious rites in the public hospitals and armed services, the Irish Catholic

population seemed to have no other choice than to create a parallel network
of social institutions in which they could place their trust. In retrospect,
it seems fair to say that by maintaining their churches, schools, orphanages,
hospitals, savings and insurance societies, political clubs, nationalist associations, taverns, fire companies, and street gangs, the Irish Catholics in
Philadelphia were both responding to their new environment and shaping
it. Catholic historian T. Thomas McAvoy has argued that the American
Catholic clergy deliberately kept its flock as separate as possible from the
institutions of the dominant Protestant culture, both to insulate the
immigrants from the rigors of cultural transition and to preserve the hold
of the church on this newly arrived mass of followers.[13] For the most
part, their efforts, combined with those of the laymen themselves, succeeded. Even where the typical immigrant Irishman lived in the backyard
of an upper-class Protestant-owned home in the center city, he very likely
maintained closer communication with his Catholic compatriots on other
blocks than with the Yankee who lived a few feet away.

In Philadelphia, Irish Catholic separatism was given its main direction
through the local parish church. While the bishop of Philadelphia spoke
with a single voice for all the city's Catholic communicants on doctrinal
and theological questions, it was to the neighborhood church and its circle
of activities that immigrant Irish families turned for their ties to the past
and to one another. In working-class neighborhoods especially, the parish
church served as a social, educational, and welfare center for local Catholics.
The parish priest, by many contemporary reports, was the single most influential person in Irish districts. He officiated at every important rite of
passage from birth to death. His literacy enabled him to help with letters
to kin in the homeland, while the sacraments he administered reminded his
listeners of Old Country customs and memories. His control over the
parish Sunday school gave him a role in raising the young. In short, the
local priest was a constant reminder of things Catholic and things Irish.
The church building itself served as a Catholic community center, a site
for meetings and rallies, a home for voluntary associations, a holy place
in which to voice shared religious convictions and take communion with
one's fellows, and, in times of emergency (such as in the nativist agitation
of 1844), even the scene of secret military drills by armed Catholic
volunteers.[14]

Just as the local parish united Irish Catholic neighborhoods, so the
Philadelphia diocese brought together the different social and economic

levels within the wider Irish community. There were more than enough distinctions among the various classes of Irish Catholics in the city so that, under the less embattled conditions of the post-Civil War period, the community developed several distinctive subcommunities at the expense of universal cohesion. But the hostile atmosphere of the Jacksonian era afforded Philadelphia's Catholics, Irish and non-Irish alike, no such luxury. Despite the fact that a significant number of Philadelphia's Irish Catholics were already two, three, or more generations removed from the Old Country by the 1840s and that some of their ancestors had served proudly with Washington or in the Continental Congress, the diocese never permitted the more fortunate members of the community to neglect the defense of their less fortunate compatriots. When the working-class Irish came under attack from political nativists in the 1840s, it was the diocese, through its leader, Archbishop Francis Patrick Kenrick, who spoke up in their defense. When Irish workingmen were arrested for their part in the 1844 Kensington riots, it was prominent Catholic attorneys, Irish and non-Irish alike, who defended them, most likely foregoing their accustomed fees. To help remove some of the grounds for nativist criticism of the Irish lower class, the church served as the organizer of the various Catholic temperance associations in the city, such as the Father Matthew Total Abstinence Society (which, despite its title, argued for voluntary temperance rather than total avoidance of alcoholic drink). Through the parochial school building program, wealthy Catholics supported religious education for thousands of poor and immigrant children, although even the poorest Irish laborers contributed a share in this massive educational effort. Finally, the diocese increasingly administered to the wants of its needy, sick, and elderly through a growing network of charitable soup societies, asylums, orphanages, and, in the 1850s, hospitals.[15]

The archdiocese particularly supported one movement that united the Irish community in Philadelphia in a common effort: the Repeal movement. The goal of Repeal was the legislative revocation of the Act of Union of 1801, which had abolished the independent Parliament in Dublin and created a minority representation for Ireland at Westminster in its place. The leader of the Repeal effort, Daniel O'Connell, known to his countrymen as "the Liberator" since his successful efforts to lift the ban on Catholics holding seats in Westminster in 1828, had managed to weave the political and religious threads of Irish nationalism into a movement to restore the Irish Parliament, a step that most Catholics viewed as a prelude

to the lifting of all disabilities on Catholics and, possibly, even Irish independence. While this last seemed only a far-off dream to most, O'Connell's agitation inside Parliament and out appeared for a time to have brought him to the brink of victory on the question of revocation of the Act of Union during summer 1843. Thousands of transplanted Irishmen and American Catholics flocked into branches of the Repeal Association in the cities of the United States, hoping to create enough public agitation and raise enough funds to convince the British that Irish home rule, or at least parliamentary separation, was diplomatically and politically wise. Although the American Catholic church generally frowned on secular reform and political movements as useless, it threw its full weight behind O'Connell's crusade for parliamentary autonomy. In Philadelphia, the diocesan newspaper avidly reported news of the Liberator's activities, permitted its pulpits to be used for fund raising, and allowed its priests to take the podium at Repeal rallies.[16]

The association's American branches bore two primary responsibilities: raising money to cover the association's expenses in the homefront campaign and applying some sort of pressure on the American government to intercede with the British on behalf of Irish liberty. When success seemed imminent in summer 1843, especially, the Philadelphia association perked with energy: it held meetings and rallies nearly every week at various halls around the city, sponsored balls and fund-raising events, invited speakers to address the public on the subject of Irish freedom, and shipped substantial sums of money overseas to support O'Connell's propaganda. The movement in Philadelphia took on the fervor of a crusade, unintentionally mirroring the raucous emotionalism of the evangelical Protestant revivals which had been sweeping the city at the same time. It was the very depth of the Repealers' convictions and their willingness to sacrifice for the cause that led many of these same evangelicals and patriotic native American citizens to charge that the Irish of Philadelphia retained greater loyalty to Ireland than to their adopted homeland. Even the normally reserved and antinativist *Public Ledger* took exception to the Repealers' practice of sending money to Ireland, which the paper feared would be used to buy arms for an insurrection. In June 1843, the editor said of Philadelphia's Irish: "As *Irishmen* they have no rights on our soil. All their rights here are those of *men* and *Americans;* and among these rights is not included that of violating *our* laws or disturbing *our* peace."[17]

The worst fears of those who doubted the Repealers' loyalties were realized in fall 1843 when word reached the United States that the British

planned to arrest O'Connell on a charge of sedition. The Philadelphia association convened a highly charged emergency meeting at which the outraged members proposed, among other things, to attack Canada should the beloved Liberator be taken. One member, the owner of a packet boat, volunteered it for any invasion that might be undertaken. Nativists, and even some of those who previously had cared little about the activities of the Repealers, were appalled by this blatant threat to filibuster the United States into war with Britain. Nothing came of the Repealers' sabre-rattling rhetoric in the end, except to further provoke the already agitated native Protestant community. Facing the charge that as Catholics they retained ultramontane loyalties to Rome, the Irish of Philadelphia added grounds for the belief that they also harbored ultramontane political loyalties to their old homeland. Reviewing the causes of the Native American riots as the smoke was clearing from Kensington, a leading nativist politician would blame the "Repeal agitation," which he claimed had been the leading source of friction between the Irish and natives in Philadelphia.[18]

From the perspective of the present, it seems clear enough that nativist fears of Irish immigrant disloyalty to the United States were grossly exaggerated. The history of American ethnic groups since the 1840s has shown repeatedly that the continuance of emotional ties to the old country is perfectly compatible with loyalty to the new. But this hindsight had not yet been granted to antebellum Americans. The Irish were the first large, self-conscious ethnic minority in the United States to engage in transnational politicking, and the unprecedented sight of Repealers scheming to embroil the United States in internal British affairs, or sending American gold to Ireland, or keeping the Irish community in Philadelphia at a near-constant emotional peak through nationalistic tub thumping—and all with the good wishes of Catholic religious leaders, no less—convinced many Americans that a perpetually unassimilable community of foreigners had come to their shores.

Still, appearances often deceive, and Americans were soon to learn, especially in Philadelphia, that Irish-American solidarity with O'Connell was not monolithic. The Liberator almost lost his support in Philadelphia by attacking American Negro slavery. In New Orleans, in fact, his attack on slavery led the Repeal chapter there to disband in protest. In February 1842, O'Connell proclaimed that Ireland could not be free until all men were free—black as well as white, in the New World as well as the Old. This pronouncement sundered the Philadelphia Repeal Association in two. In a series of raucous meetings during June 1843, the majority of association

members denounced his speech and subsequent observations on abolition
as an unwarranted intrusion into American affairs. Following the lead
of Democratic wheelhorse William A. Stokes, the Philadelphians proclaimed
O'Connell incompetent to speak for them on all but strictly Irish questions.
In the wake of these strong resolutions, a group of O'Connell loyalists
seceded from the organization to form the Association of the Friends of
Ireland and Repeal, nicknamed the "new" or "loyal" Repeal Association.
This new group's loyalty to O'Connell was definitely a qualified one, however,
since it too admitted that the Liberator's intervention in American questions
was politically unwise. Yet the harsh rejection by the old Repeal association
went further than the loyalists were willing to go. They argued that any
criticism from Repealers would serve above all to diminish O'Connell's
luster, thereby setting back the main cause of Irish home rule. The main
focus, they argued, had to be solidarity with O'Connell.[19]

Despite the hubbub he caused by his condemnation of slavery, it appears
in retrospect that O'Connell's words had little if any effect in moving
America's Irish Catholics into the abolitionist camp. Most Irish leaders,
according to Oscar Handlin, considered abolition nothing less than non-
sense, a bleeding-heart "niggerology."[20] Still, O'Connell's speeches against
slavery provided grist for the nativist mill, offering yet further "proof" that
the immigrants' attitudes in domestic politics were controlled by European
forces. Whigs as well as nativists were willing to harp on O'Connell's
attempt to intervene in domestic American affairs, since his actions had
so clearly embarrassed their common political enemy, the Democratic
party. Tied to the Irish as well as southern slaveowners and northern anti-
Negro native workingmen, the Democrats were stunned by the impact of
O'Connell's words on their fragile coalition. Although Irish Democratic leaders
publicly rejected O'Connell's presumptuous advice, his actions infuriated
the militant Democrats of the South nonetheless, just as it furthered the
growing distrust between the Irish and native working classes in the cities
of the North.

It was to the Democrats that Philadelphia's Irish Catholics looked on
the local level for their political leadership and recognition. The Jackson
party had a reputation as the more proimmigrant (and, importantly for
the Irish, anti-British) party in American politics. In Philadelphia County,
the Irish Catholic vote was so loyal to the Jacksonians that in heavily
Irish districts such as First Ward, Moyamensing, and Third Ward, Kensington,
the Democratic candidate occasionally ran unopposed. Irish voters in the

populous industrial districts helped the Democrats control the county board of commissioners as their turnout more than counterbalanced the heavy Whig majorities in the city. Because their 10 percent of the population formed a crucial swing bloc, the Democratic political leaders ardently courted the Irish. William A. Stokes, a Catholic, non-Irish Democratic boss, served as the president of the Philadelphia Repeal Association. His successor in 1845 was another Protestant, Robert Tyler, son of Democratic President of the United States John Tyler. In turn, the Irish supplied more than a few Democratic leaders in the county, and their counsel was listened to intently within party circles. This alliance between the Jacksonians and their immigrant retainers raised the ire of Whigs and nativists alike. As the Irish population increased, they warned, the Democratic grip on the county would probably become unshakable, and the Jacksonians would then be free to neglect the public good. Even as they complained, however, the Whigs themselves occasionally courted the Irish vote by nominating an Irish candidate or two in closely contested districts. Such actions would justify the founders of the nativist American Republican party, who were able to claim that both major parties had sold themselves and their country in exchange for the crucial Irish vote.[21]

In return for their loyalty, the working-class Irish rank and file asked little of the Democrats, at least in Philadelphia. They were satisfied to receive a few places on the ballot for Irish leaders and some patronage jobs on the night watch or public works. When they asked so little, the Irish were quick to be offended if it was not delivered. In spring 1842, for example, native-born, protemperance Kensington Democrats refused to vote for Irish Catholic Hugh Clark, the regular party nominee for alderman, and he was defeated. The insulted Irish retaliated soon afterward in the county-wide election by staying home or voting for Protestant Irish Whig Morton McMichael for sheriff. These Irish votes tipped a close race to McMichael, who under normal conditions would not have been expected to win. For the first time in recent memory, the Democrats even failed to carry the district commissionerships in Kensington.[22] Their lesson learned, the regular Democrats were careful to provide a number of places for Irishmen on their tickets and provide them with ample support. Those native Democrats who could not accept party discipline either joined the Whigs or helped found the new American Republican party.

If Democratic politics was a source of cohesion for the Irish community as a whole and a way of uniting with at least some elements in

the non-Irish and non-Catholic population, it was also a means of upward mobility and prestige for a small group of Irish Catholic leaders. Some elected officials collected fees and emoluments for the performance of their duties, but at the very least their prominent place in neighborhood politics was good for business. Most Irish politicians (and one might add most politicians in Philadelphia as a whole) tended to combine their electoral activities with a law practice, an officership in the state militia, or a tavern or grocery store proprietorship. Hugh Clark, a master weaver notorious for opposing the economic interests of his Irish Catholic journeymen, still managed to retain their gratitude by using his political position to defend the cultural and religious interests of the wider Catholic community. As a constable, he actively tried to put down the weavers' strike of 1842; but in another of his political capacities, that of Kensington school director, he authorized a public school teacher to suspend the reading of the Protestant Bible in her classroom, since the departure of conscientiously opposed Catholic children from the room disrupted the lesson. Clark's action, coming as it did at the height of a controversy over whether to permit the Catholic Bible into the public schools, endeared him to his fellow Catholics but proved more than exasperated evangelicals and nativists in Kensington could bear. A succession of Protestant rallies to "save the Bible in the public schools" led to violent confrontations, which in turn sparked the great Native American riots. Clark remained a hero in the Kensington Irish community for many years to come, despite the fact that in the aftermath of the riots he was one of several employing weavers who lowered the wages of his workmen to a bare subsistence level.

In sum, cohesion in the Irish community stemmed from several sources: the church's efforts at separatism; the nationalist agitation of the Repeal movement; Democratic politics; civic and charitable involvement on the part of the Irish and Catholic middle and upper classes; and an Irish Catholic sense of common destiny nourished by the hostile Protestant world around them. While the general Irish Catholic response to political slights or public school discrimination indicates that a broad internal consensus existed within the community, indirect evidence suggests that the tightest bonds were forged within the largest subgroup of Irish Catholic Philadelphians: the wage earners and laborers of the industrial suburbs. These were the men and women closest to the front lines in the day-to-day confrontation with nativists and organized nativism. Such groups as

Kensington's handloom weavers and dockworkers, or the street gangs and fire companies of Moyamensing, paid a price for their isolation from the outside world and solidarity with each other which was measured in bloody heads. Irish wage earners in Philadelphia took part in numerous violent episodes during the Jacksonian era, some pitting them against the city's armed and angry nativists, others matching them against the sheriff's posse or the black community or even their fellow-Irish employers. As Sam Bass Warner, Jr., has suggested, it was not so much that the Irishness or the Catholicism of the Irish working classes was central to the issues involved in each of these clashes but rather that the tendency of the Irish to disturb the city's peace—and especially to attack law-enforcement officials—"turned the Irish into legitimate targets for violence" perpetrated by self-appointed guardians of the social order, such as the nativist political associations.[23]

The riots in which the Philadelphia Irish participated during the 1830s and 1840s illustrate some persistent themes that reveal a good deal of information about the sources of cohesion in working-class Irish Catholic neighborhoods. In most of these incidents, the Irish were notable for the fearless way in which they resisted authority, a trait that they had developed over the hundreds of years in which they had been defying Anglo-Irish Protestant rule in the homeland. The three best examples of Philadelphia Irish fearlessness in the face of authority are the attack on black temperance marchers in 1842 that spilled over into two days of generalized attacks on the black ghetto, the sporadic attacks between 1840 and 1842 on work crews attempting to lay railroad tracks down the center of a main street through the weavers' neighborhood in Kensington despite protest to the legislature from neighborhood residents, and the violence during the weavers' strike in the winter of 1842-1843. In each of these series of riots, gangs of Irish men and women attacked a sheriff's posse in angry defiance and during the weavers' strike even administered a humiliating personal beating to the sheriff himself. During a riot in 1828, the weavers of Kensington once held a celebration "in token of . . . victory over the civil power" when they dispersed some night watchmen who had come to arrest some of their compatriots.[24] While they might have been an outnumbered minority in Philadelphia, the immigrant Irish were not passive or submissive. Their history had taught them to honor resistance, even against superior power, and they carried this lesson with them into the summer of 1844.

An equally telling theme in the Irish-centered riots of the 1830s and 1840s was the willingness of the Irish to avenge in blood insults to their ethnic origins or religion. The 1828 incident referred to above began when a family of Irish bartenders beat a German patron to death for calling them "bloody Irish transports." In 1831, several hundred Irish Catholics turned out to stone the Protestant participants in an anniversary celebration of the battle of the Boyne. Catholic anger at the boldness of this Protestant display led them to attack the celebrants with stones and missiles as well as to exchange pistol shots and inflict knife wounds. Despite their injuries and the fact that more than thirty of their number were arrested and convicted for disturbing the peace, the Catholic Irish had the satisfaction of completely disrupting the celebration.[25]

A third theme emerging from the pattern of Irish collective violence is the tendency of the Irish to use disruption, destruction, and intimidation to compensate for their political or economic weakness in the bargaining process by which Jacksonian Philadelphia distributed its material rewards to various groups. During the prolonged strike of 1842-1843, for example, the weavers used "collective bargaining by riot," as Eric Hobsbawm has characterized it,[26] in which the strikers destroyed the skeins of their employers, or invaded their factories to smash looms, or forced their compatriots who continued to weave at home to join the strike, in hopes that the material destruction would persuade their employers that holding out for a favorable settlement would be much more expensive than meeting the weavers' demands. The Irish also tended to use physical force to intimidate their competition, such as the black longshoremen who at one time dominated the waterfront labor market in Philadelphia but who were being replaced during the 1830s and 1840s by the influx of immigrant Irish labor. During the 1842 anti-temperance riot in the black ghetto, attacks against Negroes spread to the Schuylkill wharves, where black and Irish coalheavers had been engaged in a struggle for control over day labor unloading the barges arriving from western Pennsylvania. It was at the Schuylkill docks that a sheriff's posse, sent to rescue some black coalheavers before they were trapped and burned alive in a warehouse, was dispersed by an angry crowd of Irishmen and chased all the way back to the edge of the black ghetto on the other side of the city. There were Irish in the crowd that burned Pennsylvania Hall in protest over the abolitionist agitation of the 1830s. In fact, the only persons arrested for burning the hall had Irish-sounding

names, although this fact probably tells more about law-enforcement biases than it does about the actual composition of the crowd of rioters itself.[27]

No group of Irishmen in Philadelphia exhibited more bravado and esprit de corps than the handloom weavers of Kensington. Because they were so centrally involved in the Native American riots of 1844—it was *their* neighborhood in which the riots began—it seems wise to spend some time looking at their violent strike of 1842-1843 for what it says about the weavers' behavior patterns and sense of solidarity. The mutually reinforcing ties of class and ethnicity bound the group together. Evidence suggests that the working-class weavers were so tightly knit that the traditionally powerful distinction between Protestant and Catholic carried little, if any, weight among them. These men and their families seemed to live in a cultural universe of their own, rejecting any intrusion from the outside world, be it in the form of the law or the city's network of Protestant voluntary associations and reform movements. This Irish universe was centered in Third Ward, Kensington, and in the eastern portion of Moyamensing, a suburb adjoining Southwark. (It was at the Nanny Goat Market in Third Ward, Kensington, for example, that the Native American riots began. When nativists tried to enter the open shed to hold a political rally, someone among the Irish residents is supposed to have yelled, "Keep the damned natives out of *our* market!" and the fighting erupted.) This was Irish weavers' turf, a place in which they could feel secure. The market served as a social center for the community, a place for political and union meetings, and a stronghold for resistance to the sheriff's posse or bands of hostile nativist rioters. David Montgomery has suggested that the solidarity among the weavers was so great that when the Native American riots broke out, Protestant Irish weavers fought not on the side of the nativists but rather with their Catholic "brothers of the loom."[28] The widespread and extended strike over wages that began two years before the great riots demonstrates the weavers' solidarity with equal if not greater impressiveness.

The protracted dispute between the journeymen weavers and their Irish employers illustrates all the themes of working-class Irish separatism: resistance to authority; a willingness to use violence as a means of persuasion in their own behalf; and a hypersensitivity to their ethnic isolation. The dispute grew out of a breakdown in the negotiating process in fall

1842 by which the weavers' piece rates were set. Twice each year, the journeymen's union and the employers' association negotiated new rates, with the Kensington and Moyamensing branches of the union each reaching its own settlement. When hard times set in during the depression years from 1837 to 1843 and competition from the power looms of New England drove down textile prices, the city's employers felt compelled to lower the rates paid to their employees. With a large number of new Irish immigrants to Philadelphia not yet absorbed into the handloom weavers' union, the employers found that they could draw on a pool of unorganized employees willing to work at near-subsistence levels. The union was barely able to hold its own members by the winter of 1842, and a peaceful strike to restore a wage cut initiated by the employers in August made no headway in the face of all the newly arrived "scabs" in the city. In order to compensate for their weakness vis-à-vis their employers, the strikers adopted tactics of violence and intimidation against both employers and scab weavers. The weavers destroyed the woolen skeins that the employers distributed to their outworkers and smashed the looms in workshops and houses. The strikers also used violence and intimidation to convince scabs that it was dangerous to their personal well-being to take work while the strike was on. On one occasion, the weavers even tried to burn down a cotton mill in suburban Manayunk that "manufactured, by a much cheaper process, an article of cotton goods . . . hitherto . . . made by the handloom weavers." Forewarned of the attempt, the sheriff and mill owner frightened off the attack, but the weavers' hostility to machines and factories persisted until the handloom industry was completely replaced by power looms after the Civil War.[29]

The first phase of the strike lasted from August 1842 to January 1843, when outside intervention settled it. Typically, the weavers would march to reinforce their own solidarity, break into scabbing weavers' homes and pour acid on their wool or break their looms, or enter an employer's workshop and smash his equipment. By fall 1842, the weavers had shut down nearly every handloom in the city, and their success actually persuaded most of the employers to accede to their demands. When some Kensington employers persisted in paying the lower rate when the harder winter season set in, the weavers rallied there in mid-January. After a rally on January 11, 1843, the weavers set about breaking furniture and looms in weavers' homes. Alderman Hugh Clark, as noted previously, was one of the peace officers who arrested the strikers. Two others, aldermen Potts and Lukens, were beaten when they tried to stop some

loom-smashing. The defiant weavers issued a proclamation warning all elected officials not to interfere with what they considered to be an internal weaving community affair. The sheriff hastened to Kensington and asked permission to address a weavers' rally then in progress at the Nanny Goat Market. When he was hooted down, he huffily resolved to bring back a posse to punish the strikers. On their arrival, the unarmed deputies found themselves faced by three to four hundred irate weavers pouring out of Nanny Goat Market, many armed with paving stones and guns. All but three of the sheriff's friends fled, leaving the sheriff and his remaining companions to receive an exemplary beating, although none of the four as seriously injured. The bruised and humiliated sheriff called in the state militia, which occupied Kensington. The weavers and their employers settled the piece rate dispute at the direction of the deputy sheriff under the shadow of the guns of the militia.[30]

The strike broke out again in the fall of 1843, with very much the same scenario. This time, however, since prosperity was slowly returning to Philadelphia, the weavers actually negotiated a raise. But when the Native American riots swept through Kensington and destroyed the neighborhood, leaving the impoverished weavers at the mercy of their employers, the rates dropped an average of two dollars per week, and the handloom weavers never really gained back their strength. An unsuccessful strike in 1846 was conducted without any violence, and increasingly charitable and temperance-minded middle- and upper-class citizens sought to alleviate the weavers' plight through poor relief. This time, the weavers were unable to launch a powerful defense of their own cause. Although handloom weaving persisted longer in Philadelphia than in the other major textile centers of the United States, the reason for this survival probably had more to do with the low wages the city's handloom weavers accepted than their ability to resist the power loom or outperform it.[31]

In the riotous years of the early 1840s, before their weakness became apparent, the handloom weavers presented to their nativist contemporaries the image of a nation within a nation, contemptuous of authority, anarchic with a vengeance. But the weavers provided only the most dramatic example of what the nativists perceived to be the generalized undesirable tendencies of the Irish Catholic immigrant. Not that Catholicism had any necessary connection to the causes of Irish violent behavior or that the Irishness of the rioters was a necessary ingredient of, say, the handloom weavers' strike or the antirailroad disturbances of 1840-1842. It was simply that the Philadelphia Irish (most of whom were Catholics) were

seemingly at odds with some group or other, or public officials, all through the 1830s and 1840s. Increasingly, as organized nativism grew stronger after 1842, the nub of controversy between the Irish and other groups in the city seemed to be religion, especially when the school Bible controversy flared into a consuming conflagration. As in any conflict, however, the provocations and excesses were never all on one side. In their own way, the nativists, and especially the working-class elements among them, possessed equally exclusivist, equally belligerent, equally aggressive, and equally disruptive cultural values, traditions, and cultural patterns. Like the working-class Irish, native artisans were quick with their fists or paving stones in debates over religion, politics, economics, or personal and group "honor."

NOTES

1. Philadelphia *Public Ledger,* April 17, 1844.

2. Ray Allen Billington, *The Protestant Crusade, 1800-1860: A Study of the Origins of American Nativism* (Chicago: Quadrangle, 1964); Carroll John Noonan, *Nativism in Connecticut, 1829-1860* (Washington, D.C.: Catholic University of America Press, 1938); John Gilmary Shea, *History of the Catholic Church in the United States* (New York: J. G. Shea, 1886-1892); Sister M. Theophane Geary, *Third Parties in Pennsylvania, 1840-1860* (Washington, D.C.: Catholic University of America Press, 1938); Hugh Joseph Nolan, *The Most Reverend Francis Patrick Kenrick, Third Bishop of Philadelphia, 1830-1851* (Philadelphia: American Catholic Historical Society, 1948); Vincent P. Lannie and Bernard C. Deithorn, "For the Honor and Glory of God: The Philadelphia Bible Riots of 1844," *History of Education Quarterly* 8 (Spring 1968): 44-106.

3. For a discussion in analytical form of minority relations with the dominant American majority, see Minako Kurokawa, *Minority Responses* (New York: Random House, 1970), passim, and especially section 1.

4. For a discussion of the particular animus of Philadelphians against the immigrant Irish, see Max Berger, "The Irish Emigrant and American Nativism as Seen by British Visitors, 1836-1860," *Pennsylvania Magazine of History and Biography* 7 (1946): 147-148.

5. William Forbes Adams, *Ireland and the Irish Emigration to the New World from 1815 to the Famine* (New Haven: Yale University Press, 1932), 413-414; Dennis Clark, "The Adjustment of Irish Immigrants to Urban Life: The Philadelphia Experience, 1840-1860" (Ph.D. diss., Temple University, 1970), 29-30.

6. The two most readable accounts of the south Irish culture that the immigrants brought to America are Oscar Handlin, *Boston's Immigrants, 1790-1880* (New York: Atheneum, 1970) and William V. Shannon, *The American Irish* (New York: Macmillan, 1963).

7. Shannon, *American Irish,* 27.

8. Ibid., 6-7.

9. Ibid., 17.

10. Ibid., 20

11. For a discussion of religious fatalism in nineteenth-century Irish-American Catholicism, see Handlin, *Boston's Immigrants,* 130-132.

12. Clark, "The Adjustments of Irish Immigrants," chaps. 4-5; John J. Kane, "The Irish Immigrant in Philadelphia, 1840-1880" (Ph.D. diss., University of Pennsylvania, 1950), chap. 1.

13. T. Thomas McAvoy, "The Formation of the Catholic Minority in the United States, 1820-1860," *Review of Politics* 10 (January 1948): 13-34.

14. The role of the parish priest is not easily reconstructed from conventional historical documents. Billington, *Protestant Crusade,* 198, repeats the widely held nativist belief that priests could start or stop Irish riots with a nod of their heads. McAvoy, "Formation of the Irish Catholic Minority," places great emphasis on the role of the clergy in leading the Irish community down the path of separatism. Taken together, the evidence is, ultimately, little more than impressionistic. Still, it seems logical enough that priests should have formed one of the main foci for the retention of Irish culture and consciousness.

15. For the role of the Philadelphia diocese in uniting the city's Catholic community, see Clark, "The Adjustment of Irish Immigrants," chap. 4.

16. For a sketch of the American Repeal movement, see Thomas N. Brown, *Irish-American Nationalism, 1870-1890* (Philadelphia: J. B. Lippincott, 1966), chap. 1. For Repeal in Philadelphia specifically, see Peter B. Sheridan, "The Immigrants in Philadelphia, 1827-1860: The Contemporary Published Report" (M.A. thesis, Georgetown University, 1957), chap. 6.

17. *Public Ledger,* June 15, 1843.

18. Ibid., June 23, 28, 1843. John H. Lee, *Origin and Progress of the American Party* (Philadelphia: Elliot and Gihon, 1855), 105-106.

19. *Public Ledger,* June 28, 1843; Sheridan, "The Immigrants in Philadelphia," 197. It was not very long before such questions as the Irish attitude toward American slavery and even the issue of loyalty to O'Connell were dwarfed by a cruel trick of nature. In 1845, Ireland was decimated by the Great Famine, and the two Repeal associations reunited

to fight the menace of starvation in the homeland; agitation for Irish parliamentary autonomy was relegated to a back burner.

20. For the ties between the Democracy and the Irish on the question of black rights see Handlin, *Boston's Immigrants,* 132-133; 190-193.

21. For a detailed discussion of the reasons for Irish adherence to the national Democratic party throughout the Jacksonian period, see Lee Benson, *The Concept of Jacksonian Democracy: New York as a Test Case* (Princeton: Princeton University Press, 1961), chap. 7.

22. *Public Ledger,* October 8, 1843.

23. This interpretation of the significance of Irish rioting is offered in *The Private City: Philadelphia in Three Periods of Its Growth* (Philadelphia: University of Pennsylvania Press, 1968), 141.

24. For the attack on the black temperance marchers, see *The Private City,* 140-141. For the railroad riots, see Michael Feldberg, "Urbanization as a Cause of Violence: Philadelphia as a Test Cast," in *The Peoples of Philadelphia: A History of Ethnic Groups and Lower-Class Life, 1790-1940,* ed. Allen F. Davis and Mark H. Haller (Philadelphia: Temple University Press, 1973), 58-61. For the strike, see David Montgomery, "The Shuttle and the Cross: Weavers and Artisans in the Kensington Riots of 1844," *Journal of Social History* 5 (Summer 1972): 418-419. For the weavers' riot of 1828, see Bruce G. Laurie, "The Working People of Philadelphia, 1827-1852" (Ph.D. diss., University of Pittsburgh, 1971), 17-19.

25. Laurie, "Working People of Philadelphia," 17-19. Details of the Boyne anniversary riot have been abstracted from *A Full and Accurate Report of the Trial . . . on the Thirteenth of October, 1831 . . . in Which the Contending Parties Were Protestants and Roman Catholics* (Philadelphia: Jesper Harding, 1831).

26. Eric J. Hobsbawm, *Labouring Men: Studies in the History of Labour* (Garden City: Doubleday, 1967), 8.

27. *Public Ledger,* August 1-22, 1842. For the loss of dockworking jobs among Philadelphia's blacks, see Theodore Hershberg, "Free Blacks in Antebellum Philadelphia," in *The Peoples of Philadelphia,* 127. For the Pennsylvania Hall affair, see Warner, *Private City,* 132-137.

28. For the unity of Catholic and Irish Protestant handloom weavers, see Montgomery, "Shuttle and Cross," 433-434.

29. For the attempted mill-burning, see *Public Ledger,* September 26, 1842. For the persistence of handloom weaving in Philadelphia, see Sam Bass Warner, Jr., "Innovation and the Industrialization of Philadelphia," in *The Historian and the City,* ed. John Burchard and Oscar Handlin (Cambridge: MIT Press, 1963), 66-68.

30. Montgomery, "Shuttle and Cross," 418.

31. Ibid., 418-419.

3
The Nativists

Until recently, most historians assumed that the efflorescence of nativism in the 1840s represented little more than another outburst of anti-Catholic prejudice historically endemic in the great mass of American Protestants. This narrowly religious interpretation of nativism in the 1840s was first propounded by several Catholic scholars, but given its most widely read and accepted formulation in Ray Allen Billington's *Protestant Crusade: A Study of the Origins of American Nativism.*[1] After reviewing the reams of anti-Catholic literature generated by Protestant writers and lecturers in the 1840s, Billington concluded that the rise of nativism "could never have occurred had not the American people been so steeped in antipapal prejudice." Their hatred of Roman Catholicism "had been well grounded before the first English settlement and was fostered by the events of the entire colonial period." In order to explain why nativism flourished in the 1840s in particular, Billington had to concede that the arrival of Irish and German immigrants, rather than religious hatred in itself, rekindled the old fires of intolerance. The newcomers, he noted, were resented for a number of reasons: their poverty, their high crime rates, their poor sanitary habits, and their tendency to clannishness. Despite this social dimension to the anti-immigrant upsurge, however, Billington's analysis of nativist complaints against the new arrivals convinced him that the social arguments were simply rationalizations for the religious bigotry Protestant native Americans harbored in their hearts.

> Fundamentally, the aliens were opposed because they were Catholics rather than because they were paupers or criminals. The preponderant number of papal adherents among the Irish and Germans coming to the United States made Americans wonder again if their land was safe from Popery and fears were current that this immigration was a means by which Romish power could be transferred to America.[2]

This religious interpretation of 1840s nativism reigned unchallenged until the 1950s, when a newly emergent interest in the social and psychological roots of prejudice stimulated historians to undertake a reevaluation of antebellum bigotry.[3] Billington and the Catholic scholars simply assumed the existence of religious prejudice and used the phenomenon itself to explain the behavior of Protestant nativists. The later studies of the nativist phenomenon have taken the analysis one step further, identifying the social characteristics of the nativists as a means for explaining the sources, rather than the symptoms, of their prejudice. Interestingly enough, the historians, sociologists, and psychologists who undertook these re-visionist studies reached a conclusion similar to Billington's: that nativist complaints had little to do with the intrinsic character or behavior of the immigrants themselves. But these newer explanations of nativism go well beyond the simplistic one offered by the older religious interpretation. According to scholars such as Richard Hofstadter, David Brion Davis, and Seymour Martin Lipset (for convenience they will be referred to here as the pluralist analysts of nativism),[4] the immigrants served as a symbolic scapegoat onto which the nativists displaced their own social and psycho-logical anxieties. The problem, as the pluralists saw it, was not to identify what it was about the immigrants—their Catholicism or their crime rates—that provoked the rise of nativism, but rather what it was that troubled the nativists themselves to cause them to respond so excessively to the presence of the immigrants.

Perhaps the most widely read analysis to come out of the new psycho-social history of American nativism was Richard Hofstadter's influential article describing "The Paranoid Style in American Politics." In Hofstadter's estimation, a "paranoid style" rhetoric (as opposed to a clinically paranoid rhetoric) persistently creeps into American political discourse. Its users, while not necessarily "certifiable lunatics" in most cases, have tended to speak with "heated exaggeration, suspiciousness, and conspiratorial fantasy" to describe the world around them. Like true paranoiacs, persons who employ the paranoid style in their political discourse are subject to delusions of persecution and exalted visions of their own greatness. But a "vital difference" exists between the clinical paranoiac and the political variety: "The clinical paranoiac sees the hostile and conspiratorial world in which he feels himself to be living as directed specifically *against him;* whereas the spokesman of the paranoid style finds it directed against a nation, a culture, a way of life whose fate affects not only himself alone but millions of others."[5]

In general, political paranoiacs attribute these attacks on the nation's political system and cultural institutions to "alien" and "subversive" forces that they see as secretive, morally bankrupt, and not widespread, yet at the same time all-powerful, ever-present, and never flagging. The basic image employed by paranoid-style rhetoricians has tended to remain constant over time: the "alien force" is a powerful, foreign-based secret organization or movement that desires to overthrow the Constitution and enslave the American people under a brutal despotism. Although separated by a century or more in some cases, radical right-wing spokesmen tend to draw on the same imagined conspiracy to account for social problems and protests; Samuel F. B. Morse in the 1830s insisted that the Society of the Illuminati, a supposed liberal republican underground in monarchist Europe, was behind the immigration of Catholics to the United States, while Robert Welch in the 1960s swore that the Illuminati were sponsoring a communist conspiracy to conquer the West. After reviewing more than two centuries of the long and not-so-venerable history of paranoid-style rhetoric in American politics, Hofstadter concluded wearily that "while it comes in waves of differing intensity, it appears to be all but ineradicable."[6]

Historian David Brion Davis has refined Hofstadter's insight into the general phenomenon of paranoid-style politics and applied it specifically to the nativism of the 1830s and 1840s. Davis has discerned a connection between the flux and uncertainty created by the social and economic developments of the Jacksonian years and the emergence of a widespread fear that evil forces had set a conspiracy afoot to undermine conventional American values and institutions. In Davis's words:

> If [the Jacksonian] doctrine of laissez-faire individualism seemed to promise material expansion and prosperity, it also raised disturbing problems. As one early anti-Mormon writer expressed it: What was to prevent liberty and popular sovereignty from sweeping away "the old landmarks of Christendom, and the glorious common law of our fathers?" How was the individual to preserve a sense of continuity with the past, or identify himself with a given cause or tradition? What, indeed, was to insure a common loyalty and fundamental unity among the people?[7]

To restore some of that fundamental unity and provide themselves with new social ties in place of those sundered by the rapid pace of change, three organized nativist[8] movements emerged in the antebellum period:

anti-Masonry in the 1820s, anti-Mormonism in the 1830s and 1840s, and anti-Catholicism in the 1840s and 1850s.

According to Davis, each of the three movements, although distinct from one another, attempted to cope with a common set of uncertainties. The sources of change and anxiety were legion. Above all, social rank and standing changed constantly in Jacksonian America as material success came to have greater importance while birth had increasingly less. The rapid economic expansion and stress on individualism so prevalent in Jacksonian America upset forever the carefully elaborated social hierarchies of the seventeenth and eighteenth centuries. In addition, the political system appeared threatened by the "problem of assuring public consensus and solidarity in the face of uncontrolled, irreverent, and questioning media, and among people who value novelty and experimentation." In an era of geographic expansion and Manifest Destiny, many people "groped for a sense of national identity."[9] These notes of insecurity about the state of American institutions and the validity of the national purpose reflected a characteristic inability on the part of many to cope with the growing complexity of political and economic reality in Jacksonian society. Rather than believe that the nation and its institutions could accommodate several cultures and reconcile its conflicting economic interests and political ideologies, the purveyors of Jacksonian paranoid rhetoric argued that any divergence from homebred traditional culture or political values constituted not only treason to the past but a step in the direction of national suicide. By irrationally rejecting all nonconformity as illegitimate, the Jacksonian nativist, be he anti-Mason, anti-Mormon, or anti-Catholic (some individuals were probably all three), reaffirmed his own attachment to a set of core values that transcended his personal existence. "In a rootless environment shaken by bewildering social change the nativist found unity and meaning by conspiring against imaginary conspiracies."[10]

It was left to a pluralist sociologist, Seymour Martin Lipset, to identify the specific American social groups most susceptible to the appeal of paranoid, conspiratorial explanations for the untidy, pluralistic character of reality. In his *Politics of Unreason*,[11] co-authored with Earl Raab, which summarized over a decade of his thinking about nativism, Lipset hypothesizes that two American groups in particular have tended historically to see the world in conspiratorial terms: displaced elites anxious to reassert their declining prestige and the less-educated working classes who characteristically possess the lowest tolerance for ambiguity and cosmo-

politanism. Applying this analytical construct to the 1840s, Lipset and Raab assert that it was two "displaced strata" of Jacksonian society, the puritan upper classes of New England and the skilled artisans of the seaboard cities, who saw the immigrants as "the main threat to their values or position." While both of these groups had suffered severe displacement caused by the transition to industrial manufacturing and the rise of an *arriviste* industrial capitalist elite, the threat posed by the immigrants was not generally perceived in economic terms, "particularly among those who were intensely religious." (The authors avoid the question of what made certain Jacksonians intensely religious.) These deeply committed Christians saw no threat to their pocketbooks or their control of the political process, but they believed that "their values, their concept of the good life and the good society were being undermined by the open society."[12]

Lipset and Raab added several important sociological touches to the portrait of anti-Catholic nativism Hofstadter and Davis painted. They noted that the anti-immigrant movement of the 1840s was the first conservative movement in American history to operate from a mass urban base. (Both the anti-Masons and the anti-Mormons operated primarily in rural districts.) Lipset and Raab also pointed out that the nativist movement of the forties provided a channel through which native-born, working-class Democrats could pass into the Whig, then Know-Nothing, and finally the Republican parties, all three of which the authors characterize as the party of elite economic interests. These conservative, business-oriented parties used extremist nativist rhetoric to distract the native-born artisans from their preoccupation with issues of economic self-interest and thereby divided the working classes along ethnic lines. A second elite, the evangelical clergymen and moral reformers who attached themselves to the conservative political parties or created parallel "reform" movements such as the temperance and Sabbatarian crusades, tried to exploit the nativism of the working classes as a vehicle to carry themselves back into a position of social and moral dominance. This hoped-for return to prominence would have halted the status decline of the Protestant clergy in the Jacksonian era brought about by the democratization of religion among the fundamentalist sects and the growing irreligiosity among the population as a whole.[13]

While they spent some time analyzing the changing roles and status of nativist elites, in reality Lipset and Raab were far more interested in demonstrating the historical propensity of the American working class

to participate in nativist movements. This preoccupation grows out of the authors' disgust with the excesses of McCarthyism in the 1950s, which they see as a mass movement built on the shoulders of less-educated Catholic working people in the industrial centers of the Midwest and Southwest. Admittedly presentist in their historical concerns, Lipset and Raab have projected their analysis of nativism in the 1950s onto the events of the 1840s, perceiving in that earlier movement the presence of a working-class "authoritarian personality" that was cynically manipulated by displaced elites to forestall the emergence of a pluralist American culture and an increasingly modernized, industrialized society.[14]

Of late, revisionist historians more sympathetic to the problems and aspirations of America's lower classes have challenged the pluralist view of nativism as a pathological recrudescence whose symptoms appear primarily among the masses. The antidemocratic bias that lurks beneath the surface of Lipset's and Hofstadter's works has been brilliantly exposed by Michael P. Rogin, who, in his analysis of the pluralist reaction to McCarthyism, has established that the 1950s movement was a conservative, middle-class, small-business, ethnic-German phenomenon rather than a populistic, mass-base, working-class urban revolt. In another vein, influential historian John Higham has criticized the purely psychological "status anxiety" approach to nativism because it fails to account for the social and economic uses to which nativism has been put. Higham argues that historically ethnic discrimination was used less to relieve psychic discomfort than to define a hierarchy among ethnic groups in the race for wealth and the social rewards it brings. Nativism, in other words, has been a convenient justification for the oppression and exploitation of unfortunate immigrant, ethnic, and religious minorities. Finally, two historians of Jacksonian Philadelphia's working people, David Montgomery and Bruce Laurie, have offered an original and persuasive interpretation of nativism in the 1840s, which, while it does not deny the disproportionate presence of skilled artisans in the movement, tries to understand the motives of those who joined in attacking the immigrants by examining their relationship to the severe dislocations imposed by technological change and a depression on Philadelphia's craft economy. While not condoning the excesses of the nativist movement and in fact bemoaning its power to destroy the class-conscious labor movement in Jacksonian Philadelphia, Montgomery and Laurie have attempted to explain rather than simply condemn working-class complicity in the anti-immigrant crusade.[15]

Montgomery and Laurie see the nativism of the 1840s as merely one of the native skilled artisan's responses to his own victimization. Hand craftsmen were the group most displaced by the technological innovations of the 1820s and 1830s, which introduced mass production and inexpensive machine-made manufactures to American industry. The artisans were also severely stung by the depression that began in 1837 and lasted in Philadelphia well into the mid-1840s. Before the depression, Philadelphia's working people had resisted the inroads made elsewhere by power-driven machinery and shoddy production methods by retaining their network of strong craft unions and by organizing a highly effective citywide General Trades' Union (GTU). In the years of its greatest power, the GTU, a central council of the city's craft unions, financed and organized several hundred successful strikes for higher wages, shorter hours, job protection, and the maintenance of quality standards. Even more significantly, the GTU embraced workers from every skill level and every ethnic background (except the blacks) in Philadelphia. The demand for labor in the affluent 1830s coupled with the workingmen's hostility to any industrial arrangements not of their own choosing—be that excessive hours or excessive mechanization—welded various elements of the Philadelphia working classes into a single, self-conscious working class. This unity developed despite the ethnic and religious differences between native and immigrant workmen, and despite the traditional disdain that Philadelphia's "superior" artisans felt for lesser-skilled male and female workers. In Laurie's words, "The Union's most outstanding quality was class solidarity," and nativism had no place in such an organization.[16]

The remarkable Philadelphia working-class unity of the early 1830s was most clearly demonstrated by the 1835 general strike for the ten-hour day. The refusal of Irish day laborers to unload boats on the Schuylkill river wharves precipitated a general uprising of the city's working people against the excessive number of hours they were compelled to toil. When the unorganized, unskilled immigrant Irish "stood out" for shorter hours at equal wages, the highly skilled unionized native craftsmen of the city rallied to their support, much to the surprise of experienced observers of the Philadelphia labor scene. The GTU contributed money to the strikers' support, organized rallies and marches to demonstrate solidarity, and eventually declared a general strike in sympathy with the dockworkers' demands. Even the cordwainers, who a decade later were to prove themselves implacable foes of the Irish, declared on June 3, 1835, "We are all

day laborers," and vowed to work no more than ten hours per day. Reinforced by sympathetic allies in the middle class, particularly shopkeepers
and politicians, the dockworkers won their point by the end of June.
Soon afterwards, the city councils announced that all municipal employees
would also work no more than a ten-hour day. By the fall, ten hours comprised the standard work day for a majority of Philadelphia's working
people. Guided by the solidary leadership of the General Trades' Union,
the strikers succeeded, Laurie concluded, because "occupational divisions
and ethnic prejudice melted."[17]

With the onset of a depression in the late 1830s, however, high wages
and job security evaporated for Philadelphia's skilled artisans. The depression meant fewer jobs and more hands to fill them. Wages soon
dropped, yet many workers, both native-born and immigrant, gladly accepted them. Bereft of funds, the union collapsed. Workingmen found
themselves with little if any ability to protect their wages, the ten-hour
day, or any other conditions of their labor. Economically disabled, searching for a means to protect their wages and their jobs, hoping to stem the
influx of yet more hands into an overcrowded labor market, skilled, native-
born craftsmen turned to both evangelical Protestant religion and anti-
immigrant politics to make their stand against personal oblivion. In
Montgomery's words:

> It was precisely by making strikes futile, destroying the Trades' Union
> beyond even hope of resurrection, and stimulating [a] new emphasis
> on self-improvement that the depression opened the way for the rise
> of nativism among the artisans. By magnifying the importance to
> artisans of the temperance and public education movements, these
> developments set their aspirations on a collision course with those of
> the Catholic immigrants.[18]

Temperance in particular, with its stress on self-repression as a means
of economic and moral uplift, promised to raise the native artisan above
the unskilled, hard-drinking, improvident, and therefore impoverished
immigrant. Once his reputation was established as a sober, reliable em-
ployee, the native craftsman hoped to guarantee his place in the produc-
tive system. Acceptance of the ethic of self-denial might even demonstrate
the readiness of the native American worker to enter the middle class. As
Joseph Gusfield argues in his impressive study, *Symbolic Crusade,* during
the 1840s

abstinence was becoming a symbol of middle-class membership and a necessity for ambitious and aspiring young men. It was one of the ways society could distinguish the industrious from the ne'er-do-well; the steady worker from the drifter; the good credit risk from the bad gamble; the native American from the immigrant.[19]

According to Montgomery, the native artisan embraced anti-immigrant politics for much the same reason that he embraced evangelical religion and temperance: each promised in its way, to some degree at least, to restore to the artisan some measure of personal control over his economic destiny. The American Republican party built its platform around two issues, restriction of the immigrants' political rights, and Protestant control of the public schools. The first was intended, in the minds of working people at least, to discourage the continuous flow of unskilled hands from abroad; the latter appealed to the skilled craftsmen because they had traditionally viewed the public schools as a means of upward mobility by which their children could rise out of the working classes. As Montgomery notes, an "artisans' convention of 1839 demanded a 'levelling system of education' in the belief that 'intelligence is a passport to everywhere.'"[20] If the schools showed preference to Protestant children either in policy or practice, then the sons of native craftsmen would have a competitive advantage over their Catholic rivals. Throughout the depression era, the city's skilled craftsmen resisted their economic displacement and exploitation by whatever means were available, and nativist politics was just one of the methods of resistance. In the view of Robert Ernst, an early student of "economic nativism": "To one who earned poor wages or lost his job, whatever the reason, the foreigner became a plausible scapegoat. The worker's natural desire for self-preservation nourished the nativist movement . . . during the forties."[21]

If the goal of economic nativism was resistance to displacement and exploitation by the emerging industrial capitalist class, then the methods the movement chose must be considered inappropriate to the ends. Ironically, by dividing the working classes of Philadelphia along cultural and ethnic lines, native craftsmen who had supported the General Trades' Union in the 1830s were now systematically excluding the immigrants from membership in the surviving craft associations, thus leaving the newcomers more than ever without leaders to fight against the subsistence wage levels proffered by the owners of factories and sweatshops. A majority of the employees in the new spinning and weaving mills of suburban

Manayunk and Kellyville, for example, were immigrants, and almost half of these were women and children. By refusing to accept foreign workers or their families into their unions or even to organize them separately, the Protestant journeymen who were fighting against mechanization delivered to their capitalist enemies a welcome supply of cheap, unskilled labor in the form of the immigrants. A second irony emerges from the fact that, while the native working class embraced evangelical values to differentiate itself from the unacculturated immigrant Irish, these values helped to accommodate the artisans to the very same patterns of behavior required by the hated industrial system. Temperance, Sabbatarianism, obedience to authority, and the suppression of "lewd and tumultuous conduct" that the evangelical churches taught to their working-class following were attitudes "urgently needed by the new industrialists," according to Montgomery, "for it promised them a disciplined labor force, pacing its toil and its very life cycle to the requirements of the machine and the clock, respectful of property and orderly in its demeanor."[22]

My own examination of the nativist movement in Philadelphia tends to confirm many of the insights Montgomery and Laurie offered, but not to the exclusion of those that Lipset, Hofstadter, or Davis suggested. It is not that the truth simply lies half-way between their respective sets of views, for what separates the pluralist scholars from the left-oriented historians is not the facts they have gathered but their sympathies (or lack of sympathy) for the Jacksonian working classes. To cite but one example, Lipset and Raab accused the nativists of the 1840s of unremitting hostility to industrialization, which the authors themselves perceive as the basic economic precondition for the smooth absorption of ethnic minorities into the middle class. In their view, the nativists were at bottom psychological Luddites, reactionary obstructionists who refused to accept modernization since it led to a cosmopolitan pluralist society. Montgomery and Laurie, on the contrary, see the working-class nativism of the 1840s as part of a wider effort by Philadelphia's artisans to guarantee themselves a fairer share of the fruits of the new industrial system by protecting themselves against the importation of cheap foreign labor.[23] The differences in interpretation here stem primarily from conflicting ideological preconceptions rather than contradictory data.

Some of the pluralist assumptions can be tested through quantitative research, and one at least does not stand up in light of the research for this study. It does not seem true, as Lipset and Raab argue, that 1840s

nativism was a marriage of convenience between an elite leadership and a working-class rank and file.[24] The movement was composed of an alliance, but not one between an elite and a mass. Rather, there was a pronounced distinction between the well-organized American Republican political party, made up of what can best be called a petit bourgeois leadership element, and an unorganized nativist rank and file, mostly working class, which followed the party's lead in politics and voted for its candidates but was never subject to its discipline. This latter group, known only from police reports and newspaper accounts, appears to have been composed disproportionately of boys and young men, many of whom were apprentices, much the same human material that filled the ranks of the city's violent volunteer fire companies and street gangs. This distinction between the unprestigious but essentially "respectable" members of the American Republican party on the one hand and the more turbulent and youthful working-class nativist rank and file on the other weakened the appeal of the movement among the upper-middle and upper classes. While trying to battle what they perceived as a vast and amorphous conspiracy headed by alien Catholic forces, American Republican leaders also had to cope with the rowdy and destructive actions of their own undisciplined following.

The leading members of the Philadelphia American Republican party are most easily identified by their occupations. Of the 464 most active American Republicans for whom occupations could be established, the Philadelphia *City Directory for 1844* listed fully 15 percent as merchants, grocers, shopkeepers, or with the term "drygoods" after their names. Of these sixty-nine individuals, forty-one were classified as "merchants," a title that carried more prestige than "shopkeeper," but evidence indicates that none of these "merchants" conducted major enterprises in the grand tradition of Robert Morris, Thomas P. Cope, or the other well-known Philadelphia merchant princes.[25] However appropriate their title, these neighborhood businessmen who guided the American Republican party, much like the tavernkeepers active in party affairs (the survey uncovered twelve of the latter in the upper reaches of the party hierarchy), were admirably placed for exercising leadership on a neighborhood level. Their almost daily contact with residents, the modicum of prestige that proprietorship offered them in working-class neighborhoods, and their extension of credit to many of their customers afforded them influence and made their premises convenient political headquarters.

Among the professional men in the party hierarchy, lawyers and doctors were the most frequently represented. Attorneys accounted for nineteen, or 4 percent, of the most active American Republicans, while eleven physicians entered the party's higher circles. With few exceptions, American Republican attorneys and doctors were marginal members of these two prestigious professions. Few of the lawyers belonged to the distinguished Philadelphia Bar Association, the nation's most honored legal fraternity at that time. The best-known lawyers among the nativists were Peter A. Browne, who had served as mayor of Philadelphia in the 1830s; David Paul Brown, a respected Whig politician and public prosecutor; and A. DeKalb Tarr, who combined his practice with evangelical Protestant activism and who had been arrested for fighting in the Gideonite (Catholic versus Orange Irish) riot of 1831. More typical of American Republican-ism's legal contingent, however, was Lewis C. Levin, a converted Jew who gave up the law to edit a temperance newspaper, thump a tub on the temperance lecture circuit, and finally become a full-time politician and member of Congress. Another attorney of influence in the party but clouded reputation at large was Charles J. Jack, an elderly gentleman who depended more on contacts in the Pennsylvania militia than on a reputation for legal acumen for his clientele. During the trials that followed the nativist riots of 1844, Jack was himself charged with trying to influence a jury sitting in judgment on the rioters, hardly a judicious role for a practitioner of the law.[26]

Like the lawyers, the physicians active in nativist politics were a motley lot. Among members of the medical fraternity, the most deeply involved was Dr. Joseph B. Strafford, who spoke at party rallies and even ran for minor public office on the American Republican ticket while still maintaining a respected practice. The best-known medical man in the party, however, was Dr. David Jayne, whose income stemmed from the sale of a popular patent remedy. It is difficult to decide whether Jayne should be listed as a physician or entrepreneur.

Another title that usually conferred prestige in Jacksonian Philadelphia was "manufacturer," and the *City Directory* listed some American Republican leaders in this category. But these, too, were a very mixed group, none of whom possessed superior wealth (according to surviving tax lists) or seemed to have had high status. The *Directory* turned up three "ship manufacturers" whose names graced the American Republican movement, but none of them left any record in the tax ledgers of owning a

shipyard. The lone "carpet manufacturer" owned a small weaving shop in Kensington. Similarly, there were three "dockbuilders" in the movement; one, Thomas Grover, was a man of some wealth. His real estate was valued at an impressive $75,000. He financed the nativist *Daily Sun* under the editorship of Lewis Levin despite its constant losses, and held several public offices as a Democrat in the 1830s and 1840s. Eventually, Grover became the boss of Southwark's American Republican machine. The two other dockbuilders, however, did not come near equalling Grover's wealth or stature, and they may well have been carpenters who specialized in dock work.

Significantly, none of the city's important industrialists, such as locomotive magnate Matthias Baldwin, iron foundry owner Samuel V. Merrick, or cotton mill proprietor Joseph Ripka associated in any way with organized political nativism. As an essentially backward-looking movement that glorified the simpler days of an earlier, more homogeneous republic, Philadelphia American Republicanism was hardly calculated to appeal to the progressive instincts of the new class of industrialists. Baldwin, Merrick, and Ripka each staffed their mills and shops to varying degrees with immigrants, and while they encouraged temperance and self-discipline among their workers as a means to develop their reliability and productivity, the industrialists apparently were not willing to use moral or cultural issues as a political stick with which to beat their workers. While they supported some of the same reforms as the American Republicans, particularly temperance, Sabbatarianism, and public schooling, it was for the much subtler goal of indoctrinating the foreigners with the so-called Protestant ethic rather than for the personal satisfaction to be gained from proclaiming the superiority of native American life styles. The industrialists, unlike the nativists, wished to "improve" the immigrants, not discourage them.[27]

At the upper reaches of the party hierarchy, newspaper editors and publishers were highly influential. Lewis Levin, editor of the *Daily Sun,* served three terms as an American Republican congressman from Southwark. Philip S. White, a lawyer and temperance lecturer, supplemented his income by publishing a nativist weekly. Thompson Westcott, lawyer, publisher, and historian, similarly tried his hand at a weekly nativist magazine. Yet it appears that none of the publishers associated with the party was the proprietor of a major press. Some doubled as their own editors. Like Ben Franklin in an earlier day, an individual with the capital

for a printing press could set himself up as an "editor and publisher." A survey of American Republican activists identified eleven publishers and nine editors, some of whom ran bookshops. Since there were never more than five nativist newspapers in Philadelphia and no more than three after 1845, it seems safe to conclude that the bulk of the nativist "editors and publishers" were probably printers who gained a certain degree of satisfaction from adopting a glorified title.[28]

Although there were some professional men in its ranks, the American Republican party did not comprise anything resembling the elite Lipset characterized. Reflecting on his own occupational survey of American Republicans, David Montgomery concluded that the party was "decidedly not upper class in leadership or following."[29] Its members came from the second rank socially and economically, and it seems quite possible that many members who belonged to the middle class had entered it from the artisan ranks, or from families whose head had been an artisan. What, then, if not a cynical class interest (as Lipset and Raab imply) motivated these lesser individuals to adopt nativist political beliefs and devote their time to organizing and propagandizing for the party? Was it, as the pluralists suggest, a sense of status displacement or a threat they perceived to their tenuous social rank that led middle-class nativists to see the Irish immigrants as mortal enemies of the republic? Were these men unable to come to grips with the growing cosmopolitanization, industrialization, and depersonalization of antebellum America? Did they seek to forget their own sense of inescapable decline by fighting against any symptom of change and disruption in the society around them and focus on the Irish as a convenient symbol of the deterioration they abhorred? Or were the nativists men on the make, petit bourgeois in habits and aspirations, who saw in their own attacks on the Irish a reflection of a self-perceived superiority inbred in native-born Americans? Were some, like Thomas Grover, simply reacting against the increased influence of the Irish in the Philadelphia Democratic party after the Democracy had for so many years been under the domination of native American workingmen? It was, after all, native Democrats such as Grover, Lemuel Paynter, and Lewis Levin who led the "Incorruptible" revolt against the regular Democratic candidacy of Hugh Clark in 1842. Yet, while these native leaders were locked in a political power struggle with the Irish for control of their party, there is no evidence that the upper ranks of the American Republican hierarchy was brimming with displaced or threatened

Democratic regulars. Impressionistic but consistent evidence points to the conclusion that most of the American Republican leadership was comprised of "new" men.[30] Does the presence of these political initiates indicate a sudden, desperate search for a means of retaliation against alien forces driving native Americans down to the bottom of the middle class or even back into the working-class ranks, or does it indicate, as Joseph Gusfield suggests, that nativist politics in the 1840s represented the "efforts of urban, native Americans to *consolidate* their middle-class respectability?"[31] And what is one to make of the status anxiety of the working-class members of the American Republican movement who proudly proclaimed their social origins and wished only to protect their position for the future? Conclusive data with which to answer these questions simply do not exist. There is as yet no evidence to indicate that either the middle- or working-class nativists who populated the American Republican hierarchy were experiencing a greater social or economic decline (or rise) than the substantial number of native-born Protestant Philadelphians who stayed loyal to the Whig and Democratic parties. Until such a comparative study is completed (if one is possible), generalizations about status change and status anxiety must remain in the realm of suggestive speculation.

The ambiguity surrounding the status and the consciousness of the petit bourgeois shopkeepers and professionals in the upper ranks of American Republicanism equally shrouds our knowledge of the party's working-class leaders. Approximately 55 percent of the activists in the American Republican organization were craftsmen, well out of proportion to the 20 percent or so of the Philadelphia population whose occupations were classified as artisan. Like their fellow-nativists from the middle class, at least some of these artisans probably blended their working-class backgrounds with petit bourgeois aspirations and self-images. The sampling technique by which American Republican craftsmen have been identified for this survey almost guarantees that they were master craftsmen who ran their own shops with one or more journeymen and apprentices in their employ.[32] As working proprietors with a touch of middle-class entrepreneurial status, these master employers were particularly susceptible to the Jacksonian siren song of upward mobility through capital accumulation. As Stuart Blumin has suggested, however, by the 1840s movement upward and out of Philadelphia's working class through the mechanism of artisan proprietorship was growing increasingly difficult. The narrowing of opportunity for the traditionally independent master craftsman might well

have been a cause for resentment that could draw frustrated native artisans into a scapegoating, anti-immigrant movement. To the degree that status decline was involved in the movement of master craftsmen to the ranks of American Republicanism—and here the status anxiety hypothesis seems to stand on more solid ground—it can best be understood through an examination of the impact of what George Rogers Taylor calls the "transportation revolution" of 1815-1860 on the skilled mechanic.[33]

Taylor used the term "revolution" to describe the impact of the network of canals, turnpikes, and railroads constructed between the War of 1812 and the Civil War. These internal improvements, as they were known, created a wider market than ever before for manufactured goods such as shoes, clothing, tools, and housewares. By the late 1860s, the demand for manufactures would be met for the most part by factories with their large labor forces and power-driven machinery. In the 1830s and 1840s, however, before the factory system came to dominate the national economy, the bulk of manufacturing was still done in smaller workshops and primitive mills, much of it by handcraftsmen. Yet, while the means of production had not yet changed a great deal to meet the demands of the transportation revolution, the nature of the market for manufactured goods had been altered radically. No longer were high quality handmade goods at a premium. Since many of the new consumers lived in the countryside or west of the Appalachians, far from the centers of production or homes of skilled workmen, they were more interested in easily replaced and inexpensive goods rather than those that were durable and repairable. The skilled shoemaker or tailor found that the demand for his highest art was slackening.

Compounding this declining demand for quality goods was the discovery by local employing craftsmen in urban manufacturing centers such as Philadelphia that they did not command direct access to the expanding nationwide marketing network. In the newly accessible rural and western markets, goods needed to be sold on consignment or long-term credit, something that took capital only rarely commanded by the typical local master employer. Thus a new type of entrepreneur, the "merchant capitalist," emerged to supply this deficiency. Here was a merchant who cultivated relationships with store owners and custom peddlers throughout the West and South who could afford to ship on credit and wait several months for payment. He obtained his supply of inexpensive, or "shoddy," goods from the master craftsmen's workshops in eastern manu-

facturing centers. Technically no more than a middleman between the craftsmen of the East and the merchants of the rural South and West, the merchant capitalist entrepreneur functioned in effect as the employer of the master employers whose shops produced most of the nation's manufactures in the 1830s and 1840s.[34]

The merchant capitalist controlled the masters through the use of mass-production contracts. Merchant and master agreed, for example, that a certain number of shoes or shirts or skillets or washboards would be delivered on a certain date for a fixed price. The master, in turn, hired journeymen and apprentices to produce the number of items called for in the contract. Since the price paid for the total lot was fixed in advance by mutual agreement and the cost of raw materials was governed by market forces of supply and demand beyond the control of the master employer, the only way he could keep his production costs within his profit margin was through adjusting the wages he paid his workers. He accomplished this in one or more of several ways: a cut in the piece rate which "sweated" his journeymen by forcing them to work longer hours or at a faster pace in order to take home the same pay; an increase in the number of youthful apprentices hired in place of skilled, more highly paid journeymen; or an increase in the number of unskilled immigrant men, women, and children who, like the native-born apprentices, worked for less pay while producing a lower quality product. Wherever master employers adopted any of these methods to reduce expenses they placed themselves in opposition to the interests of their journeymen. Many Philadelphians poignantly recalled the "old days," when there purportedly existed a sense of harmony, or at least mutual self-interest, in the city's tradition-bound crafts. Now the masters and "jours" were clearly on opposite sides of the fence.[35]

The transportation revolution and the rise of merchant capitalism, then, signaled a crisis for both the master craftsman and the superior journeyman mechanic. Both were losing control over the conditions of their labor while watching their own relationship deteriorate. As masters turned away from employing skilled journeymen and offered their places to apprentices and immigrants, the future of the skilled craftsmen grew bleaker. Some employers began the practice of hiring a new crew of learners every few weeks, turning out onto the labor market several sets of semiskilled young workmen and immigrant families every year to compete with more established hands. By no coincidence, artisans from

occupations most disrupted by the rise of merchant capitalism were disproportionately represented in the American Republican ranks. Thirty-seven carpenters, twenty-nine shoemakers, and thirteen printers and an equal number of tailors were counted among the leaders of the party. The first three crafts in particular long stood out as preserves for militant and proud native-born mechanics with historic traditions of self-respect and solidarity, many of whose members demanded the respect paid to middle-class merchants and professionals.[36] Now these men were being squeezed by the pressures of a shoddy-goods market and the influx of unskilled foreign and female hands into their occupations. For the master craftsman, the pressure was particularly intense. Caught between the contractual demands of the merchant capitalist and his traditional sympathy for his "jours," the master might well have felt that his own rise out of the ranks of the journeymen was more a disappointing anticlimax than the happy culmination of a lifetime of upward struggle. Here then might be one source of the belief, criticized as "paranoid" by the pluralist historians, that the world as the mechanics had known it was being "subverted" by sinister "alien" forces.

If any generalization about the social origins of Philadelphia's organized political nativists can be formulated with some assurance, it may at most claim that the American Republican leadership probably represented an alliance between second-rank professionals and shopkeepers of diverse and ambiguous social standing and master employers and their journeymen groping for a means to restore their sense of self-determination through a mutual campaign against a common enemy. It would be an oversimplification, however, to attribute the rise of political nativism exclusively to class or economic conflict.[37] The intense anti-Catholic rhetoric of nativist leaders, the fervor roused by the temperance and Sabbatarian movements, and the violence spawned by the school Bible issue cannot be dismissed as windowdressing for more latent economic discontents. A distinctive set of nativist cultural values, reflected in blatant Protestant dogmatism, superpatriotic Americanism, an insistence on abstemiousness and good order, and an exaggerated reverence for the power of public education to effect moral improvements, marked the members of the American Republican movement. While some of these values, most notably the nativist belief in temperance, bore a relationship to the economic competition between native working people and the immigrants, they had a vitality and life of their own independent of their economic component.

The variety of anti-immigrant appeals aimed at Philadelphia's nativists and potential nativists skillfully blended blatantly scurrilous anti-Catholic rant with large doses of reasonable-sounding political and economic rhetoric. (Reasonable, that is, once a set of nativist assumptions, discussed below, was accepted.) Cultural, political, and economic nativism in Philadelphia cannot be neatly divided into separate categories. The American Republicans borrowed freely at times from the arsenal of the city's cultural crusaders and evangelical Protestant Bible thumpers, especially when they called on the city's board of school directors to require Catholic children to read the Protestant version of the Bible in the public schools. Similarly, religious, Sabbatarian, and temperance leaders who declared cultural or theological war on the American Catholic Church and its followers did not hesitate to enlist the support of nativist politicans in their efforts to close taverns on Sundays or enforce liquor licensing restrictions. Despite this cooperation, however, there did apparently exist a line dividing the American Republican party from such cultural nativist organizations as the Sabbatarian associations, the Bible societies, and the temperance clubs. For the most part, the American Republicans limited themselves to the question of immigrant political rights. The only major exception to this generalization was the party's involvement in the school Bible issue, but this did not become a serious American Republican preoccupation until winter 1844, well after the movement was under way. Nativism in Philadelphia, because it blended politics, economics, religion, and culture, was not a monolithic movement in either its social composition, its beliefs, or its practices.

The American Republicans left most of the agitation against the Catholic Church and the lax enforcement of the city's blue laws to a hard core cadre of evangelical Protestant clergymen who remained outside the party organization. These reverend gentlemen belonged instead to the American Protestant Association (APA),[38] a body of evangelical ministers whose propaganda and publishing activities are discussed in Chapter 4. Not that the secular American Republican press was devoid of attacks on the Roman Catholic clergy, for indeed it was not, but most often political nativists attacked Catholic priests for their politics and not their theology. The outright slanders heaped on Catholic religious beliefs spewed forth mostly from the pulpits and religious presses of the city rather than from its political soapboxes. The survey of American Republican activists referred to earlier uncovered only three Protestant ministers who were openly

enrolled in the ranks of the party: John H. Chambers, John H. Gihon, and John Perry. While other well-known Protestant divines and founders of the American Protestant Association of Philadelphia occasionally shared a podium with nativist politicians, especially at the height of the school Bible campaign, these clergymen never signed their names to American Republican documents. The party tried at all times to project a purely nonsectarian, secular image.

To avoid the label of a proscriptive religious party, the American Republicans claimed simply to stand for "good government." In their own view, they opposed neither Catholics, immigrants, priests nor popes *as such.* Rather, the nativist press attacked each of these groups for their respective roles in corrupting the republican political institutions of the United States. In their founding statement of principles, the American Republicans claimed that "without any distinction as to political creed or religious faith . . . we invite the stranger, worn down by oppression at home, to come here and share with us the blessings of our native land— here find the asylum for his distress and partake of the plenty a kind providence has given us." They attached one proviso to this invitation: the new arrivals had to leave behind any loyalties to their old homelands and old values. According to the nativists, the immigrants refused to abandon their ancient habit of obedience to aristocratic and autocratic forms of government. Immigrants represented a potential fifth column for monarchy and popery. Quite possibly, Americans faced the cruel irony of seeing their republican institutions undermined by the nation's liberal naturalization laws. As the party's founders put it:

> The day must come, and, we fear, is not too far distant, when most of our offices will be held by foreigners—men who have no sympathy with the spirit of our institutions, who have never sacrificed aught to procure the blessings they enjoy, and instead of governing ourselves, we shall be governed by men, many of whom, but a few short years previously, scarcely knew of our existence.[39]

The problem, then, as American Republicans saw it, could be resolved only through government by the native-born or, as they put it, the "purity of the ballot box." Since they assumed that the United States was a democracy in which all power rested with the people, the American Republicans considered that all institutions touching on the life of the

populace were ultimately subject to political control. Management of the schools, for instance, or the process of tavern licensing, or the leadership of political parties, could be wrested from the hands of corrupt elites, alien conspirators, or venal politicians simply by the native majority's exercise of its inherent right to make laws for the general good. Logically, such an act of self-determination seemed simple enough, but the democratic system, while the most ingenious ever devised by man, was also the most vulnerable to subversion by the forces of tyranny. The price of the people's liberty was eternal vigilance. Unless it jealously guarded its rights, the majority would find elections stolen by well-organized, willful, strategically placed minorities. Given the proper information and a full range of choices, the people (read "native-born majority") would invariably choose the moral path in politics. But should the intelligence or instinctive good judgment of the people be thwarted through the machinations of "alien" influence or should voters other than inherently virtuous native-born Americans be given a voice in the decision-making process, the system could quickly be destroyed.

From such a view derived the *political* opposition of the American Republican party to priests and rum-sellers in politics, heavy drinkers (read "Irishmen") at the polls, aliens in the inner councils of the major political parties or holding elective office. Given the need to make informed, responsible judgments in the never-ending process of self-government, citizens who were held in thrall by rum-selling politicians or told how to vote by "priestly dictation" could not be allowed to participate in the electoral process. A clear head and free will were the basic elements of self-determination and moral accountability.

Equally necessary for participation in the political process, the American Republicans claimed, was experience in the exercise of the rights of citizenship. The immigrants often came from nations in which politics was limited to the aristocracy or wealthy elites. Yet these uneducated foreigners were allowed naturalization and the right to vote in American elections after a mere five years. Native-born citizens, by contrast, had to wait twenty-one years before they were considered experienced enough in the ways of the political system to be permitted the right of franchise. Because this obvious injustice was permitted to continue, "tens and tens of thousands who were neither born nor reared with us . . . who know nothing of the principles of our government, of its history, its requirements, or even the questions at issue . . . deposit their votes as if they would throw stones in the river."[40]

Although opposed to universal suffrage for immigrants, the nativists, contrary to what the pluralist historians argue, were neither elitist nor thoroughly antidemocratic. They opposed full political privileges for foreigners but proclaimed a great faith in the democratic political *process,* which they believed was based on a strict majoritarian principle. Furthermore, the American Republicans possessed a high degree of faith in the virtue and intelligence of their fellow-citizens of native birth. They even included in this category the children of the immigrants themselves, and nothing in their rhetoric ever contemplated disfranchising those immigrants already naturalized. Political ability was assumed to be a transmittable national trait available to all who were raised as Americans.

Like many of their contemporaries, party spokesmen were struggling toward a definition of American nationality. They experimented with the notion that birth and nurture in American society endowed the American race with its own unique national character. Lewis Levin, for example, argued that the American people had by themselves "advanced the cause of human civilization ten centuries," while the New York daily *American Republican* argued that our citizens "have all the elements of becoming a greater people, a mightier nation, and a more enduring government than has ever held a place in the annals of time." Philip S. White argued that the nation was already perfect in its defense, agriculture, and manufactures and nearly so in its literature, and therefore needed no further immigration to build its fortunes.[41] While immigrants were not needed in future, however, neither White nor any of his fellow-nativists suggested that those already here be returned, nor that their children were in any way disqualified from becoming fully assimilated.

It was the saving grace of Jacksonian nativism that scientists had not yet "discovered" the theory of natural selection and hereditary superiority employed with such devastating effect by later nativist and totalitarian movements. Advocating immigrant disfranchisement seems far more benign than advocating eugenics. The American Republican argument for the uniqueness of the American people derived from a purely environmental theory: the republican institutions in which they were nurtured had elevated their political and moral capacities beyond those of the common people of Europe. Thus, if the nation should someday fail to achieve its full potential for moral and political leadership in the world, it would happen because those same republican institutions were inadequately safeguarded from alien subversion. America's schools, her churches,

and her ballot boxes—but not her bloodlines—had to be kept pure of foreign taint. When American Republican party spokesmen attacked real or imagined political interference by foreign despots or the pope, their focus was on the antirepublican character of their enemies' political views or on the low level (as the nativists understood it) of their personal morality and not their race or nationality.

In fairness to the American Republicans, their rhetorical excesses in praise of the nation's political institutions sounded not so very different from (although at times it seemed a good deal more voluble) the patriotic blather indulged in by the Whigs and the Democrats. In an insightful article, historian Klaus Hansen has challenged the notion that nativism in antebellum America was limited to fringe parties or certain sections of the country. Instead, he points out that the idea was transplanted by the first English Protestant settlers of the seventeenth century and incorporated into the classic American nationalism of the eighteenth. By the Jacksonian era, white Protestant American chauvinism had become an integral part of the political and cultural rhetoric of all geographic sections and among all political elements.[42] In one respect, however, in their fixation on a foreign *conspiracy* to overthrow America's political institutions, the nativists of the 1840s went well beyond the ardent patriotism of their Whig or Democratic contemporaries.

The nativist conspiracy theory of the 1840s revolved primarily around the pope, who supposedly was coordinating a wicked alliance of the crowned heads of Europe to destroy American freedom. Nativists believed that the autocrats of the Old World were plotting to capture the New as a place of refuge against the unavoidable day when their thrones would be overturned by liberal forces in Europe. Nativists fantasized that the impoverished and criminal immigrants arriving from Catholic Europe were one day to rise on the pope's signal and take over the American continent. Even more disconcerting, tyranny and popery might come to rule the United States without a shot ever being fired if contemporary demographic trends were simply to continue. As long as the Constitution granted foreigners the right to vote, it was merely a matter of time before Catholic immigrants could elect themselves to positions whereby they could either capture the present machinery of government or vote to alter the form of government itself. Nativists assumed that the Catholic clergy, and especially the "wily" Jesuits, were sent here to convey the wishes of the pope to his subservient lackeys. Should it become necessary,

the priests would lead a bloody alien conquest; if takeover were possible
through a peaceful capture of the regular political parties or the formation
of a Catholic party in politics, priests would be there to direct the immigrant vote. Many nativists feared that the subversion process had already
begun through Catholic efforts to tamper with young Protestant minds
in the public schools, while others predicted the demise of the American
spirit through the liberal distribution of Catholic-supplied rum.

Obviously, fighting such a conspiracy would take a greater effort than
the purely political exertions of the American Republican party. Doubtless many of the party's leaders would have liked to cast their nets beyond
the realm of election reform and into the temperance crusade, as did
Lewis Levin, or into the Sabbatarian movement, as did the Reverend John
Chambers. Yet the reason that official American Republican agitation on
cultural and moral issues remained so circumscribed can probably be
traced to the polyglot nature of the party's following. To hold together
its electoral coalition, the American Republicans had to draft a platform
neutral enough to embrace both temperance-oriented, middle-class professionals and master craftsmen on the one hand and hard-living, volatile,
class-conscious journeymen on the other. The party's position on the issues
of the day had to be anti-Catholic enough, at least by implication, to
maintain a close relationship with the city's evangelical ministers while
not so violently anti-immigrant that Irish and German Protestants became
alienated from the movement. The party had to wed working-class Democrats with middle-class Whigs and even an occasional patrician reformer
who took at face value the party's claim to be, at bottom, no more than a
nonpartisan, good government movement.

As a result, the party evolved a simple, three-plank platform. It
promised:

To extend the period of naturalization—

To elect none but natives to office—

To reject foreign interference in all our institutions, social, religious,
and political.[43]

The three principles have little if any class or economic content; it would
have been difficult to create a single program of native economics that
could please the entire body of diverse American Republican voters. The

one economic measure that might appeal to both middle- and working-class nativists was the protective tariff, but the American Republicans did not make this a central issue in their campaigns until *after* 1844. When they were trying to build their strength in the earlier period of their growth, they focused almost exclusively on the elimination of political corruption and electoral abuses. By avoiding a call for immigrant exclusion, the party hoped to escape the appearance of hostility to immigrant Protestants, even though such a stand might well have been popular with some native workingmen. Similarly, by veiling their attacks on the Catholic hierarchy behind a more vague phrase, "foreign interference," the American Republicans hoped to shun the label of a "proscriptive movement," that is, one intolerant of a minority religion. Party apologists continued their protestations of religious neutrality even after their undisciplined followers had gone directly from an American Republican rally to burn two Irish Catholic churches.

If we take the American Republicans at their word, however, if only for a moment, their three demands do possess a kind of logic and respectability that support their protestations of religious and ethnic neutrality, at least by their own standards. By demanding an extension of the naturalization period, the party could claim to be asking for nothing more than equality between the immigrants and native-born citizens. If the latter had to spend twenty-one years learning the political system and civic values of the United States before they were entrusted with the vote, then why not apply the same standard to those who had to *unlearn* the lessons of their European backgrounds in order to appreciate the American form of government? American Republican party spokesmen denied any intention to disfranchise those immigrants already naturalized. Newcomers arriving in the future, however, would be obliged to serve the same length of apprenticeship as native-born sons before receiving the vote. Other than the franchise, none of the immigrants' civil rights or liberties would be impaired. Voting, as the nativists saw it, was neither a right nor a liberty but a privilege.[44]

So, too, was the holding of an elective or appointive office. If the founding fathers had prohibited foreign-born individuals from becoming president or vice-president of the nation, then by the same logic should not the offices of senator, congressman, judge, or even tax assessor be reserved for native-born Americans as well? All offices in the gift of the people were held in sacred trust. If a foreigner was unfit for one re-

sponsibility, he was unfit for all. Again, no current office-holder was to be deprived of his post, but if the American Republicans were entrusted with power, no immigrant in the future would be allowed to run for or hold public office.[45]

The third demand, the extirpation of foreign influence from American institutions, entered the American Republican litany long before the school Bible issue flared up in winter and spring 1844. More than any other, the demand reflected the conspiratorial mentality of the nativist movement in Philadelphia. Since the late 1830s, vigilant nativists had been detecting wholesale illegal attempts to naturalize boatloads of landing immigrants in order to use their votes at the polls. The American Republicans attributed this abuse to both the Whigs and the Democrats. Nativists repeated unfounded stories to each other about parish priests who had the power to start and stop Irish rioters by means of a pre-arranged signal. Most nativists were thoroughly convinced that Rome wanted to overthrow the Constitution and replace it with a monarchy. Some saw the local parishes as a network through which subversion and armed attacks were to be carried out. Some believed that the pope was stirring Catholic Mexico to war on Texas and the United States. The notion of foreign interference with the American way of life was infinitely adaptable, and it could be used to explain what was wrong with the American economy, the quality of social relations, or the unmanageable nature of electoral politics. The notion of foreign interference came ultimately to rest on a question far more basic than that of Catholic interference in the schools, voting abuses, or even diplomatic policy; this question was rarely explicated, and bore only indirectly on politics. At bottom, nativists were asking themselves whether or not immigrant values, beliefs, social systems, and behavioral patterns should be granted equality, or at least autonomy, with those already prevalent in the United States. They answered themselves with a resounding "No!" Cultural pluralism was unacceptable. The anti-immigrant movement insisted not only that the Catholic clergy keep out of the public schools in particular and politics in general but that they let their flocks become "*Americanized* . . . instead of being kept distinct as a clan."[46] With characteristic optimism about the transforming power of the environment, however, most American Republicans called for the ultimate total absorption of the immigrants, not their expulsion or segregation.

While the sketchily preserved historical record has permitted this speculative excursion into the American Republican mind, the sources are thinner still for exploring the consciousness of the rank-and-file nativists who followed the party's lead at the polls but remained outside its discipline. These obscure men can be known now only through arrest records and newspaper accounts of their riotous behavior. From these sources, two facts become clear: first, of the nativist rioters and demonstrators whose occupations could be established, thirty-seven of fifty-two, or fully 71 percent, were journeymen or apprentices. Second, almost all accounts agree that these turbulent nativists were boys and young men in their twenties. Whether their anti-immigrant animus was motivated primarily by social and economic competition, a religious hatred of Catholicism, an intolerance of pluralism stemming from their inadequate education, or just a love of the competitive rough and tumble that makes so many of the ethnic fire company and gang fights of the 1840s appear in retrospect as little more than a form of recreation, cannot be finally determined. It would be unsafe simply to assume that a rank-and-file nativist uncritically accepted the American Republicans' political solution to the immigrant question, limited as it was for the most part to narrowly defined electoral reforms. Although young, these nativist artisans were heirs to several traditions and ideological preconceptions that rendered them hostile to European immigrants of any religion or class and likely to express their animus in bursts of occasional violence.

Artisans had long played a central role in the life of the city. By the 1830s they had made Philadelphia the nation's leading manufacturing center. The sheer number of skilled hands, rather than the value of invested capital, had given the city this preeminence. There are no reliable statistics telling just how many skilled workers plied their trades in Philadelphia during the Jackson era, but the best estimates place the figure at between 15 and 20 percent of the work force, or as many as twenty thousand men. Most of these artisans worked in small- and medium-sized shops, often without machinery or with only the simplest mechanical devices, producing wares of the highest quality found in the United States. Philadelphia was especially known for producing shoes, cabinets, carriages, textiles, and leather goods. Most journeymen took pride that "the name PHILADELPHIA MECHANIC [had] become synonymous with skill and superiority in workmanship." Skilled urban craftsmen

in Philadelphia and elsewhere "enjoyed the highest income and status of any wage earners and were psychologically the most firmly wedded to the social values and practices of the traditional artisan." Intellectually, "the mechanics proudly preserved an ideological heritage blended of Ben Franklin's maxims and Tom Paine's 'Rights of Man.'" Ethnically, except for significant pockets of German tailors and Irish handloom weavers, most Philadelphia artisans were native-born Americans with family roots from pre-Revolutionary times. Sam Bass Warner, Jr., has characterized these men as "intensely patriotic, white equalitarian, anti-Negro, anti-foreigner, in short, strong followers of the old radical Revolutionary tradition."[47]

The Revolutionary heritage left the city's "labor aristocracy" with more than narrow prejudices; it also provided them with a rewarding sense of pride. The self-esteem of these craftsmen contrasted sharply with the reality of their declining social and economic standing. Still clinging to remembrances of a preindustrial past, each craft thought of itself, in words used by the city's butchers, as "a fraternity of men essential and indispensable to the body politic."[48] Working people still expected a degree of deference, however formalistic, from the rest of the general public. During campaigns candidates for public office competed for the title "workingmen's friend," and on the Fourth of July rhetoricians praised the skilled craftsmen as the city's "backbone" with the same obligatory enthusiasm with which they praised the nation's farmers, few if any of whom lived or voted in Philadelphia. Yet at this very time, thanks to the transportation revolution described above, many Philadelphia journeymen were suffering painfully from a series of wage reductions, a loss of social prestige in the eyes of their employers and the community, a loss of control over entry into their industries, and a loss of control over their individual working conditions. This disjunction between ideology and reality must have been clear to many artisans; in part at least, this gap between proud tradition on the one hand and hardship and decline on the other helped to draw the native workingman into the orbit of organized anti-immigrant politics and spontaneous anti-immigrant violence.

A portion of the Philadelphia artisan's Revolutionary heritage seemed—to him at least—to justify an occasional resort to collective violence. Long after the middle and upper classes had rejected as unworkable the Revolutionary notion of the people's right of resistance to unjust authority (they argued that all authority in a democracy was by definition legitimate),[49]

spokesmen for the skilled mechanics continued to invoke the principles of popular sovereignty and natural justice to explain working-class protests and violent strikes. These Jacksonian heirs to the radical tradition declared themselves in legitimate defiance of public officials when, for example, mayor John Swift convened a posse to protect the property of wealthy employers during the general strike of 1835 or when a posse was ordered to guard the work crews when the Philadelphia and Trenton railroad sought to lay its unwanted tracks in Kensington. In these instances and many others, angry protestors resisted the posse and often as not dispersed it with rocks and clubs. It took only a slight transformation of the same populist logic to apply collective force in situations where the *absence* of government action led to "injustice" or some perceived violation of community norms or majority rights. If, for example, the sheriff and other officials could not protect the city from the subversive actions of the abolitionists, then the white majority simply had no choice but to act in its own defense. Armed with such notions, the crowd burned Pennsylvania Hall. In July 1844, when some Irish leaders armed St. Philip de Neri Roman Catholic Church, nativists in the neighborhood decided to disarm the building on their own when Sheriff Morton McMichael was slow to do so. In sum, the minority had to abide by the standards of the majority even if elected officials were unwilling to recognize the legitimacy or legal force of popular opinion. Ultimate authority was reserved, according to the radical Revolutionary tradition in its Jacksonian working-class form, not to elected authorities but to the people themselves.

Philadelphia's native-born journeymen were also receptive to certain radical social doctrines. In religion, many were deists, and more than a few were outright atheists, especially the leaders of the General Trades' Union of the 1830s.[50] Unfortunately, the exact number of deists and skeptics in the artisan ranks can never be known, but a search of Protestant church membership lists during the Jacksonian decades reveals that middle-class men, and especially women, seem to have outnumbered artisan men and women by a large margin. David Montgomery has suggested that ephemeral storefront churches might have predominated in Jacksonian Philadelphia's working-class neighborhoods,[51] but there is no way to know exactly what doctrines were being taught in them or whether the men attended. The imprecision of historical knowledge in this area makes it impossible to know how many artisans endorsed nativism because of their religious convictions, although there is no necessary correlation

between church attendance and religious convictions. Interestingly, however, as mentioned previously, the Protestant clergy was conspicuous by
its *absence* from the American Republican party hierarchy. The best-
known minister in the movement, John H. Chambers, appears to have been
a bit of a maverick; he pastored an "independent" church no longer af-
filiated with the regular Methodist denomination to which he had once
belonged. It may well be possible, arguing intuitively from a sense of the
evidence, that the working-class leaders in the American Republican
machine advised the party that the organized religious character of the
movement should be played down even if its generalized Christian or
Protestant character needed to be maintained.

In much the same regard, the relative absence of temperance leaders
from the party's upper ranks has already been noted. Here, too, the
sensibilities of workingmen might well have played a role in the separation
of the nativist and temperance organizations. Granted, some important
temperance men like Lewis Levin and Philip S. White were active in both
movements, and Levin even went to Congress for three terms from a
heavily working-class district in Southwark. But in the rough-and-ready
communities of Philadelphia's workingmen, it would be surprising indeed
if a substantial majority were willing to give up alcohol for an extended
period of time.[52] Temperance activists continually complained throughout
the 1840s that some employers were still paying a portion of the daily
wage in rum, and there is no sign that the neighborhood tavern declined
as a center for community sociability. The number of unlicensed "oyster
cellars" throughout the city reached beyond a thousand, indicating that
despite the temperance fervor someone besides the Irish was drinking.
As the temperance movement drifted closer toward prohibition through
its efforts to shut down the unlicensed drinking places (and all drinking
places on Sunday), it seems probable that many workingmen who endorsed voluntary abstinence backed away from the movement. Recent
investigations have shown that many workingmen in the 1840s did embrace the moderate Sons of Temperance and other voluntaristic temperance
societies, and even the Irish had their church-sponsored voluntary temperance societies.[53] Moderation was an obvious virtue to those who saw the
lives of so many around them ruined by excessive drinking. Still, the im-
pression one receives from evidence for the 1840s is that the total abstinence stand taken by the more intense reformers failed to enlist a majority
of the city's native artisans. The American Republican party did not
assign the liquor question a central place in its political program.

Instead, the party proposed to take care of its rank and file's economic interests by other means. While far from radical on economic issues, the American party adopted antimonopoly, antielitist, anti-Bank, pro-hard money positions. It is hardly surprising that the American Republicans sounded a good deal like the Jacksonian Democrats, since party leaders such as Thomas Grover, Lemuel Paynter, and Oliver P. Cornman had been virulent anti-Bank Democrats during the rechartering campaign of the 1830s. Unlike the national Locofocos, however, the working-class Democrats of Philadelphia were high tariff men; unlike the Whigs, they were not interested in protecting "infant industries," but rather in protecting the jobs of American workers from an influx of cheap manufactures. The *Daily Sun,* edited by Lewis Levin, roundly denounced the Democratic Walker tariff of 1846, which lowered rates on some imported manufactures, and Levin and Thomas Grover organized a mass rally of Philadelphia workingmen to protest Congressional passage of the measure.[54]

To meet the economic needs of nativist journeymen on a day-to-day basis, John Botsford, Oliver Cornman, and other leaders of the General Trades' Union who had turned to nativism founded the United Order of American Mechanics (UOAM). The order functioned primarily as a benevolent society, paying sick benefits and funeral allowances to its members. It also served as a clearinghouse for native craftsmen seeking employment. Finally, the UOAM benefitted the parent American Republican party by keeping the nativist rank-and-file actively involved in an ongoing nativist organization that could be mobilized at the polls. To stimulate its members' interest, the order sponsored lectures on the immigrant question and other subjects, such as making and saving money. It also kept a reading room and marched its members in parades on patriotic holidays. In the later 1840s, the order increasingly introduced temperance principles into its affairs, but there is no evidence to show that it stressed the liquor question when the American Republican party was at the height of its electoral influence in 1844 and 1845. Unlike the party itself, the leaders of the United Order of American Mechanics were drawn strictly from the ranks of workingmen.[55]

Insofar as the American Republicans appealed to the economic interests of the native working people of Philadelphia, editorially attacked the "aristocracies" of Europe and the American banking industry, and stressed the innate virtue and intelligence of the "people," they fall within the populist tradition that Hofstadter, Lipset, and the other pluralist historians have perceived as an important wellspring of American

nativism.[56] Their association with the masses clearly lowered the American Republicans in the eyes of the city's upper-class elements, especially when the rank and file rioted in Kensington and burned two Catholic churches. The nickname "church burners party" stung the American Republicans, many of whom had seemingly joined the movement to at least partially satisfy their search for petit bourgeois respectability. Yet, the party's ideology and its positions on various issues could not help but attract a large working-class constituency with a violent tradition and strong preconception of its own popular rights.

If the pluralists were accurate in describing the populist tinge to Jacksonian nativism, how well do their other hypotheses and assumptions hold up in light of the evidence and suggestions offered here? Were the nativists of the forties paranoid, or at least paranoid in the style of their rhetoric? They were, especially in their perception that the Jesuits were hatching a plot to "capture" America for the pope. But there was some realistic validation for nativist fears in the fact that large numbers of Catholics were migrating to the United States and remaining self-consciously isolated in their living arrangements, cultural patterns, and political allegiances. Protestant nativists also saw around them a vigorous worldwide effort by the Roman church to make converts, especially among the American Protestant population. Were the American Republicans status anxious? At present the evidence remains inconclusive, but it suggests that the answer is at best "only somewhat" or "in some cases." Was the movement comprised of what Lipset and Raab called "an elite leadership and a mass base?"[57] If such a description applies, it does so only for the temporary alliance between Philadelphia's Whigs and American Republicans on election day 1844 and 1845. (As Chapter 8 will indicate, however, this ploy by the elite Whigs, if indeed there was one, redounded mostly to the benefit of the American Republicans.) If there was an elite that benefitted from the rise of nativism in the 1840s it was, in David Montgomery's view, factory owners and industrialists. These entrepreneurs gained indirectly from the ability of the evangelical temperance crusade to teach the virtues of sobriety and self-discipline to the working masses. Montgomery acknowledges, however, that the industrialists themselves never took a direct part in promoting or leading temperance organization, while Bruce Laurie even suggests that working-class nativists might well have started their own temperance organizations in rebellion against the values of the industrial elite.[58]

Finally, there remains a major interpretive difference between the pluralist historians of Jacksonian nativism and historians of the working classes such as Montgomery and Laurie: Hofstadter, Lipset, and Davis have tried to explain most of the behavior of the nativist movement by analyzing its members' cultural attitudes and sociopsychological characteristics, while Montgomery and Laurie, by contrast, stress the power of economic forces to activate the nativist crusade. Can these two interpretive approaches be reconciled? This will be the first question addressed in Chapter 4.

NOTES

1. Ray Allen Billington, *Protestant Crusade: A Study of the Origins of American Nativism* (Chicago: Quadrangle, 1963).

2. Ibid., 1, 36.

3. This reawakening was sparked primarily by the work of sociologists Gordon W. Allport, particularly his *Nature of Prejudice* (Reading, Mass.: Addison-Wesley, 1954), and Theodor W. Adorno, et al., *The Authoritarian Personality* (New York: Harper and Bros., 1950).

4. In his *The Intellectuals and McCarthy: The Radical Specter* (Cambridge: MIT Press, 1967), 14-15, Michael Paul Rogin offers an insightful summary of pluralist thinking. According to Rogin, pluralist sociologists and historians value the proliferation of all interest groups that stay within the liberal tradition, be they corporate elites or university intellectuals, while at the same time they fear the rise of mass-based popular movements such as the Populist party or McCarthyism. In the pluralist schema, "Groups provide individuals with specific channels for realizing their demands, focusing their members on the practical desires that can be realized in ordinary democratic politics. At the same time, even nonpolitical groups provide isolated individuals a home, integrating them into the constitutional order. Moreover, when an individual belongs to many groups he cannot act in an extreme fashion in support of one group without threatening his commitment to another. He thus becomes committed in general to the society and is unable to threaten that commitment through the support of particular extremism." Pluralists value a liberal, multigroup society because mass movements such as the nativism of the 1840s "arise from the desperation, rootlessness, and irrational longings of isolated individuals. Their targets are scapegoats, and the

solutions they propose are either harmless but pointless panaceas or else threaten to destroy the constitutional regime."

5. Richard Hofstadter, *The Paranoid Style in American Politics* (New York: Alfred A. Knopf, 1965), excerpted in David Brion Davis, ed., *The Fear of Conspiracy: Images of Un-American Subversion from the Revolution to the Present* (Ithaca: Cornell University Press, 1971), 2-9.

6. Ibid., 3.

7. David Brion Davis, "Some Themes of Counter-Subversion: An Analysis of Anti-Masonic, Anti-Catholic, and Anti-Mormon Literature," *Mississippi Valley Historical Review* 47 (September 1960), 205-224, excerpted in Richard O. Curry and Thomas M. Brown, eds., *Conspiracy: The Fear of Subversion in American History* (New York: Holt, Rinehart and Winston, 1972), 65.

8. Davis uses the term "nativist" in the generic sense to indicate "defenders of native traditions" who "identified Masonry and Mormonism [as well as Catholicism] with forces alien to American life." Ibid., 64.

9. Davis, *Fear of Conspiracy,* xx, xxii.

10. Davis, "Themes of Counter-Subversion," 77.

11. Seymour Martin Lipset and Earl Raab, *The Politics of Unreason: Right-Wing Extremism in America, 1790-1970* (New York: Harper & Row, 1970).

12. Ibid., 47-48.

13. Ibid., 58-62.

14. Ibid., 194-195, 234-235, 478-481.

15. Rogin, *Intellectuals and McCarthy;* John Higham, "Another Look at Nativism," *American Catholic Historical Review* 44 (July 1958): 147-158; David Montgomery, "The Shuttle and the Cross: Weavers and Artisans in the Kensington Riots of 1844," *Journal of Social History* 5 (Summer 1972): 411-446; Bruce Laurie, "The Working People of Philadelphia, 1827-1852" (Ph.D. diss., University of Pittsburgh, 1971).

16. Laurie, "Working People of Philadelphia," 48.

17. Ibid., 49.

18. Montgomery, "Shuttle and Cross," 421.

19. Joseph Gusfield, *Symbolic Crusade: Status Politics and the American Temperance Movement* (Urbana: University of Illinois Press, 1963), 5.

20. Montgomery, "Shuttle and Cross," 423.

21. Robert Ernst, "Economic Nativism in New York City during the 1840s," *New-York History* 29 (1948): 184.

22. For Kellyville's population see Dennis Clark, "Kellyville: An Immigrant Success Story," *Pennsylvania History* 39 (January 1972): 44-45. Montgomery, "Shuttle and Cross," 411.

23. Discussing the pluralist attitude toward industrialization, Michael

Paul Rogin observes that "the intellectual heritage of pluralism suggests that the theory is not simply a defense of diverse groups sharing power but also an analysis and defense of tendencies within modern industrial society. Pluralism requires more than diversity; it requires as well the consensus and orientations of modern industrial society to protect and limit that diversity." *The Intellectuals and McCarthy,* 15.

24. Lipset and Raab, *Politics of Unreason,* 47.

25. The *City Directory,* published annually by James McElroy, was a business directory rather than a house-by-house census. McElroy's inflation of titles was probably intended to flatter potential purchasers among those listed and at the very least reflected the title offered by the respondents themselves when McElroy was conducting his survey.

26. David Paul Brown served briefly as county prosecutor under a nativist Whig sheriff in 1846. For a biographical sketch of Levin, see American Council of Learned Societies, *Dictionary of American Biography* (New York: Charles Scribner's Sons, 1946).

27. Philadelphia industry in the 1830s and 1840s often employed immigrants, but none did more than the cotton factories. See Pennsylvania Senate, *Report of the Select Committee Appointed to Visit the Manufacturing Districts of the Commonwealth* (Harrisburg, 1838). Manufacturers were active in the modernizing movements of the period, such as administrative consolidation and reform of county government, expansion of public schooling, and temperance, but they steered clear of organized nativism.

In his *"Gentlemen of Property and Standing": Anti-Abolition Mobs in Jacksonian America* (New York: Oxford University Press, 1970), chap. 5, Leonard Richards observed that abolitionists in the 1830s often earned incomes derived from newer, industrial occupations, while the antiabolitionists more likely made their fortunes in commerce and the free professions such as medicine and law. Richards accounts for this contrast by hypothesizing that abolitionism—in this instance the radical position—appealed to the more innovative, experimental types who were drawn to the burgeoning industrial forms of economic enterprise. Antiabolitionism, the status quo position, was more congenial to the "gentlemen of property and standing" involved in the older, tradition-bound, more stable forms of business. As another status quo position, like antiabolitionism, American Republicanism failed to attract Philadelphia's manufacturers.

28. The nativist press included Levin's *Sun,* Samuel Kramer's *Native American,* Hector Orr's *Native Eagle,* Cephas G. Childs' *North American,* and Peter Hay's *American Sentinel.*

29. Montgomery, "Shuttle and Cross," 428.

30. For a parallel discussion of the "new" men in the nativism of the 1850s, see Michael Fitzgibbon Holt, "The Politics of Impatience: The Origins of Know-Nothingism," *Journal of American History* 60 (September 1973): 309-331.

31. Gusfield, *Symbolic Crusade,* 36-37.

32. As a business guide, the *City Directory* listed only those artisans who owned shops—that is, master employers.

33. George R. Taylor, *The Transportation Revolution, 1815-1860* (New York: Holt, Rinehart and Winston, 1964).

34. For a discussion of the rise of merchant capitalism and its impact on Philadelphia craftsmen, see Stuart Blumin, "Mobility in a Nineteenth-Century City: Philadelphia, 1820-1860" (Ph.D. diss., University of Pennsylvania, 1968), chap. 1.

35. Ibid. Cf. Laurie, "Working People of Philadelphia," chap. 1.

36. Ibid., 6-8.

37. For a discussion of economic reductionism, see Gusfield, *Symbolic Crusade,* 57.

38. On the APA, see Billington, *Protestant Crusade,* 183-186.

39. John Hancock Lee, *Origin and Progress of the American Party in Politics* (Philadelphia: Elliot and Gihon, 1855), 15.

40. Philadelphia *Daily Sun,* July 17, 1846.

41. Ibid., January 2, 1845. Lee Benson, *The Concept of Jacksonian Democracy: New York as a Test Case* (Princeton: Princeton University Press, 1961), 115-116. *Public Ledger,* June 26, 1844.

42. Klaus Hansen, "The Millennium, the West, and Race in the Ante-Bellum Mind," *Western Historical Quarterly* 3 (October 1972): 373-390.

43. Philadelphia *Native American,* April 23, 1844.

44. Lee, *Origin and Progress of the American Party,* 22-23.

45. Ibid.

46. Philadelphia *Banner of the Cross,* July 27, 1844.

47. Edwin T. Freedley, *Philadelphia and Its Manufactures* (Philadelphia: E. Young and Co., 1867), 72-73. David Montgomery, "The Working Classes of the Pre-Industrial City," *Labor History* 9 (Winter 1968): 21. Sam Bass Warner, Jr., *The Private City: Philadelphia in Three Periods of Its Growth* (Philadelphia: University of Pennsylvania Press, 1968), 88.

48. *Public Ledger,* July 19, 1836.

49. For a discussion of the "natural rights" and "popular sovereignty" doctrines as a justification for American collective violence, see Richard Maxwell Brown, "The American Vigilante Tradition," *Violence in America: Historical and Comparative Perspectives,* ed. Hugh D. Graham and Ted R. Gurr (Washington, D.C.: U.S. Government Printing Office, 1969).

50. Laurie, "Working People of Philadelphia," 42-44.

51. Montgomery, "Shuttle and Cross," 430.

52. Both Bruce Laurie, "'Nothing on Compulsion': Life Styles of Philadelphia Artisans, 1820-1850," *Labor History* 15 (Summer 1974): 337-366, and Paul Faler, "Cultural Aspects of the Industrial Revolution: Lynn, Massachusetts Shoemakers and Industrial Morality, 1826-1860," ibid., 367-394, argue that temperance gained a strong foothold among the skilled workers of Philadelphia and Lynn, respectively. Neither can establish the number of artisans who adhered to the movement, either in absolute terms or as a percentage of their socioeconomic class. The estimate here, based on Laurie's and Faler's inferences as well as my own, is that somewhat less than half of the skilled artisans, and a much smaller percentage of the lesser skilled, adhered to strict temperance principles.

53. Laurie, "Working People of Philadelphia," 125, and "'Nothing on Compulsion,'" 354. Catholics organized the Father Matthew Temperance Society, named after a beloved Irish priest who came to the United States in 1849 to preach the virtues of abstinence.

54. In 1846, the *Sun* waged a constant editorial campaign against the repeal of the tariff of 1842 on the ground that American mechanics would lose their jobs. Despite protests by both Whigs and American Republicans, the Democratic administration and Congress did lower the tariff.

55. For the United Order of American Mechanics, see Laurie, "Working People of Philadelphia," 146-149.

56. Lipset and Raab, *Politics of Unreason*, 13.

57. Ibid., 49.

58. Montgomery, "Shuttle and Cross," 411. Laurie, "'Nothing on Compulsion,'" 365-366.

4
Patterns of Conflict

As the previous chapters have attempted to demonstrate, much of the conflict between the native-born and immigrant Irish populations of Philadelphia arose from economic competition. The immediate disputes that led to violence in summer 1844, however, were strictly cultural. More specifically, the Native American riots arose out of the incompatibilities between the Irish Catholic and native Protestant systems of moral behavior and religious training characteristic of the 1840s. To a degree, the nativist rejection of immigrant Irish moral values can be explained by pointing to the nativists' own self-interest. By advocating temperance, for example, native-born workers were hoping to persuade employers that they were a better risk than their Irish or Catholic fellow workers, who were presumed to be heavy drinkers. But most of the other cultural conflicts that marked the 1840s had little or no economic content. Rather, they seem to have reflected for the most part the desire of each side to assert the superiority of its own system of values. In no issue was this clearer than the debate over the use of the Bible in the public schools. Technically, the issue revolved around whether Catholic schoolchildren in Philadelphia would be required to read the Protestant King James version of the Bible as part of their regular school exercises, read their own official Catholic version in its place, or simply be excused from Bible reading altogether. In and of itself, the issue had only minimal pedagogical, much less economic, relevance. But the question took on extraordinary symbolic importance.[1] For Protestants to allow a Catholic version of the Bible in public, tax-supported schools or even to permit Catholic children to refrain from reading the Protestant version would have been granting a measure of equality to the Catholic religion. In other words, by making the King James version optional as a school text, the Protestant majority would have been admitting that it could no longer

set itself above the Irish Catholic minority whose culture it considered inferior. The battle to "save" the King James Bible in the public schools was part of a wider war against the first appearance of the cultural pluralism now so much a part of the social and political climate of the United States.[2]

Most historians and social scientists have long since abandoned the theory that American society was a melting pot in which immigrant and ethnic groups were turned into a "totally new blend, culturally and biologically, in which the new stocks and folkways of Europe, figuratively speaking, were indiscriminately mixed in the political pot of an emerging nation and fused by the fires of American influence and interaction into a distinctly new type."[3] Instead, the dominant theory of ethnic dynamics now accepted in scholarly circles stresses the importance of cultural pluralism, a model that accounts for the degree to which the various immigrant groups and their offspring retain goodly amounts of their Old World traits out of a mix of both pride and self-defense. These retained traits are supposedly blended, though only in part, with the values acquired from contact with other ethnic groups as well as the core culture of native American society to add a healthy diversity and richness to American life.

While agreeing that from the perspective of cultural richness and freedom pluralism has been a positive good, scholars have recently begun to note that, historically, the heterogeneity of American ethnic groups has caused an extraordinary amount of conflict, disruption, and violence.[4] When asked to define the exact relationship between ethnic conflict and the structure of American society, or how ethnic conflict compares with other forms of conflict such as class or economic struggles, historians have yet to reach substantial agreement. In general, the major interpretive disagreements have been spurred by reactions to the "consensus" history of the 1950s. The consensus historians were among the first to appreciate cultural and ethnic conflict as an important indicator of basic American values and as a tool by which one could study the functioning of the nation's political system. Of late, however, their estimates of the significance of conflict and violence in the American past have been seriously challenged, at least in part out of a misunderstanding of the notion of "consensus." In recent years, the consensus historians have been accused of neglecting the many forms of class, economic, ethnic, racial, political, and cultural conflict dotting the pages of the American past. But the leading theoreticians of consensus history, such as Richard Hofstadter and

Louis Hartz, have not denied the prevalence of serious discord and violence among groups in our society; it is rather that in their understanding of the past conflict has attained a particular and limited significance. Consensus historians are deeply impressed by the degree to which the particular kinds of violent conflict that have arisen appear to demonstrate the limits to conflict in general in the United States. Richard Hofstadter summarized those limits in the following way:

> It is generally recognized that American politics has involved, among other things, a series of conflicts between special interests . . . and that it has not shown . . . many signs of a struggle between the propertied and unpropertied classes. . . . The fierceness of the political struggles has often been misleading; for the range of vision embraced by the primary contestants in the majority parties has always been bounded by the horizons of property and enterprise. However much at odds on specific issues, the major political traditions have shared a belief in the rights of property, the philosophy of economic individualism, the value of economic competition; they have accepted the economic virtues of capitalistic culture as necessary qualities of man. . . . The sanctity of private property, the right of the individual to dispose of and invest it, the value of opportunity . . . have been staple tenets of the central faith in American political ideologies.[5]

Building on this premise, Lee Benson, in his influential *Concept of Jacksonian Democracy,* argues that basic agreement by all groups on the fundamentals of the economic system has not meant political peace in the United States but has merely provided a wider latitude for disagreement on a variety of other issues of less fundamental importance. As Benson puts it, "Rather than deduce that agreement on fundamentals will necessarily produce harmony, it seems more logical to deduce that agreement on fundamentals will permit almost every kind of social conflict, tension, and difference to find political expression."[6] Since the United States was socially and ethnically so heterogeneous in the nineteenth century, so decentralized administratively and politically, and peopled by so many individuals with high levels of personal aspirations, it is not surprising that a great variety of conflicting *values* managed to work their way into the public arena. Put another way, the presence of tumult and disorder in American politics did not necessarily indicate any disagreement over

fundamental (read "economic") values and in fact may have been possible only because fundamental agreement already existed.

To support his argument, Benson offers the case of nativism in the 1840s as an example of a movement that attacked its enemies in the political arena almost exclusively on cultural, rather than class or economic, grounds. Not just nativism, according to Benson, but all the major party battles of the Jacksonian era—anti-Masonry, the Bank War, the Free-Soil movement, Sabbatarianism, internal improvements, even the tariff— reflect above all a concern for cultural rather than class interests. Party personnel were not differentiated along class lines. Whigs, Democrats, Free-Soilers and American Republicans, according to Benson, were all basically middle class; what distinguished the adherents of one party from another was a set of attitudes toward certain pressing cultural questions of the day: the relationship between church and state and the role of the state in enforcing public morals, the role of the federal government, as opposed to private enterprise, in fostering national economic growth, and the attitude of each party toward the perpetuation of discrimination against the two groups at the bottom of American society, the slaves and the immigrants. In his study of voting patterns in New York State during the 1840s, Benson reached a conclusion that might well be applied to Jacksonian Philadelphia: despite local variations from ward to ward and neighborhood to neighborhood, the Whigs, and even more clearly the American Republicans, tended to attract evangelical Protestants regardless of class or income, especially those who were willing to impose their puritanical moral standards on others through state action.[7] The Whig acceptance of government intervention in the economic sphere extended into the moral, and it was this attitude toward state power above all that differentiated the party of Webster and Clay from their Democratic opponents.

Cultural issues—religious and moral value conflicts—are the stuff of ethnic consciousness. According to Benson they were the chief source of social conflict in the Jacksonian period. He argues that the easiest way to understand the impact of cultural conflict on political behavior in the antebellum years is through the concept of "negative reference." This sociological theory assumes that in the realm of moral and cultural preferences "men behave according to patterns set by groups to which they do *not* belong, or by certain individuals whose patterns influence them in determining their own."[8] One can imagine that Develin, an Irish Catholic, voted Democratic in Southwark in 1844 on the assumption that Smith,

his evangelical Methodist neighbor, voted American Republican; Smith, noting from the returns that Develin and his countrymen in the next ward voted Democratic, was simply reinforced in his tendency to favor the American Republicans, or, more importantly, disfavor the Democrats. Neither man necessarily voted out of a positive regard for his own party's stand on any particular issue, although the Democrats, the Whigs, and the American Republicans each took noticeably different positions on some issues. Of greater importance to both Develin and Smith was the fact that the Democratic party was traditionally identified as the immigrant party, and thus a vote against it was a symbolic act reflecting distrust of or dislike for the Irish. Benson uses the negative reference hypothesis to support his belief that, ultimately, cultural issues in the Jacksonian era were stronger determinants of political behavior than class or economic issues.[9]

The historical interpretation that sees ethnocultural conflict as a re-flection of consensus on class and economic issues has reigned since the mid-1950s, and few historical monographs have had as much influence on American historians in the last decade as Benson's.[10] Criticism of the consensus approach has never been lacking, however. In an important critique of his own intellectual history of American nativist ideology, John Higham called for a more thorough consideration of the functional role of ethnic hostility in perpetuating the economic and social status quo in the United States. Implicitly, Higham was criticising both the "paranoid" and consensus interpretations of nativism for viewing the phenomenon from a narrowly psychological or cultural viewpoint. While nativism might have been a refuge for psychologically disturbed individuals or a socially acceptable means by which one group differentiated itself from another group in order to reinforce its collective ego, Higham considered that ethnic prejudice has been a major force in assigning ethnic and racial groups to either a high or low place in American society. Put differently, preju-dice has not only been cathartic but remunerative for native-born groups because it justified their exploitation or repression of latecomers. Higham calls upon other historians to examine the ways in which ethnic rivalries and tensions have reinforced the "basic structural realities" of class and status in American society.[11]

David Montgomery has made a start toward analyzing the relationship between ethnic rivalries and the structure of economic inequality in Jacksonian Philadelphia. He has concluded that the demands of evangelical politics on native Protestant workingmen, especially in the areas of

temperance and religious education in the public schools, had distinct ramifications in furthering the economic decline of the skilled native craftsman:

> Such moral policing as evangelists demanded was in turn urgently needed by the new industrialists, to be sure, for it promised them a disciplined labor force, pacing its toil and its very life cycle to the requirements of the machine and the clock, respectful of property and orderly in its demeanor.[12]

But the psychological impact of ethnocultural agitation was only one of the benefits gained by the new class of American industrialists. Ethnic conflict tended to divide the working class along lines of birth or religion. Thus, when skilled native craftsmen were displaced by factories and machines and arriving immigrants found their only economic opportunities in the dehumanizing setting of labor gangs and the very same factories, the two groups were unable to overcome the centrifugal pull of separatist agitation launched simultaneously by nativist politicians and evangelical divines on the one hand and Irish-American nationalists and Catholic clergymen on the other. According to Montgomery, the irony of the industrial transformation of the 1840s was that "the pattern of cultural politics generated by the religious impact of industrialization . . . *attached* workers to the political leadership of the middle classes of their particular ethnic groups." Harangued by importuning temperance preachers and nativist politicians, Protestant workingmen had to choose between loyalty to the working class or faith in the rightness of their own religion over that of their Catholic fellow workers. Since the depression of the late 1830s had effectively destroyed the class-conscious labor movement in Philadelphia, the choice of nativism over labor militance was a foregone conclusion. But, according to Montgomery, the fact that ethnic consciousness was chosen by default, under great duress, and with no reasonable alternatives in the economic conditions of the times does not mean that economic issues were not important to American workingmen in the 1840s or that their class consciousness was completely forgotten. In parting words for the consensus historians, Montgomery concludes, "By their very nature, evangelical demands fragmented the working class as a political force in antebellum Philadelphia and thereby created for historians the *illusion* of a society lacking in class conflict."[13]

Whether nativism in the 1840s represents the absence of class conflict, as Benson would have it, or a displaced manifestation of it, as Montgomery suggests, is a question of emphasis rather than fact. Many causes of the conflict between the Irish and native workingmen were indeed closely related to the role of the unskilled immigrant in furthering the American industrial revolution at the expense of skilled native artisans. Furthermore, the immigrants did compete with native residents for housing, public services, and the other social benefits. At the same time, the consensus historians are correct in pointing out that all the manifest areas of complaint by nativists seem to fall in the area of cultural and ethnic rather than economic complaints. The issue of the Bible in the public schools, the movement for Sunday closings of bars, the assertions that the pope was trying to subvert the Constitution, have precious little class or economic relevance.

Rather than trying to assign primacy to cultural and psychological explanations of nativism, as opposed to an economic interpretation, it might be more useful to suggest that various kinds of conflict were at work in the nativism of the 1840s but that only certain aspects of the overall struggle led to distinct forms of behavior by one side or the other. More specifically, the fight for jobs and housing stirred resentments between the Irish and the blacks who lived in the city's southside slums. These conflicts encouraged the working-class elements in the respective ethnic groups to isolate themselves in the emotional as well as physical ghettoes of neighborhood, church, workshop, firehouse, and tavern. Yet, at the same time, these struggles were not sufficient to activate the entire native or Irish population to organize and mobilize against each other in the streets or at the polls. The middle-class elements of both communities were drawn in by the cultural issues of the day. While the places that the Irish filled in the factories, the almshouses, the jails, the crowded back alleys, and the weaving shops alerted the native population in the upper and middle as well as the working classes to the danger of receiving an unskilled and uneducated foreign mass at its gate, actual contact and competition between natives and immigrants occurred most frequently at the working-class level. So long as the heat from this friction did not radiate up to the higher reaches of native Protestant society, the issue of the immigrants did not generate much political excitement. But when these same reviled foreigners began to put forth demands for cultural parity, either by asserting their right to drink on the Sabbath or to read their own Bibles in the

publicly supported school rooms of Philadelphia, then natives from every rung on the social ladder were provoked into defending against any "alien" assaults on their position as the guardians of the dominant culture. It was not so much a question of whether economic rather than cultural conflict was more basic as a source of nativist attacks on the Irish in the political arena. Rather, cultural issues proved more effective in mobilizing massive anti-immigrant sentiments than were the more narrowly working-class concerns of economic nativists.[14]

Group conflict that arises out of cultural issues is easily translated into organized movements in the United States precisely because cultural values tend to cut across class lines. Hence, thousands of Protestant Philadelphians, regardless of differences in their wealth, occupations, neighborhoods, political affiliations, education, or other socioeconomic characteristics, could unite in response to the unsubstantiated but emotional charge that the city's Catholics had set afoot a conspiracy to "kick the Bible out of the public schools." As coreligionists, Protestants of all denominations and classes shared a common heritage in the King James version of the Bible. Because the nativists interpreted the Bible fight in terms of a Catholic challenge to the Protestant religion rather than as the simple demand for recognition of Catholic rights in the schools, the anti-Catholic crusade was able to create a broad base of support in both the middle and working classes. For the working-class nativists, perhaps, the Bible issue was just one more in a series of challenges that the immigrants had been raising since the late 1830s, a cumulative addition to their already deep economic and social antipathies toward the new arrivals.

While the constellation of cultural issues that divided natives and immigrants in Jacksonian Philadelphia revolved around religious issues, they were not strictly religious in a doctrinal sense. Rather, most of them had to do with the definition of public morality. The nativist demand that the King James Bible be used exclusively in the city's public schools embodied a widely held Protestant belief that the nation's primary moral values were based on the teachings of Protestant religion. Similarly, the evangelical injunctions against drinking, swearing, gambling, and fighting were related more to preferences in public decorum than they were to the scriptural teachings of Christ, who had little if anything to say about the drinking habits of Irishmen. While all of these issues were tied to preferences in moral systems, they were well suited for exploitation in the political arena. Questions of public morality in the United States

move from the realm of personal preferences to the province of politics and law enforcement because those who have wished to regulate the behavior of others have often come to see the power of the state as the only effective means for enforcing their standards. The era of prohibition in the 1920s was the most notable example of this tendency. Just as Jacksonian Philadelphia's evangelicals, supported to a degree by nativist politicians, tried to make the regulation of drinking in the city the responsibility of elected officials and law-enforcement personnel, so too they tried to politicize the school Bible issue and bring it into the realm of public regulation and prescription. They hit upon the argument that the Protestant majority had the democratic right to set its own educational standards and that the elected representative officials of the Philadelphia public school system had the right to designate the curriculum used by teachers in those schools.

It was at this intersection of morals and politics that nativists and Irish Catholic partisans collided in Jacksonian Philadelphia.[15] Politics is an arena in which "face" plays an important role, and no party to a political drama can easily accept the appearance of total defeat or even appear to have compromised its principles overmuch. The school Bible issue evolved into a particularly volatile political affray since it brought into the battle evangelical spokesmen who strongly believed that the mission of the Protestant United States was to save the world from sin in general and Roman Catholicism in particular. For their part, ardent Catholics tended to accept their church as the one true church, and they prayed fervently that Protestants would some day see the errors of their apostasy. Such convictions are not the stuff from which political compromises are easily shaped.

As noted in Chapter 3, earlier interpretations of nativism in the 1840s attributed its rise almost exclusively to the agitated rantings of Protestant clergymen caught up in a scurrilous anti-Catholic Protestant crusade.[16] While this interpretation minimizes the importance of economic and social tensions as a source of nativism, it does point up the role Protestant churches played in legitimizing the anti-Irish prejudices native-born Americans harbored. Evangelical clergymen exploited the repressed sexuality of their followers by repeating the false "revelations" of priestly abuses of innocent nuns and female parishioners in the confessional. Even respected clerics such as New York's Henry Ward Beecher and Philadelphia's Joseph F. Berg trotted out tales of nuns kept as concubines by priests and of children born from these matings slaughtered in the secret

passageways buried beneath convents. Like the image of the black stud that pervaded the southern imagination after the days of slavery as a justification for racism, the Catholic priest was invested with great sexual powers by many imaginative and sexually guilt-ridden nativist Protestants in the antebellum period as a justification for their anti-Catholicism.[17]

Philadelphia produced one of the nation's strongest local crusades against Catholics. In 1842, more than fifty local clergymen united in the American Protestant Association, which dedicated itself to alerting the public to the evil teachings of popery through lectures, publications, Sunday schools, revivals, and the reinstitution of the Sabbath as a day of piety. The association gained attention through a series of popular lectures, especially those by the charismatic renegade ex-priest, Reverend William Hogan, who spread incredible lies about the Catholic church after leaving it in the 1830s. Truth was never at a premium among the members of the American Protestant Association; its leading members offered a hearty welcome to the somewhat deranged Maria Monk, a former convent student turned prostitute who spread fantastical tales about her sexual encounters with priests, after the young woman had fled New York City rather than face some challenges to her credibility raised there by respected Protestant clergymen. Some American Protestant Association members, such as the reverends Joseph F. Berg, Albert Barnes, and George H. Burgin, later became fellow-travelers of American Republicanism.[18]

Capitalizing on the popular reaction against the "papal threat" in the schools, Philadelphia's evangelical clergy used the political environment to promote puritanical Protestant morality in public life and social institutions. Working hand in hand with secular temperance leaders and nativisit politicians, clergymen such as Reverend John Chambers (himself an important American Republican as well as a temperance preacher) launched a lobbying crusade to improve observance of the Sabbath. These leaders deplored the decline in decorum and respect that had once marked Sundays. A major Sabbatarian convention held in Philadelphia in 1843 urged a series of measures to restore the sanctity of the Sabbath, including a request to the city's railroads to suspend Sunday train service to the countryside because the excursions competed with the churches for patronage. Through pressure on senators and congressmen, the Sabbatarians attempted to convince the federal government to terminate Sunday mail delivery. They also called on local officials to chain off any street on which a church was holding Sabbath services so that the noise of fire carriages and

trucks would not disturb sacred devotions. Finally—and this was the most pressing aspect of the campaign in the Sabbatarians' own minds—they attempted to pressure Philadelphia magistrates into enforcing the laws against Sunday liquor sales. A series of neglected eighteenth-century local ordinances forbade the sale of liquor on Sundays in all places except hotels and travelers' inns. These same laws also provided that liquor not be sold in units of less than a gallon, thereby making it illegal to sell glasses of beer or whiskey over the counter or in units small enough for working people to afford. By forcing local officials to resurrect these regulations, Sabbatarians and temperance advocates hoped to move the city toward prohibition of all alcohol sales.[19]

The antiliquor faction was aiming especially at the unlicensed oyster cellars and dram shops that sprouted like mushrooms in every nook and cranny of working-class districts in Jacksonian Philadelphia. There may have been more than a thousand such places in the city, all unlicensed and all dispensing liquor, wine, and beer by the glass to their patrons. Because these cellars were often the headquarters for prostitutes, pimps, thieves, and street gangs, the evangelical reformers hoped to raise the moral climate of the city in more ways than one through closing down the cellars and dram shops.

Then as now, the zeal with which public officials enforced moral legislation depended on the amount of public pressure brought to bear on them. To mobilize support for their crusade, the Sabbatarians found it necessary to create a political movement so that right-minded magistrates got placed in office and wrong-minded ones changed their thinking. By focusing primarily on the liquor question, however, the Sabbatarians had chosen an issue incapable of stirring up an overwhelming moral majority at the polls. The presence of so many unlicensed drinking places in the city indicates that many more persons than the Irish immigrants were still enjoying their daily ration of alcohol. As mentioned earlier, some "Incorruptible" native Democrats had withheld their votes from Irish leader Hugh Clark in a Kensington district election because (among other things) his brother Patrick ran a pub attached to Hugh's house. But this foray into moral politics was a failure, as the Irish more than retaliated in the succeeding county elections by helping provide the margin of victory for Whig Morton McMichael in the race for sheriff. Temperance Democrats had a similar experience in Southwark during the 1843 elections when they were forced to vote for the Whig candidate rather than their own "spoiler" because the great mass of regular Democratic voters in that

district would not abandon Irish Democrat Thomas McCully in his race
for the First Congressional District seat. Only by combining with the
Whigs could the antiliquor nativists defeat McCully.[20]

Neither the Sabbatarians and temperance enthusiasts, with their narrow
moral concerns, nor the political nativists, with their concern about the
power of the Irish bloc vote in the Democratic party, had identified an
issue capable of energizing widespread support for their respective movements. Fortunately for both the evangelicals and nativist politicians,
however, a series of events created the perfect vehicle—the question of
the Bible in public schools—through which to bring both moralism and
anti-immigrant sentiments into Philadelphia politics.

The controversy over religion in Philadelphia's classrooms was part of
a broader Catholic resistance to the Protestant denominationalism of
the city's public institutions. Catholic clergymen were not permitted to
administer rites in public charity hospitals and Catholic sailors were
forced to attend Protestant religious services when in port. But worst of
all, at least in the eyes of Catholic Bishop Francis Patrick Kenrick, was
the clear Protestant bias in the Philadelphia public schools. Catholics supported the schools with their tax monies but their children were forced to
partake in sectarian Protestant prayers at the start of each day. They were
also forced to read the Protestant Bible. Normally a quiet man, conservative by temperament and apolitical by preference,[21] Bishop Kenrick chose
to make a public stand on the school issue since, of all those whose souls
were charged to his care, the children were the most vulnerable to seduc-
tion by Protestantism.

From 1790 until 1834, tax-assisted education in Philadelphia had been
reserved for the children of the indigent. In 1834, however, the state
legislature required Philadelphia county to provide enough schools for
every child in low-income families, not just the indigent, through direct
taxation, and in 1837 the county board announced that grammar schooling
would thenceforth be open to every child regardless of family income. As
early as 1834, Catholics had complained that the public schools for the
poor were using materials that portrayed the pope as antichrist. Not
surprisingly, the Protestant bias of other public institutions had infiltrated
the schools as well. In 1834, responding to Bishop Kenrick's complaints,
the county board of school controllers, an appointive body with authority
over local elected boards in each district, forbade the introduction into
the public schools of any books with religious content without its express
permission.[22]

The 1834 prohibition on unauthorized anti-Catholic school books would have met one of the points of Kenrick's complaint if it had been well enforced, but it was not. Furthermore, the denominational nature of the schools was reflected in more than just the texts. Most teachers in the public schools were Protestant. Religion, or at least conventional Protestant moral training, pervaded the curriculum. The school day opened with prayers and hymn singing. The Bible was used as a textbook for the students' reading lessons. Because the schools were dominated by Protestants, the King James version was the standard Bible chosen by the teachers. Catholics found this latter practice offensive because they recognized only the authenticity of the Douay version with its authoritative papal annotations. In 1838, the legislature guaranteed that the state's public schools would have a religious orientation by passing a law requiring the Bible as a reading text in schools where it was not already being used. The legislature reasoned that the Old and New Testaments contained "the best extant code of morality in simple, clear, and beautiful language." No one doubted that the legislature referred to the King James version when it passed the law.[23]

Bishop Kenrick objected to the use of scurrilous anti-Catholic texts and the forced reading of an unauthorized version of the Scriptures. He also rejected the practice of Catholic children saying opening prayers with Protestant children. Kenrick politely explained in 1843 that while he embraced all men in "the sincerity of Christian affection" and offered prayers for their souls, "it is not consistent with the laws and the discipline of the Catholic church for her members to unite in religious exercises with those who are not of their communion." Thus his objections to the public schools were placed on three distinct foundations: bad texts, a Protestant Bible, and forced ecumenism. While he wished to correct all three situations, he had to move carefully. In the years between 1834 and 1842, he was most concerned about the Bible question, asking only that Catholic children be permitted to read the Douay Bible rather than the King James during reading exercises. In a conciliatory letter to the school controllers, he registered his opposition to the Douay's exclusion and asked that all antipapal reading matter be removed from the classroom. Meanwhile, in the diocesan newspaper, the *Catholic Herald,* he warned his flock to be vigilant on school matters. The controllers responded with a reaffirmation of their 1834 decree requiring their approval of all texts so that anything offensive to Catholics might be avoided, but they never permitted the introduction of the Douay Bible. Most likely, they feared a nativist

reaction if Catholic Bibles were let into the schools where Protestant children would be able to sneak a look at them. Nor would they abandon the opening prayer. Before they would do that, they would have to abandon the generalized belief held widely by both Protestants and Catholics that the schools were not meant to be godless. The question was rather one of finding the proper means to bring religion into the schools.[24]

In 1841, the quiet dialogue between Kenrick and the school controllers was drowned out by the sound and fury of the public school controversy in New York City. Catholics there represented a much larger percentage of the population than Philadelphia's Catholic community (which was only 10 percent of the city), and their political power was stridently voiced by their outspoken leader, Bishop John Hughes. Faced with school practices similar to those in Philadelphia, Hughes demanded that New York's sectarian Protestant school controllers (inaccurately known as the Public School Society even though it was a private body) return to the New York archdiocese any tax revenues collected from Catholics to support the public schools. Those funds could then be used to build and staff parochial schools for Catholic children. Hughes argued that the use of Protestant materials in the schools violated constitutional separation of church and state as well as Catholic rights of conscience, and if the public schools could not be nonsectarian then Catholics should not be forced to contribute to their support. When the Public School Society and Protestant city officials turned down his request for funds in 1841, Hughes organized a "Carroll Hall" slate of candidates to run for the city council. Because it took enough votes from the Democrats to permit a Whig victory and thereby forced the Democracy to champion Catholic demands in the future, Hughes' plan must be counted a success. But the presence of a "priest-chosen" ticket in a secular election confirmed the worst fears of many nativists that "in ten years [Jesuits] will threaten and in twenty years rule" America if immigration and naturalization were not limited or cut off completely.[25]

After the New York controversy captured national headlines, Philadelphia's evangelicals and nativists paid closer attention to Bishop Kenrick's pronouncements on school questions. In 1842, the increasingly nativist-leaning district school board in Southwark dismissed a Catholic teacher who would not comply with the state law of 1838 by reading the Protestant Bible to her students. The city waited for Kenrick's response. In an impassioned but tightly reasoned letter to the county board. Kenrick

objected to the sectarian character of Philadelphia's public schools. While
not directly referring to the Southwark incident, Kenrick generally opposed
the exclusive use of the King James Bible as a reading text. He reiterated
his complaint that, contrary to the 1834 board ruling, anti-Catholic books
were still appearing in public classrooms. On both questions he demanded
equality for Catholics.[26] Increasingly, influential Catholics were lining up
behind the bishop, and pressure was mounting on the controllers from
evangelicals and Catholics alike to resolve the various school issues in
favor of one side or the other.

Seeking a compromise that would placate the bishop and his followers,
as well as the board's Catholic members, yet not provoke Protestant
displeasure, the board narrowly passed a compromise resolution affirming
the right of "those children whose parents prefer or desire any particular
version of the Bible, without note or comment," to be furnished one by
the schools. The board also resolved that "no child be required to attend
or unite in the reading of the Bible in the public schools whose parents
are conscientiously opposed thereto."[27] Thus, while only Protestant Bibles
(those without "note or comment") were to be allowed in the public
schools, Catholic children were excused from reading them during lessons.
The board stopped short of permitting the Douay Bible in the schools or
forbidding opening devotions, but they at least recognized that members
of minorities could not be forced into practices offensive to their personal
religious principles.

The compromise satisfied Kenrick somewhat in that it marked an
improvement over what existed previously. Although he did not say so in
public, he would have preferred the schools to dispense entirely with
religion rather than promiscuously mix Catholics and Protestants in school
prayers and Bible reading exercises. Excusing the Catholic scholars from
reading the King James version was at least a step in the right direction.
Still, he had the political acumen never once to say in public that he
preferred religion left out of the school curriculum. Despite Kenrick's
reticence on this question, evangelicals howled loudly on hearing the board's
plan, claiming that the decision to permit Catholic children to miss Bible
reading played into the hands of the bishop, who was plotting to subvert
religion in the schools. The Southwark teacher's refusal to read the Bible
in class, they warned, was part of a master plan to "remove the Bible from
the schools" altogether. The disruption that would result from Catholic
children leaving the room during reading period was intended to nullify
any value that the exercises might have. Even worse, by leaving the room,

Catholic children who needed it the most would be allowed to escape
exposure to the basic teachings of American morality contained in the
Protestant Bible. Schools, evangelicals feared, were being converted into
dens of atheism; once disrupted, they were ripe for use by the Catholics
as agencies of papal propaganda. Furthermore, religious right overlapped
with the fundamental political principle of majority rule. As the Philadelphia weekly *Presbyterian* put it, "Protestants have founded these schools
and they have always been a majority." They therefore had a right to
order whatever books they deemed fit. The nativist daily *North American*
complained that "for years and years the schools have been in operation,
planned by Protestants, and almost wholly supported by Protestants, and
now come the 'Bishop of New York' and the 'Bishop of Philadelphia' to
interfere in the management of them, creating confusion within their walls
and excitement without."[28]

The Protestant counterattack on the bishop's plan to make the schools
more acceptable to Catholics peaked in January 1844 with the publication
of Navy Chaplain Walter Colton's *Reply* to Bishop Kenrick's 1842 epistle
to the school controllers. While not particularly profound or exciting, the
pamphlet appeared at a time when public attention was riveted on the
battle to "save the Bible" in the schools, and it served as a rallying point
for the Protestant allegation that Kenrick was trying to remove the Bible
from the schools rather than simply asking equality for the Douay version.
Despite its triteness, the pamphlet received wide circulation from the
American Protestant Association and was distributed gratis to every public
school teacher. While Colton's *Reply* contained nothing new or true, the
school controllers deemed it necessary to reissue its 1834 directive that
no literature on religious subjects should enter the schools without their
permission. They did not specifically demand that Colton's pamphlet be
removed.[29]

An incident occurred just one month after Colton's pamphlet was
circulated that seemed to confirm the worst Protestant fears about
Catholic intentions. Late in February 1844, Kensington school director
and evangelical Henry Moore burst into a prayer meeting at the Methodist
church at Queen and Bedford streets to inform the congregation that
Hugh Clark, among other things a Kensington school director, had forced
a district teacher to suspend her class's Bible reading. The outraged gathering
listened to Moore's account of the teacher's bravery: how she offered to
resign rather than capitulate to the Catholic Clark's command. Moore
angrily insisted that Philadelphia's Protestant majority had tolerated enough

popish dictation in their schools. The time had come for concerted defensive action. Unsubstantiated accounts of Clark's outrage as reported by
Moore were carried in most Philadelphia newspapers.[30]

More than two excited weeks passed before the truth was finally
learned, and by then it was too late to stop the train of consequences
that followed. It seems that while Clark was on routine inspection as part
of his board duties, the school's principal teacher, Louisa Bedford, complained to him that Catholic children leaving the room during Bible
reading disrupted the entire class, rendering the reading almost useless.
She asked Clark to help restore order. Volunteering to take personal
responsibility for countermanding the state law requiring the exercise,
Clark recommended to Miss Bedford that she suspend the reading until a
more practicable method for excusing Catholic children was devised. But
he left the ultimate decision with her. Miss Bedford's testimony to this
effect before the county board exonerated Clark.[31]

In quieter times, Clark's vindication might have closed the affair. But
evangelicals such as Henry Moore, as well as political nativists like the
leaders of the American Republican party, refused to let the issue drop.
Even before Bishop Kenrick's letter to the school controllers in 1842,
a small group of Protestant enthusiasts had insisted on misperceiving
Catholic demands in the school debate. They failed to see any difference
at all between the quiet protest of Kenrick and the overt politicking of
Hughes in New York. Perhaps this blindness was deliberate. Cultural
and religious nativists probably believed that *any* acquiescence to Catholic
school demands would symbolize far more than the end of the exclusive
use of the King James Bible in the seats of learning. The Protestant cultural
monopoly itself would be severely threatened if Catholics were permitted
to achieve recognition for their own Bible in the schools. To the self-
righteous enunciators of a Protestant American millennium, the thought
of Catholics planting a cultural foothold on the soil of the New World
must have been galling indeed. But the emotional reacton of the political
nativists somehow comes across as more opportunistic than heartfelt.
Because the Bible issue involved the public schools and because the elected
or politically appointed school officials were all public servants, the controversy was ideally suited for those willing to exploit it at the polls. To
their three-part platform of extended naturalization, native Americans
only in public office, and separation of church and state, the American
Republican party suddenly added a fourth plank after the Hugh Clark
incident: "Resolved, that the Bible, without note or comment, is not

sectarian—that it is the fountainhead of all morality and all good government, and should be used in our public schools as a reading book."[32]

Nativist ideologues now raised an elaborate defense of the Bible on
political—never religious or anti-Catholic—grounds, as was their usual custom.
In the aftermath of the Clark affair, Lewis Levin explained that "the
Declaration of American Independence is but a transcript from the Bible,
which is the original fountain of human liberty and the rights of man."
Protestantism was, after all, connected intimately to the political purposes
of the founding fathers when they established the nation. Peter Sken Smith,
editor of the *Native Eagle and American Advocate* weekly magazine
declared that American Republicanism did not wish to interfere with any
other man's religion—he "may be a Turk, a Jew or a Christian, a Catholic,
Methodist or Presbyterian, and we say nothing against it"—but at the
same time reminded his audience that "when we remember that our
Pilgrim Fathers landed on Plymouth Rock to establish the Protestant
religion, free from persecution, we must contend that this was and always
will be a Protestant country!"[33]

A decisive leap had been made. A series of rallies to "save the Bible
in the schools," manned by party leaders, drew a far better response than
all previous American Republican party rallies. On March 11, two weeks
after the Clark incident, a meeting led by American Republicans George
App, Sr., Lemuel Paynter, and Elihu D. Tarr in conjunction with Protestant divine George Burgin attracted three thousand persons. A second
rally on March 13 protested Catholic attempts to "trample our free
Protestant institutions in the dust." This meeting created a watchdog
committee to keep tabs on the school controllers so that they would not
give in to priestly dictation in the schools.[34]

The willingness of the American Republicans to run on a broad-based
Protestant issue returned them great dividends at the polls. The day before
the county controllers heard Miss Bedford's testimony and acquitted Clark
of any wrongdoing, local elections for ward offices were held throughout
the county, and nativist candidates won seats in Southwark and Moyamensing.
Most impressive was the clean sweep that the American Republican ticket
made in Second Ward, Spring Garden. The returns indicated that approximately thirteen hundred persons in Philadelphia County had voted for
nativist candidates, far more than the earlier "reform" tickets had attracted.
In April, at a special election for district commissionerships in Spring
Garden—an important race because the board of commissioners appointed
the district's policemen and school board—the American Republicans fell

only seventy-seven votes short of victory. The Irish brought little sympathy
on themselves when they attacked native voters at the polls in Third Ward,
Spring Garden.[35]

Emboldened by its success in the spring elections, the party decided
to organize for victory throughout the county. By May 1844, there was
an American Republican Association in almost every ward of the city.
The few that held out were heavily populated with Irishmen. Yet, in what
it surely knew was a provocative action, the party announced its intention to form a ward association in the heart of "enemy territory," Third
Ward, Kensington, the Irish weavers' community. A late April organizational meeting at the home of John Gee had to be postponed when Irish
residents threatened to destroy any house in the ward that hosted an
American Republican meeting. The threat was hardly idle. Irishmen had
shot out the glass from the "Sign of the Ball," the emblem of a tavern by
that name in Second Ward, Spring Garden, where the local nativist association regularly held its meetings. Other party gatherings had been disrupted,
and one in Moyamensing had been threatened.[36] Spurred by their electoral
successes and a healthy dose of self-righteousness, the American Republicans of Third Ward, Kensington, refused to be intimidated. They decided
to move the meeting from Gee's house to an open lot at Second and
Master streets in the heart of the Third Ward and invited members from
outside the ward to come sustain them in their right to hold a public
meeting. The party scheduled this mass rally for May 3. The defiant
American Republicans were going to organize a chapter under the very
noses of the volatile Irish weavers. The results were not difficult to predict.

NOTES

1. The debates over the exclusive use of the Protestant Bible in the
Philadelphia public schools should be understood within the context of
the Protestant Bible movement of the 1830s and 1840s. During that
period, evangelicals placed great faith in the argument that if every human
being would but read the King James version of the Bible, the human
race would soon be converted to Protestant Christianity. Starting from
this assumption, several of the major denominations organized colportage
programs to carry the Bible to places at home and abroad where it was
not likely to be read without some urging by missionaries. These Bibles
were distributed gratis to anyone who promised to read them.

2. For a description of cultural pluralism, see Milton M. Gordon, "Assimilation in America: Theory and Reality," in *Minority Responses,* ed. Minako Kurokawa (New York: Random House, 1970), 87-94.

3. Ibid., 88.

4. See, for example, Michael Wallace, "The Uses of Violence in American History," *The American Scholar* 40 (Winter 1970-1971): 81-102.

5. Richard Hofstadter, *The American Political Tradition* (New York: Vintage, 1948), vii-viii.

6. Lee Benson, *The Concept of Jacksonian Democracy: New York as a Test Case* (Princeton: Princeton University Press, 1961), 273-274.

7. Ibid., chap. 11.

8. Ibid., 284.

9. Ibid., 286-287.

10. The annual convention of the American Historical Association in 1965 devoted a rare double session to a panel debate of Benson's book.

11. John Higham, "Another Look at Nativism," *Catholic Historical Review* 44 (July 1958): 147-158, reprinted in *Conspiracy: The Fear of Subversion in American History,* ed. Richard O. Curry and Thomas M. Brown (New York: Holt, Rinehart and Winston, 1972), 281.

12. David Montgomery, "The Shuttle and the Cross: Weavers and Artisans in the Kensington Riots of 1844," *Journal of Social History* 5 (Summer 1972): 411.

13. Ibid., 412, 439. In an important article that appeared too late for full consideration in this work, Bruce G. Laurie has argued that at least some of Philadelphia's nativists in the 1840s included class-conscious issues in their political demands. In particular, he cites an antiaristocratic and antiexploitation quality to the temperance rhetoric of the period, and thereby implicitly disagrees with Montgomery that the rise of temperance as a working-class issue detracted from the earlier class consciousness of Philadelphia's nativist artisans or made them satellites of middle-class leaders. Unfortunately, Laurie cannot say with confidence how many working-class nativists used the temperance movement to reinforce their class consciousness and he suggests that, in fact, the number might only represent a small fraction of the organized nativist movement. Bruce G. Laurie, "'Nothing on Compulsion': Life Styles of Philadelphia Artisans, 1820-1850," *Labor History* 15 (Summer 1974): 337-366.

14. For an early discussion of economic nativism that foreshadowed at least some of Montgomery's insights, see Robert Ernst, "Economic Nativism in New York," *New-York History* 29 (1948): 170-186.

15. For a discussion of nativist politics and moral issues in the Jacksonian era, see Joseph Gusfield, *The Symbolic Crusade: Status Politics and the American Temperance Movement* (Urbana: University of

Illinois Press, 1966), chap. 2.

16. Such is the argument in Ray Allen Billington, *The Protestant Crusade, 1800-1860* (Chicago: Quadrangle, 1964).

17. Ibid., 99-108.

18. Ibid., 183-184.

19. Montgomery, "Shuttle and Cross," 422-423.

20. *Public Ledger,* October 12, 1843.

21. Hugh F. Nolan, *The Most Reverend Francis Patrick Kenrick, Third Bishop of Philadelphia, 1830-1851* (Philadelphia: American Catholic Historical Society, 1948), argues that the bishop was at all times the most pacific of men in word and temperament as well as deed.

22. For a full account of this controversy, see Vincent P. Lannie and Bernard C. Diethorn, "For the Honor and Glory of God: The Philadelphia Bible Riots of 1844," *History of Education Quarterly* 8 (Spring 1968): 44-106.

23. Ibid., 48.

24. Ibid., 56.

25. On the public school question in New York, see Billington, *Protestant Crusade,* chap. 6; quotation from the Philadelphia *Presbyterian,* April 20, 1844.

26. Lannie and Diethorn, "For the Honor and Glory of God," 56.

27. Ibid., 57-58.

28. Ibid., 59.

29. Colton's *Reply to the Allegations and Complaints Contained in the Letter of Bishop Kenrick to the Board of School Controllers of the Public Schools* (Philadelphia: n.p., 1844), can be found at the Library Company of Philadelphia. Chaplain Colton later joined Cephas G. Childs as the co-editor of the Philadelphia *North American,* a nativist-leaning paper.

30. *Public Ledger,* February 28, 29, March 1, 1844.

31. Lannie and Diethorn, "For the Honor and Glory of God," 65-66.

32. *Spirit of the Times,* March 4, 1844 (reprint of letter to *North American*).

33. John Hancock Lee, *Origin and Progress of the American Party in Politics* (Philadelphia: Elliot and Gihon, 1855); *Sun,* June 6, 1845; *Public Ledger,* June 8, 1844.

34. Lannie and Diethorn, "For the Honor and Glory of God," 70.

35. *Public Ledger,* March 16, April 17, 1844.

36. Lee, *Origin and Progress of the American Party,* 39; broadside, "Origin and Cause of the Great Riot in Philadelphia" (Philadelphia: Historical Society of Pennsylvania, 1844).

5
The Kensington Riots

The fabrications and distortions surrounding the Bible dispute became the basis for serious rioting and loss of life in Kensington, May 6-8, 1844.
It seems clear enough from the perspective of the present that the bishop was not asking to have the Bible removed from the public schools. We can understand the direct interest of the evangelical press and the American Republican party in fostering the unfounded belief that Kenrick wanted to remove it, but we learn a great deal more from the fact that thousands chose to believe their propaganda despite the published evidence to the contrary. The Bible question did not manufacture anti-Catholic, anti-Irish feelings in Philadelphia; those already ran deep by May 1844. The issue served only to crystallize suspicions and focus organizing activities on both sides. By May, emotions had heated to a fever, and each side approached the Bible issue with an intense self-righteousness.

It is difficult at this remove to recapture the overwrought passions that gripped Philadelphia that spring. A single incident a week before the Kensington riot illustrates how tautly nerves were strung. On May 1, *Daily Sun* editor Lewis Levin fell into a brawl with an elderly man while strolling at Fourth and Lombard streets at the edge of the black ghetto. Levin's antagonist, John Manderfield, joined by some friends, had been taunting a Negro as Levin passed by. Referring to a provision in the Pennsylvania constitution that excluded blacks from voting, Manderfield reminded the black man that he was, ironically, a native American, but unlike the state's Irish immigrants, forbidden to vote. Levin, we are told, "turned back in a second or two and inquired what was said, and answered that he was not spoken to, or of, but that the remark was made of the black man." Taking the reference to native Americans as a personal insult, Levin suddenly exploded. He attacked the old man with such fury that several passersby were needed to pull him off the helpless fellow.

Later, when arraigned before the sheriff on assault charges, Levin was heard to regret that he had not used a knife to "cut the hog's throat." Levin's anger cooled soon afterward and he apologized to Manderfield, who then dropped the charges.[1] While this highly charged incident ended without serious injury, the next clash produced a far bloodier result.

If Levin's outburst in any way represented nativist sensibilities, it is not surprising that the American Republican leadership chose not to let the Irish disruption of the April 27 meeting at John Gee's house pass unnoticed. Their following would be scrutinizing the party's response to the Irish violation of their right of assembly. It was just such disruptive behavior that had led the party to label the immigrants unfit for American citizenship. Furthermore, if an association could be successfully launched in Third Ward, Kensington, an Irish stronghold, then American Republicanism could claim a great propaganda victory.

The Third Ward was clearly Irish territory. The neighborhood centered around the Nanny Goat Market on Washington Street, between Master and Jefferson, an open-sided shed with stalls for local food merchants (see Map 2). Here neighborhood women gathered to shop each day and men met to exchange information and greetings. The market had been the scene of the weavers' great victory over Sheriff Porter in January 1843. Surrounding the marketplace, along narrow cobbled streets, stood rows of brick and frame houses, three stories high, interspersed with empty lots. In the courtyards behind the narrow row houses were shanties and "factories," workshops that housed the local handloom weaving industry. Irish families lived in these crowded backyards as well as in the brick and frame houses. A check of local tax records shows that almost every name of the residents on these streets was Irish-sounding.[2] Many males were boarders, single men living with or near their Irish employers.

Throughout the afternoon of May 3, the date of the rescheduled meeting, an expectant mood stirred the air in the neighborhood around Second and Master streets. Nativists busily erected a platform against the schoolyard fence while local residents remained content to watch. By three P.M., the announced starting time, only a hundred persons had gathered, but more came straggling in. *Native American* editor Samuel R. Kramer, flanked by printer John Perry and William R. Craig, addressed the crowd first. The *Ledger* noted that his speech was disturbed by "noisy boys" and unrest that rippled through the mostly Irish audience, now numbering about three hundred. Kramer bravely defended the

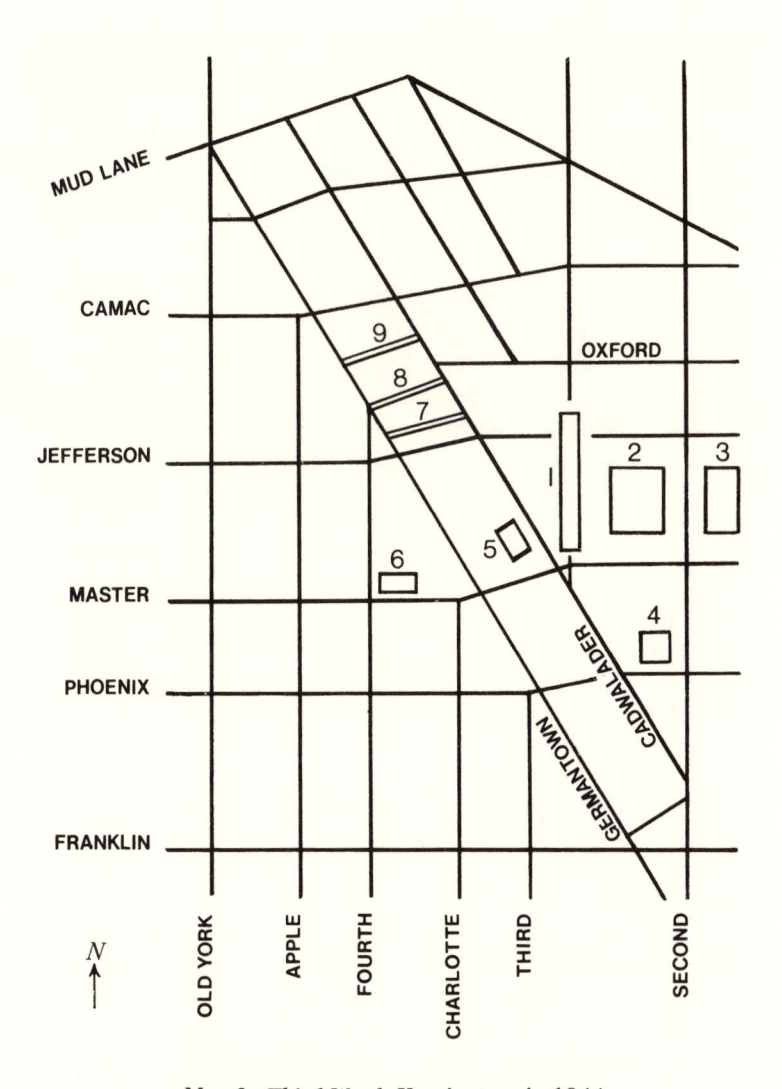

Map 2 Third Ward, Kensington, in 1844

1. Nanny Goat Market
2. St. Michael's Church
3. Schoolhouse
4. Seminary
5. Hibernia Hose House

6. Hugh Clark's residence
7. Harmony Court
8. Keyser's Court
9. Weavers' Court

party's proposed twenty-one-year residency requirement, justifying it by claiming that "a set of citizens, German and Irish, wanted to get the Constitution of the United States into their own hands and sell it to a foreign power," presumably the pope. Weaver-employer Patrick Lafferty, who had figured prominently in the 1831 Gideonite riot,[3] taunted Kramer, "Come down here, you old crocodile [one witness claimed the phrase was "you son of a bitch"] , I am a better citizen than you, for I am sworn to the country [a reference to his naturalization oath] and you may turn Tory any minute." Following Lafferty's lead, Hugh Flanagan, another veteran of the Gideonite battle, also invoked the audience's anti-English sentiments by remarking that "it was not Americans speaking but the money of British Whigs." Others spoke out as well, but the accounts record only the words "Go on, boys!" as the crowd surged forward. Perry and Craig responded by inviting any Irish spokesman present to debate the issues. The crowd hooted, resumed pushing forward, and started tearing down the stage. Choosing not to press their arguments under the circumstances, the three American Republicans ran into Northern Liberties, while several Irishmen followed in pursuit. The meeting was reconvened in the friendlier atmosphere of the George Fox Temperance Hall. Most of the Irish crowd remained behind to demolish the platform and carry it home for firewood. This confrontation, like many other of the city's past conflicts, ended without serious injury on either side. Restraint on both sides, however, soon passed. The disruption of the May 3 meeting was the first skirmish of what developed into a brutal ethnoreligious war.[4]

The American Republican party resolved to make Friday's events the pretext for a test of strength. They rescheduled the "adjourned" meeting for Monday, May 6, and placarded the city with appeals for American Republicans to come from far and wide to support the organizing effort in Kensington. Once again, the schoolyard at Second and Master was the chosen site.

Three thousand persons, ten times the number at Friday's meeting, thronged to the rally that Monday afternoon. It is easier to narrate the events that followed than to say for certain who was in attendance. Certainly not all those present were American Republicans. Doubtless some were Irishmen come to heckle the speakers. Among the nativists later wounded or prominent in the fighting, most were journeymen or apprentices not found on any American Republican membership lists. Some, it appears, came only to listen. A few carried weapons. Whether

bearing arms was common practice for Philadelphians at that time is
not known. At least some nativist participants did seem especially
prepared for violence.

Around three P.M., after a flag-raising ceremony, Samuel Kramer
briefly concluded his address, which had been interrupted the previous
Friday. Next followed Colonel Peter Sken Smith of the militia, an editor
and a temperance lecturer who had turned his talents to American Republican organizing. Smith's speech was interrupted when Irish carter John
O'Neill drove his horse and wagon through the crowd to a spot ten feet
from the platform and dumped a load of dirt or manure (the evidence is
conflicting but the insult is clear).[5] No one had ordered the "dirt,"
and O'Neill's choice of delivery time seems suspicious. In 1855, nativist
historian John H. Lee speculated that O'Neill tried to induce an attack
on himself so that his friends would have a reason to disrupt the meeting
in his "defense."[6] O'Neill's antics, however, caused only a small disturbance.
Lewis Levin, the next speaker, recaptured the crowd's attention, and
O'Neill drove off unmolested. Levin was an unlikely candidate for
leadership in a Protestant protective movement. While his credentials as
a leading temperance lecturer qualified him for a major role in the
American Republican party, his Jewish birth at first glance seems a
handicap. Levin may have been a convert to Protestantism, judging from
his rhetoric. If he was not, however, the movement allowed room not
only for Jews but even Irishmen, especially if they were Orangemen.
American Republicanism, after all, claimed to be neither anti-Catholic
nor anti-Irish, merely prorepublican. Its fight to save the Protestant Bible
in the schools was incidental to its fight to preserve American institutions
from foreign subversion.

A sudden cloudburst interrupted Levin's tirade on immigrant election
abuses and religious influence in politics. Seeking shelter, the crowd ran
around the corner to the Nanny Goat Market. A *Ledger* reporter noted
that when the crowd ran toward the shelter, there was a "great deal of
hallooing and shouting." "Everyone in the street," he observed, "seemed
to be excited" but none displayed any "angry feeling."[7]

The rainstorm and decision to reconvene in the market house proved
fateful. A group of thirty or so Irish residents awaited the nativist crowd.
The story goes that as the first arrivals entered, one Irishman yelled,
"Keep the damned natives out of the market house; this ground don't
belong to them, it's ours!" Levin climbed a market stall to reorganize the

meeting and finish his speech, but Irish hecklers interrupted him. Words
turned to blows. A pushing match developed between a nativist and his
Irish antagonist at the north end of the market. One held a club, the
other a brick. At first, friends tried to part the two but then fell to fighting
themselves. A native youth pulled a pistol; an Irishman dared him to
fire; the young man did; another fired back at him; the battle was under way.
One of the unsuccessful peacemakers, Patrick Fisher, Irish and a former
Kensington constable, was shot in the face during the exchange, his reward
for intervening. Soon bricks, clubs, and several pistols were brought into
play. Since the natives in the market house outnumbered the Irish, the
former soon controlled the building. They drove the Irish from the en-
closure and into Master Street about a block toward Germantown Road,
hurling paving stones and bricks at them.

The first nativist victory was soon reversed by the Irish who had the
advantage of fighting on home territory. Like some of the nativists, a number
of Irish residents seemed ready for mayhem. A rain of musket fire poured
down from the houses along Cadwalader Street and up Master. The guns
were mostly located in the Hibernia Hose House on Cadwalader Street
across an open lot from the market. Without walls, the market shed
offered the nativists little real protection. First to fall wounded from the
ambush was George Schiffler, an eighteen-year-old apprentice leather
worker. He died soon after. Three others fell victim to Irish gunfire under
the market eaves: Joseph Cox, a Kensington stonecutter's son, who died
of his wounds three weeks later; Henry Temper, a Kensington barber's
apprentice, who recieved a hip wound; and Thomas Ford, who received
a less serious wound.[8]

Persons in the marketplace found themselves stationary targets for
Irish gunners, so they fled the shed in all directions. Irish adversaries
awaited them in the streets with bricks and stones. Among the leaders in
this operation were weavers Patrick Lafferty (once again), David Funk,
and Robert Quillan. Unable to escape the neighborhood, the natives regrouped in the comparative safety of the market house. Retired tavern-
keeper and militia officer Peter Albright, his hands covered with blood
from carrying Schiffler, escaped to his home in Northern Liberties,
gathered eighteen of his friends with muskets and rifles, and returned to
the fray around four-thirty P.M. These guns gave the natives a measure of
equality with the Irish. While there is no record of any Irish woundings
or deaths from native marksmanship, the intensity of Irish shooting
diminished after Albright's return.[9]

This reinforcement with firepower permitted the natives to take the offensive once again. A large group of them swept up Cadwalader Street, source of the devastating Irish gunfire, armed with sticks, bricks, and pistols. They stoned Pat Lafferty's door and tried to break into his house. Next, the crowd stoned Lafferty's neighbor's home because an Irish gunner had been seen running up the adjoining alleyway. John Lavary's house received the same treatment because earlier a man with a pistol had used the doorway for cover. An Irishman fleeing up Cadwalader Street fell in weaver Edward Develin's doorway, and Develin closed his door on the man as if to dissociate himself from the latter's activities. The crowd had little time for such distinctions and broke Develin's doors and windows.[10]

The fighting and shooting raged back and forth until Sheriff McMichael and his deputies finally arrived at the marketplace around five o'clock, more than an hour after the battle had begun. With the sheriff present, the fighting ended. Guns had been used by rioters to a greater extent than ever before in the city's history. One of the implicit limits to Philadelphia collective violence had been violated. This change had come about because the fighting involved the Irish, a group not fully integrated into the values and behavioral pattern of the Philadelphia working population. But there was still much about this first round of fighting that kept within the traditional bounds established in the city's earlier episodes of collective violence. The Irish homes that were attacked were not chosen randomly; they belonged to those who were fighting the natives or who harbored Irish marksmen. The natives killed no one, confining their retaliation for the most part to attacks on houses rather than individuals.[11] Yet heavy gunfire had been exchanged, and the potential for massive bloodletting was evident.

The calm following McMichael's arrival proved uneasy at best. As dusk set in, unidentified boys lit bonfires that cast an eerie glow over the now quiet battlefield. Curious sightseers from around the city gaped at the bullet-scarred buildings. McMichael, wishing to prevent further trouble after nightfall, sent for his good friend, General George Cadwalader, commander of the city division of the First Brigade, Pennsylvania Militia. McMichael asked Cadwalader to muster his volunteers for service that evening, but Cadwalader and his junior officers balked at the request. Pennsylvania had no riot statutes. Under then-current law, victims' next of kin could sue for damages if the troops caused bodily injuries while quelling disturbances. It was not even clear that state military authorities could take action at the request of local magistrates, since some legal experts argued that only the governor could authorize their mobilization.

These questions would be settled later as the smoke cleared from Kensington. That evening, Cadwalader agreed to stay with McMichael only as an observer and advisor.[12]

Documentary evidence about that evening's happenings is somewhat vaguer than for the daytime fracas, but the main outlines seem clear. Around ten P.M., the *Ledger* reported, a nativist "mob" of unspecified proportions and composition "collected in the vicinity of Franklin and Second Streets," marched up toward Nanny Goat Market, and on the way "commenced breaking into the houses on both sides of the street, destroying the furniture, demolishing the windows, and rendering the houses completely uninhabitable." Their motive, it appears, was vengeance. Most residents along the route abandoned their homes before the crowd arrived. Only those Irishmen gathered around the Nanny Goat Market were able to put up a united defense. The others whose homes were scattered throughout Kensington were forced to flee in the face of the mobilized natives.

On their way north, the natives surrounded the seminary of the Sisters of Charity where they began throwing stones and building a fire next to its fence. Thus the crowd gave its hostility a new symbolic focus: the Catholic church. The seminary was empty, the Sisters already having removed to Iowa to take up a new assignment. A Mrs. Baker remained behind as caretaker. Unlike the afternoon counterattacks on the houses along Cadwalader Street, the attack on the seminary had no strategic or defensive purpose. It simply indicated the identity in the nativist mind between hostile Irish immigrants and the Catholic church. While the crowd swirled out front, Mrs. Baker opened the door to plead with the assailants and was struck by a flying stone. Just then, the *Ledger* recorded, "some persons," probably Irish who had been guarding St. Michael's Church, "advanced from above and fired a volley of ball and buckshot into the crowd." The natives fled, leaving two casualties behind. One of them, John Wright, supposedly an innocent bystander and son of city salt merchant Archibald Wright, died instantly. Nathan Ramsey, a Northern Liberties blindmaker, died later in the month from a chest wound. Rumor had it that St. Michael's was next on the nativists' list of targets, and many Irish defenders had already gathered at the church "with arms, determined to protect it at the hazard of their lives." The natives never attempted an attack. Throughout the night, sporadic shots were heard, but no further concentrated native forays occurred.[13]

Considering the accounts of constant gunfire, casualties and damage from Monday's two rounds of fighting seem to have been relatively light. Only one nativist, George Schiffler, was killed outright; two were to die later of wounds; John Wright, the fourth victim, was simply a bystander; and three natives were wounded. Not a single Irish death was recorded; some houses were stoned, others ransacked, and the seminary fence was scarred by flames. The only recorded Irish wounds resulted from faulty weapons exploding in the users' own hands. One Irish partisan, John McAleer, was arrested on May 8 at Pennsylvania Hospital where he had gone for medical treatment. His thumb, blown off when his flintlock pistol exploded, was discovered the next day and traced to him at the hospital. John Daley, an Irish weaver who helped break up the Friday afternoon rally, was also injured when his musket misfired. His trail of blood was traced to a friend's nearby room. Most of his native-born neighbors feared to enter, but American Republican housepainter Albert Alberger, later appointed a Kensington watchman, burst in and made a citizen's arrest of Daley and his companion.[14]

The casualty lists confirm the occupational patterns that characterized both nativist and Irish Catholic activism. Daley, McAleer, and most of the other Irish combatants whose names survived in the records were Third Ward weavers living in the Cadwalader Street, Master Street, and Germantown Road area surrounding the Nanny Goat Market. Patrick Lafferty and Edward Sherry, leaders in disrupting the Friday meeting and victims of the attack on the Cadwalader Street houses, were both employing weavers. Lafferty had fought the Gideonites in 1831. Such men possessed prestige as employers and could provide leadership for the more recently arrived Irishmen who worked in their shops and lived in their houses. Of those wounded or killed on the nativist side, all were young men, none was known to be a member of the American Republican party, and, with the possible exception of John Wright, all were employed as apprentices or journeymen craftsmen.

Tuesday's fighting was more bloody and destructive. The American Republican party must bear much of the blame for inciting the second day of violence as their attempts to capitalize politically on Monday's shooting led directly to further rioting. A small meeting of American Republicans convened on Monday evening voted a thousand-dollar reward for George Schiffler's murderers and invited the general public to meet in the yard behind the old state house yard (now named Independence Hall)

on Tuesday afternoon. Reverend John H. Gihon, one of the few clergymen active in the party, moved that the words "LET EVERY MAN COME PREPARED TO DEFEND HIMSELF" be appended to the call. The party then placarded the city with this announcement. That morning, the *Native American* proclaimed inflammatorily:

> Another St. Bartholomew's day has begun in the streets of Philadelphia. The bloody hand of the Pope has stretched forth to our destruction. Now we call on our fellow-citizens, who regard free institutions, whether they be native or adopted, to arm. Our liberties are now to be fought for— let us not be slack in our preparation.[15]

At least three thousand persons gathered for the rally by three-thirty that Tuesday afternoon. Despite the meeting's call, *North American* publisher Thomas R. Newbold tried to set the tone for a peaceful meeting in his address.[16] He cautioned his listeners to limit their activities to nonviolent political measures worthy of native-born Americans. Newbold's speech was warmly applauded, but the next speaker, Colonel Charles J. Jack, a militia officer and attorney, drew even louder cheers by making a bellicose address. Jack reminded the audience that for at least two years he had warned about "the influence of foreigners in the elections" and had urged the formation of "a regiment of Native American volunteers to sustain the native citizens and the laws against the aggressions of foreigners."[17]

Jack's speech liberated the desire for revenge harbored by many nativists. John Perry, a speaker at the May 3 Kensington rally, tried to turn the meeting from the militant spirit of Jack's words but with little success. Perry proposed a series of resolutions condemning the Irish attack on the previous day's "peaceful assembly," recommending a fund for the families of the dead and wounded and committing the meeting to peaceful redress of its grievances. While all three measures were adopted unanimously, the crowd refused to accept a fourth suggestion that the meeting adjourn until Thursday to discuss further plans. Instead, a chorus of voices shouted, "Adjourn to Second and Master now!" and "Let's go up to Kensington!" Loud approval greeted these calls. Retaking the podium, Newbold reminded the crowd of its commitment to peaceful action, but to no avail. Once again, the American Republican party could not control the forces that it had called into being. With Colonel Jack at their head, several hundred men formed a file in the state house yard, marched in military

fashion down to Second Street, turned left at the corner, and headed north toward Kensington.

As on Monday, some natives came prepared for a fight. Witnesses testified that at least a few men at the rally were carrying arms, while others who joined the line of march up Second Street had guns on their shoulders. Someone carried a torn and soiled American flag[18] with a banner attached, provocatively exclaiming: "This is the FLAG that was trampled UNDERFOOT by the IRISH PAPISTS."

Kensington's Irish also showed some degree of preparation. Many had abandoned their houses previously, taking their furniture with them, and more did so when word of the approaching march reached then. Some Irish awaited the procession with guns, clearly reflecting Irish preparedness for another confrontation. When the nativist vanguard, mostly "boys and young men,"[19] reached Master Street, it did not stop to reconvene at the Nanny Goat Market but directly attacked the Hibernia Hose House, the center of Irish firepower during the previous day's shooting. The assailants forced a side door and rolled out the hose carriage, intending to destroy it. Without hesitating, guardians stationed in the upper stories opened fire on the attackers. The natives abandoned the carriage, took shelter under the market's eaves, and returned the fire. They were joined by other armed marchers. Bullets from both sides caught the crowd in a crossfire before many could find cover.

As in Monday's fighting, the first advantage lay with the Irish who were sheltered in their homes and the Hibernia Hose House. Harmony Court, a weaver's residence off Cadwalader Street just above Jefferson, provided the most concentrated source of Irish gunfire. That morning, a shipment of muskets had been delivered to the home of weaver John Paul and he had distributed them to friends.[20] Musketballs poured into the market house from the windows and doorways along these alleys. The first native casualty, apprentice cordwainer John Wesley Rhinedollar, fell dead near the very spot where Schiffler had been shot. Three other young skilled workingmen, none of them an American Republican, also lost their lives during the first outbreak of gunfire: Kensington ship carpenter Matthew Hammitt, Southwark marble mason Lewis Greble, and Southwark rope-maker Charles Stillwell. At least eleven other nativists received wounds on Tuesday, including Peter Albright and Augustin R. Peale, the only known American Republicans who sustained recorded injuries. Peale, a dentist, was shot in the left arm and had it amputated when the wound festered. Southwark laborer George Young was shot in the back by John Daley,

prominent on the Irish side both Friday and Monday, an assault for which
Daley was later convicted. Wright Ardis, a Southwark ship carpenter, and
Kensington tavern keeper Henry Hesselpaugh were also numbered among
the injured.

The initial Irish advantage was eradicated when the nativists introduced
a new tactic: arson. Groups of nativists (none is known by name because
none was apprehended) slipped out of the market to set fire to the houses
along Cadwalader Street. In a stroke, the Irish shelters were turned into
potential traps. The frame houses in the back alleyways especially caught
fire quickly, driving out the hidden marksmen stationed there. Soon the
flames spread to the Hibernia Hose House. The *Ledger* supposed that
several persons, some perhaps wounded in their homes by nativist gunfire,
were trapped by the flames. At least one charred body was found in the
basement of a burned-out Cadwalader Street house.

As fire consumed the block between Master and Jefferson streets, nativist
gunners found Irish fugitives ready targets, and only poor marksmanship
explained why a large number of persons was not killed. The fires drove one
Irish gunman, John Taggart, out of a Cadwalader Street doorway and into
the arms of constable Bartholomew Baker. Baker attempted to bring
Taggart to alderman Isaac Boileau (a member of the American Republican
party) for arraignment, but a crowd surrounded Taggart, flailed him,
dragged him through the streets, and strung him up to a lamppost by the
neck. Finally, thinking him dead, they abandoned him. Baker revived
Taggart and preserved him for later trial. Only one Irish citizen, it appears,
was killed in the shooting: Joseph Rice, who was watching the fighting over
his front yard fence, was shot and killed instantly by a bullet from seventeen-
year-old Isaac Hare's gun. Hare escaped severe punishment at his trial because
of his youth.[21]

The shooting and incendiarism lasted until five P.M., almost an hour
after it began. General Cadwalader, Sheriff McMichael, and several militia
companies appeared at the market and the shooting ceased at once. Cadwalader
had obviously resolved in his own mind the problem of serving under a civil
magistrate. He gathered his subordinate officers earlier that afternoon and
ordered them to swear allegiance to the sheriff. McMichael was later criticized for not bringing the troops to Kensington sooner, or even better,
preventing the state house rally to begin with, but without Cadwalader's
cooperation McMichael was powerless to stop any large crowd arrayed
against him.[22]

The fires struck panic in Kensington Irish hearts, and not even the arrival of troops and firemen could allay these fears. By midnight, the area around the Nanny Goat Market was all but abandoned save for the troops. Hundreds of Irish families fled to Camac's Woods, north of Kensington. The *Catholic Herald* later gave heroic accounts of Irish refugees living for three days on nothing but berries and of one mother giving birth under a tree.[23] Fire was an especially frightening weapon in 1844 when most housing was wood framed and fire engines were primitive hand pumpers.

Despite the fact that the natives unleashed the fearsome weapon of fire on the Irish, they appeared to have only limited goals rather than wanton destruction on their minds that Tuesday afternoon. The records show that only Cadwalader Street homes that had been the center of the Irish firepower were burned. Some of the destroyed homes belonged to men prominent on the Irish side, such as Hugh Develin, James and Barney Sherry, and Pat Lafferty.[24] These fires were "defensive" in nature, used only to flush out armed Irish residents who had trapped the natives in the market house by their crossfire.[25] On Wednesday, however, the nativists went looking for vindication.

Wednesday dawned to find soldiers patrolling key points in the vicinity of Nanny Goat Market. Cadwalader assigned Captain Jonas Fairlamb to command in his absence, and Fairlamb elected to concentrate most of his men around St. Michael's Church. Someone had painted the words "POPE PROPERTY" on the rectory fence as if marking it for destruction. Father Michael Donohoe, the pastor of St. Michael's, a Repealer and highly unpopular with nativists because of his strong public stand on the Bible issue, thought it best to leave the neighborhood.[26] Before leaving in a cab, Donohoe put the keys of the church in Fairlamb's hands for safekeeping. By eight A.M. the riot area was already crowded with hundreds of visitors curious to view the destruction. While young boys pulled down tottering chimneys in the smoky ruins of destroyed houses, fire companies played water on the embers. Additional troops arrived after breakfast. The area was thus turbulent but peaceful, and the *Ledger* reporter on the scene predicted that there would be no more violence. He was wrong.[27]

Trouble began about ten that morning. Wandering the neighborhood in small bands, nativist partisans decided to search abandoned Irish houses on Cadwalader Street for arms. Invariably, soon after one of these vigilance committees visited a dwelling it caught fire. While the "searchers" worked their way into the weavers' alleys above Jefferson Street that had been a

center of Irish firepower, the military, reluctant to shoot, proved powerless
to stop the incendiarism. A military patrol, for example, intercepted some
searchers at Whitecar's Court, a carpet weaving shop with several frame
houses behind it. Captain Fairlamb was called to the scene and he persuaded
the citizens to disperse, but despite his efforts smoke was soon pouring
from a basement window. The court burned entirely before firemen could
save it.[28]

Emboldened by their success, the nativists finally decided to move against
St. Michael's in the early afternoon. They lured away the soldiers guarding
the church by setting fire to two houses around the corner belonging to
Patrick Magee. Fairlamb dispatched his men to protect the firemen fighting
the blaze. In their absence, natives invaded the church and rectory and set
fire to the furniture and woodwork. While the rectory burned, boys amused
themselves by pulling up shrubbery in the yard. Rioters invaded Donohoe's
library and sacked his books and papers; they also turned up a rusty old
musket in the basement. At least three men were arrested for turning over
gravestones in the churchyard. Flames rapidly devoured the church and
as the cross fell from the toppling steeple the crowd cheered. Someone
who came to the scene equipped with fife and drum reportedly struck up
the Orange song "Boyne Water."[29] Fire companies hurried to the scene but
judged that the crowd would never permit them to save the church. Instead,
they wet down nearby houses to protect them from flying cinders. Their
efforts were only partially successful; five houses burned.

Having destroyed Donohoe's church, the crowd moved on to the
next church-owned property, the seminary of the Sisters of Charity, scene
of the ill-fated Monday night attack. This time the building was burned
without resistance. From the seminary, the nativist crowd moved to Joseph
Corr's Catholic temperance grocery store across the street, stoned it, and
hurled his goods out the windows. On Monday, Corr allegedly had supplied
his Irish compatriots with ball and shot and the natives were taking their
revenge. The *Ledger* speculated that the crowd refrained from burning
Corr's because many American flags displayed in nearby windows indicated
that fire might spread to the homes of local patriots.[30]

Perhaps the most satisfying revenge that the rioters extracted was the
destruction of school controller Hugh Clark's home at Fourth and Master
streets. The roving crowd hurled bricks through his windows, then entered
the house and threw furniture and books into the street. According to the
Ledger, Clark's library worth several thousand dollars was completely
destroyed. The books and furniture were fed into a bonfire set in the street.

The invaders then moved next door to Clark's brother's tavern and gutted its interior as well. Finally, the crowd sacked the home and grocery of Patrick Murray who, like Joseph Corr, had supplied the Irish with ammunition earlier in the week. Merchandise worth four thousand dollars was scattered, destroyed, or stolen. Such looting was unusual. Estimates as to the total loss due to looting in the riots are not available, but the virtual absence of any other mention of stealing in the press suggests that it was minimal. Apparently revenge, not profit, was the chief motive for attacking the two groceries.

Inexplicably, Cadwalader and McMichael did not arrive in Kensington to aid Captain Fairlamb until after St. Michael's was already in flames. They brought additional troops with them. Marching up Fourth Street from the city, Cadwalader divided his men into two groups, sending some down Phoenix and then up Second Street with Colonel James Page, a Democratic politician and attorney in private life, planning to regroup again at Second and Master. While marching up Phoenix Street, Page's unit confronted a nativist group that threatened violence if the troops did not withdraw. Page "appealed to them as American citizens, upon which the crowd gave him three cheers and retired."[31] Eventually, after the nativists' attack on Clark's house and the burning of Harmony Court, the troops were able to restore order. By that time, however, there was little left worth burning in the area around Nanny Goat Market.

If the sheriff seemed remiss in failing to prevent destruction in Kensington, city Mayor John M. Scott did try to protect property under his jurisdiction. When he heard that the nativists next planned to visit St. Augustine's Catholic Church at Fourth and Vine streets in the city, Scott issued a call through the ward alderman asking citizens to "prepare themselves to patrol the streets, to resist all invasions of property, and to preserve the public peace by resistance to every attempt to disturb it." In at least two wards, residents responded by forming volunteer patrols, four men to each square block. There was no mention in the press as to whether the men were armed.[32]

By ten-thirty that night, several thousand had gathered at St. Augustine's, a crowd far larger than the mayor could hope to control. On their way from Kensington, the nativists passed a German Catholic church but did not harm it, underlining the anti-Irish basis for their actions. The crowd pressed in on the mayor, his constables, and his volunteers,[33] and when Scott mounted the church steps to ask the crowd to disperse, a stone struck him in the chest. Shortly afterward, a fire broke out in the

church vestibule, supposedly set by a fourteen-year-old boy who entered during the confusion after Scott's injury.[34] Within half an hour, the $45,000 brick structure was a total loss;[35] as the steeple fell the crowd cheered as it had at the St. Michael's fire. Again the firemen dared only hose down buildings nearby.

The burning of St. Augustine's marked the last major outbreak in the Kensington riots. The transfer of the rioting to the city, home of Philadelphia's elite, seems to have marked a turning point. For three days and nights, respectable Philadelphians had left peacekeeping in the Irish districts to the sheriff and the military. But on Thursday morning, after the violence had struck close to home, Philadelphia's leading citizens started taking measures that would not only end the Kensington riots but eventually transform the city from a preindustrial battleground to a characteristically modern, urban bastion of state-enforced order. While the transformation took several decades, the beginnings were made on May 9, the morning after St. Augustine's burned.

In an emergency session late Wednesday night, Philadelphia's Common and Select councils appropriated money to pay for troops to guard every Catholic church in the city. But the real impetus to order that halted further rioting came from Philadelphia's private citizens. Thousands attended a Thursday morning rally in the state house yard called to take measures against continued disorder. Catholic lawyer and judge John M. Read presided and ex-congressman Frederick Fraley served as secretary. Horace Binney, perhaps Philadelphia's most respected attorney and elder statesman, spoke first. He reminded his audience that they had all gathered because they believed that Philadelphia was a "community governed by laws," which every citizen, "for his own safety and the peace and order of the city," had to defend. To insure peace, Binney argued, constituted authority had to use *"whatever force is necessary . . .* to prevent the lives and property of citizens from being destroyed."[36] Binney's words were greeted with hearty cheers. By popular acclaim, order-conscious Philadelphians told military leaders that they endorsed the use of lethal force in suppressing riot and disorder. The soldiers need no longer hesitate to act for fear of being held liable for rioters' injuries. No less eminent an authority than Pennsylvania Attorney General Ovid Johnson, a resident of Philadelphia, discussing the meeting's resolution, acknowledged that the doctrine of unlimited police power during a riot was essential and proper. "I know this power has sometimes been questioned," he explained, "but without its possession, our government would be a mere shadow."[37]

The law-and-order citizenry took its resolves seriously. Hundreds of persons volunteered to serve in citizens' patrols under General Robert Patterson, commander of the Pennsylvania militia. Sheriff McMichael and Mayor Scott put their powers in his hands. The general then ruled Philadelphia County by martial law. Patterson's orders to those serving under him left little doubt of his intention to maintain tranquility even at the cost of human life. Patterson told his soldiers that they were to "use all force at their disposal to protect public and private property." They were to "clear and occupy any street, alley, or private property to prevent riot, disturbance or destruction." If they encountered resistance, the offending party was to be given five minutes to disperse; after that time, the area was to be "cleared forcibly." Patterson concluded:

> Order must be restored, life and property rendered secure. The idle, the vicious, the disorderly must be curbed and taught to understand and respect the supremacy of the law and, if they will not take warning, on their own heads be the consequences.[38]

We may take the measure of Philadelphia's new spirit of order by retelling a single anecdote. Thursday night, May 9, in Southwark, a hostile crowd of young men and boys gathered outside St. Philip de Neri Catholic Church at dusk to heckle the militia company assigned to guard it. Southwark aldermen were called, and they arrested the leaders before they provoked the soldiers into a serious clash. To the *Ledger*'s surprise, the aldermen were "promptly assisted by a large body of citizens who prevented any rescue" by the hecklers' friends.[39] Such help for constables in recent years had almost never been forthcoming. After the Kensington riots, however, enough Philadelphians seem to have been aroused to activate a new spirit in the city. Once the crisis passed, a good deal of this spirit remained alive and helped bring about the adoption of permanent measures to maintain civic order in the future.

Martial law remained in force nearly a week. No public meetings were allowed without General Patterson's approval. By Wednesday, May 15, he dismissed the last of his troops and the citizen guards disbanded later in the week. Bishop Kenrick suspended all Catholic worship on Sunday, May 12, and when the Sabbath passed without incident the city breathed more easily.[40] The bishop reopened the churches the following week. Peace had been restored, but at least six persons were known dead. Certainly twenty persons, and perhaps many more, were wounded. Property damage

was estimated conservatively at $250,000, not counting lost commerce
and man-hours of labor and the cost of military upkeep. The *Ledger*
noted that drunkenness in Kensington seemed higher than usual that first
weekend following the riots.[41] This was not the only sign of heightened
anxiety that became manifest after this first round of fighting.

NOTES

1. *Public Ledger,* May 3, 1844.

2. Kensington Tax Records, 1844 Philadelphia City Archives.

3. See above, chap. 2. If Lafferty was typical of the other immigrant
leaders in the ensuing riots, then it was likely that Kensington's Irish leaders
were not recent arrivals but rather men who had been in the neighborhood
long enough to secure recognition and a following. This pattern, which
seems likely, can be confirmed by hypothesizing that recent arrivals would
not yet have the reputation or self-confidence necessary for an active role
in community affairs, either in politics or rioting. Some of the other Irish
leaders in the fighting such as Barney Sherry, John Paul, and Hugh Develin,
while certainly not men of high social standing in the wider Irish community, were established employers who set the tone of public affairs in
the weavers' neighborhood around Nanny Goat Market. Unfortunately,
we cannot compare the list of leaders with some "typical" rank-and-file
Irish rioters because only the formers' names survive in the documents.

4. *Public Ledger,* September 20, May 4, 1844. References to September and later issues of the *Ledger* indicate that the facts cited were
gathered from trial testimony reprinted in the *Ledger,* rather than on-the-
spot accounts.

5. *Public Ledger,* May 7, 1844.

6. John Hancock Lee, *Origin and Progress of the American Party*
(Philadelphia: Elliot and Gihon, 1855), 49-51.

7. *Public Ledger,* May 7, 1844. The *Sun* identified the reporter as
Captain William W. Small.

8. Ibid., September 7, 1844. A decade later, American Republican historian John Hancock Lee retold the probably apocryphal tale that
Schiffler died while holding the American flag, despite his wounds, as a
rallying point for the nativists. This image of the expiring Schiffler supporting the tottering flag also appears in the anonymous epic poem, *Six
Months Later,* which commemorated the half-year anniversary of the
Kensington riot. Schiffler's name was later immortalized through its

adoption by a nativist hose company and several branches of the "Young Native" clubs, not to mention a street gang in Southwark. Despite this canonization, the party apparently had no claim to Schiffler before his death. None of the written records reflect Schiffler's formal membership. His age and social standing make it highly unlikely that he would have been a participating member.

9. *Public Ledger,* May 7, 1844. Albright was later cleared of all charges against him; ibid., January 31, February 1, 1845.

10. Ibid., May 7, 1844.

11. George Rudé, in *The Crowd in History, 1730-1848* (New York: Wiley, 1964), argues that one of the chief characteristics of "preindustrial" crowds was their restraint. For an application of Rudé's analytical categories to Jacksonian Philadelphia, see Michael Feldberg, "The Crowd in Philadelphia History: A Comparative Perspective," *Labor History* 15 (Summer 1974): 323-336.

12. McMichael, a Whig, was later editor of the *United States Gazette* and the *Saturday Evening Post.* Subsequently, he helped found the Union League and was instrumental in creating Philadelphia's Fairmount Park. Cadwalader, an attorney in private life, was described by his friend Sidney George Fisher as a man of "power, energy, boldness, decision of character, activity of mind . . . though not capable of thought on abstract or general topics." These qualities served Cadwalader well in his military career, and he performed bravely but ruthlessly when given a free hand in the Southwark riots. Sidney George Fisher, *A Philadelphia Perspective* (Philadelphia: Historical Society of Pennsylvania, 1967), 225.

13. *Public Ledger,* May 7, 1844.

14. Ibid., May 9, 1844.

15. *Native American*, May 7, 1844.

16. Other officers included A. DeKalb Tarr, Thomas Grover, Reverend Gihon, cooper John D. Fox, watchcase-maker John S. Warner, printer James Gihon, dentist Augustin R. Peale, and the ever-present Lewis C. Levin.

17. *Public Ledger,* May 8, 1844.

18. An Irish witness later testified that the flag had been torn and soiled when, after the rainstorm broke, the nativists dragged it through the streets in their flight to the Nanny Goat Market for shelter. The natives claimed that it was soiled when Schiffler fell trying to uphold it. *Public Ledger,* September 20, 1844.

19. Ibid., May 8, 1944.

20. Ibid., September 20, 1844.

21. Ibid., October 19, 26, 1844. Taggart also received a light sentence because the judge considered the crowd's beating sufficient punishment. Hare was later pardoned by the governor; ibid., January 23, 1845. He went

on to become a hero in the battle of Cerdo Gordo during the Mexican War, serving as a lieutenant under Captain Charles Naylor, a prominent figure in the Southwark riots. After being cited for bravery at Cerdo Gordo, Hare was convicted of killing a civilian in cold blood and sentenced to death. *Sun,* May 18, 1848.

22. The troops were later accused of failing to turn out because they were not promised sufficient pay before they started. Evidence to support this charge is lacking, however. It appears that the officers' concern for their legal liability was the cause of the military's failure to arrive quickly in Kensington.

23. The most miraculous story involved the daughter of Patrick Fisher, first man wounded in the Nanny Goat Market. On July 4, 1844, the *Herald* reported that "when the Kensington riots were raging at their heights, the house of Patrick Fisher was burned and his family, driven before the raging flames and dreading the vengeance of the mob, made a precipitous flight into the woods. A daughter of Mrs. F., 12 or 13 years of age, who from her infancy had never been able to either walk or talk, was actually frightened into speech and the power of walking by the terrible scene of battle and conflagration. The girl can now run about like other children of her age, and is in perfect possession of the faculty of speech."

24. A full list of damages appears in the *Public Ledger,* May 8, 1844. Most were able to collect awards against the county for their losses.

25. The limited nature of the nativist counterattack was well illustrated by an incident at the home of a Mr. Magee on the corner of Washington and Jefferson streets. The natives entered his home to search for weapons. When they found Mr. Magee at home ill, they left without doing any damage.

26. Bishop Kenrick, on the advice of friends, also fled the city. He was later criticized for abandoning his churches, but the Irish Catholics were a very small minority in Philadelphia and could not hope to stand up alone against the natives. Kenrick fled rather than remain either as a potential hostage or the symbolic leader of a futile Catholic resistance. For a defense of his actions, see Father Hugh Nolan's biography, *The Most Reverend Francis Patrick Kenrick, Third Bishop of Philadelphia, 1830-1851* (Philadelphia: American Catholic Historical Society, 1948), 320.

27. *Public Ledger,* May 9, 1844.

28. Ibid.

29. Ibid. The exact role of Orangemen in the Native American riots cannot be known. Some sources—especially Catholic ones—blame the Orange for precipitating the riots, but a check of various Presbyterian and Methodist congregation rolls for the 1840s and 1850s failed to turn up any rioters who were members of those denominations. Nor did the American Republicans, who doubtless would have been pleased to pro-

claim the presence of Irishmen in their ranks had Orangemen been there in any numbers, make much mention of them. On the contrary, the *Catholic Herald* proudly announced that two Orangemen and a Jerseyman fought for the Hibernia Hose against the nativists. David Montgomery believes that Orange weavers joined their Catholic workmates in resisting the invasion of Kensington. "The Shuttle and the Cross: Weavers and Artisans in the Kensington Riots of 1844," *Journal of Social History* 5 (Summer 1972): 43. Finally, the crowds of nativists were too big, and too many persons voted for the American Republic ticket, to explain satisfactorily Philadelphia nativism simply as an Orange-based movement.

30. The display of flags and *Native American* mastheads paralleled the London custom of illuminating windows to indicate the occupants' support for a popular demonstration. Persons unsympathetic to the cause did not light candles, and the crowd then retaliated by smashing their windows. Rudé, *Crowd in History,* 55.

31. *Public Ledger,* May 9, 1844.

32. Ibid.

33. According to the testimony of Joseph Sill, a Philadelphia merchant, the First City Troop was on the scene but it did not aid the mayor. Three times, by Sill's account, they galloped past the crowd at St. Augustine's but did nothing to disperse it. Sill claimed that the company wished to encourage the crowd, but judging from the First City Troop's highly respectable composition this seems unlikely. Many of the city's most affluent upper-class gentlemen served in its ranks.

34. One of those who aided in the burning of the church was eighteen-year-old John Hess, who had emigrated to Philadelphia from Europe only six years previously. Several of the rioters had German-sounding names, although no clear inference can be drawn from this fact.

35. Church trustees later collected $100,000 in damages.

36. *Public Ledger,* May 10, 1844 (emphasis added).

37. Ibid.

38. Ibid., May 11, 1844.

39. Ibid., May 10, 1844.

40. Nativists attacked Kenrick for this action, which they interpreted as a publicity stunt to draw further sympathy to the Catholic cause. Patterson himself was annoyed by the implicit doubt about his ability to keep order. He announced that "he desires to have it instantly settled that all may render their devotion to their Maker in their own way unmolested and unharmed." Kenrick and Patterson were reconciled a few days later. Letter of May 11, 1844, Cadwalader Papers, Historical Society of Pennsylvania.

41. *Public Ledger,* May 14, 1844.

6
Interlude

As the ashes settled in Kensington, the antagonists on both sides stepped back to regroup and reflect. General Patterson's prohibition on public gatherings gave the Irish and the natives some time to formulate a posture on the cataclysmic events that had just fractured the city's peace. For both parties, the question became one of placing the blame on the other side while exonerating their own. Framing the Irish and nativist responses was the new background created by Philadelphia's respectable elite. The laissez-faire attitude toward violence held by the city's ruling class was rudely shaken by the burning of the churches, especially St. Augustine's downtown.

Horace Binney's resolve at the May 9 rally to support the laws with "all necessary force" had been met by enthusiastic cheers. While his rhetoric was not new, subsequent developments indicated that large numbers of middle- and upper-class Philadelphians were sufficiently moved by the death and destruction to back their cheers with concerted action, much of it unprecedented. In the past, these people had tolerated and occasionally condoned a limited amount of political violence along the lines of the eighteenth-century Wilkite or "church and king" riots.[1] Most election riots, or an event like the burning of Pennsylvania Hall, caused little sincere anguish among the upper classes because of their sympathy with the rioters' cause.[2] But a much less tolerant attitude emerged after the Kensington riots, one that evolved into a thorough rejection by the ruling elite of any form or degree of private collective violence. The heavy loss of life and property in Kensington convinced them that violence was no longer a viable means for adjusting community conflict.

It should come as no surprise that upper-class and property-owning Philadelphians recoiled from the massive violence that had raged for three tumultuous days, and nary a voice was raised to justify the beha-

vior of either side. What seems most notable about the aftermath of the Kensington riots, nonetheless, was the intensity and purposefulness with which the elite responded and the sense of personal shame and guilt that emanated from upper-class circles for many months after the Kensington eruptions. In the days immediately following the restoration of order, the Philadelphia Bar turned out a contingent seventy strong to patrol the neighborhood around St. Mary's Catholic Church. Citizens in Dock, Delaware, and North Mulberry wards in the city formed volunteer patrols to keep their homes safe from wandering bands of rowdies. Citizens in every district walked musket to musket with soldiers during the first week of martial law, and after the troops were dismissed some of the vigilance committees continued to patrol a while longer.[3]

Not all the citizens active in the volunteer patrols were wealthy Protestant merchants, lawyers, or bankers. While the North Ward volunteer patrol, for example, was officered by Samuel V. Merrick, owner of the city's largest ironworks, and Matthew Newkirk, owner of a newspaper and full-time politician, the company included stove maker Owen Kisterbock, cordwainer James Hood, plasterer Aaron Burtis, and many other men from the humble toiling classes. It seems fair to say, however, that Philadelphia's traditional ruling elite took the lead in restoring order to the city, and they did so by rendering active personal service.[4]

Members of the elite might have disturbed their normal lives to play soldier out of the human desire to add variety and excitement to their lives,[5] but personal participation in the rigors of peacekeeping had long been one of their traditions. Their willingness to assist in maintaining order marked not only a departure from their recent past but also a return to an older heritage that had fallen into disuse.

One "Old Citizen," lamenting the breakdown of that tradition in the *Public Ledger,* reminisced about the good old days when Robert Wharton had been mayor between 1806 and 1819. Wharton, claimed the writer, had been able to quell a large collection of rowdies simply by "commanding them to disperse" and "calling upon the bystanders at the same time to 'assist the mayor,'" a call responded to "by every good citizen present, so far as was necessary to enable the Mayor . . . to arrest such as would not disperse." By the 1840s, however, deferential law enforcement rarely, if ever, worked. Almost daily, the Philadelphia press reported escapes by prisoners taken by constables who were then attacked by the offender's friends as bystanders stood gawking. The failure of the great mass of

uncommitted persons to stop the recent disorder in Kensington proved
that the typical taxpayer was willing to demand protection but not to
offer assistance in return to harried law-enforcement officials. One
Ledger reader openly berated his fellow citizens for abandoning the
sheriff and the mayor to grapple singlehandedly with the crowds in Kensington and at St. Augustine's. He proposed that all Philadelphians
swear an oath that they would "never . . . participate in any riot, and . . .
use all lawful means to prevent them," while vowing to offer aid to
public officials in whatever manner necessary. The author was ashamed
to have to remind his readers that in times past such a formal oath would
have been unnecessary.[6]

The failure of Philadelphia's upper classes to participate in peacekeeping was out of character with their other attitudes toward public service
and civic responsibility. Even in an age that glorified the "common man,"
it remained fashionable for Philadelphians of stature and wealth to serve
in public office.[7] Politically, the elite dominated the city through control of the Whig party.[8] Well-bred Democrats such as Richard Vaux, mayor of Philadelphia in 1854, and Congressman Charles Jared Ingersoll,
the only Jacksonian supporter in a family replete with aristocratic Feder-
alist and Whig ancestors, were simply viewed as misguided sheep lost from
the flock.[9] Moral uplift and reform as well as charitable community service also attracted the upper crust. The city's leading names graced the
officers' lists of innumerable charitable and soup societies, libraries, and
workingmen's institutes aimed at raising the aspirations and hopes of the
lower orders. Philadelphia's "aristocrats," such as the wealthy John Hare
Powel or the snobbish Sidney George Fisher, were not above descending
into the political cockpit or collecting wood for the poor, the sort of
pursuits that all but a few of the "best" Philadelphians of later generations would find below their dignity.[10] During the Jacksonian era, Philadelphia's upper classes still ruled as well as reigned. As time passed, the
civic duties they performed would be assigned to professionals trained
in handling the social problems of a more complex metropolis. In 1844,
however, this transfer had not yet begun.

Active involvement in civic affairs was central to the elite's tradition.
While it is difficult to generalize about any large population, especially
one that lived more than a century ago, it seems safe to say that most
prominent Philadelphians were white, of English descent, Protestant, and
the offspring of several generations of former Philadelphians. Families
whose sires had provided the nation with political and military leader-

ship during the Revolution—the Morrises, Mifflins, Biddles, Cadwaladers, Ingersolls, and Binneys—were still ruling Philadelphia in 1844. In the days before independence, the city's most prestigious citizens generally made their fortunes in commerce and banking, but over the years professions such as law and medicine had also acquired high standing in the upper circles. The Philadelphia Bar, for example, was probably the nation's most respected. Pennsylvania Hospital and the University of Pennsylvania Medical School were manned by some of the nation's leading physicians. Even Catholic business and professional men gained access to the city's social and political elites through their learning and wealth. Newer industrial fortunes could also buy a place in high circles. In short, Jacksonian Philadelphia's elite had either breeding, wealth, or both.[11]

More than tradition led Philadelphia's establishment to arrive at a consensus against further collective disorder. The Kensington riots had illustrated more powerfully than ever before the great danger such eruptions posed to property and persons. Especially as the city grew in size and its factories and warehouses expanded in number, disorder and destruction harmed those most who had their fortunes invested in real property. Riot proved expensive to property owners in yet another way: an 1841 county ordinance provided for the reimbursement of mob victims from the public treasury. In an age that viewed even the smallest taxes as an unbearable burden, the cost of compensation became an explicit incentive for suppressing public disorders. In addition, more than one observer noted that the prevalence of disorder in Philadelphia cost the city untold millions each year because out-of-town investors were doubtless hesitant to venture their capital in such an unstable setting. When measuring costs, city spokesmen were well aware of the public relations problem the riots and nativism were causing. The Democratic daily *Spirit of the Times* scolded:

Philadelphia is utterly and irremediably disgraced. Her high pretensions to Christianity and morality may well become a mockery and a by-word of reproach in the mouth of millions. To think that she should be the first to trample, not only on the principles of republicanism, but on the first principles of Christianity itself.[12]

The *Spirit of the Times* was not alone in berating Philadelphians for the failure of their behavior to live up to the past traditions and present pretension of the "City of Brotherly Love." Many critics went even fur-

ther, questioning whether the massive riots in Kensington indicated some serious malady in the body politic, whether the fragile organism of American freedom was being overcome by a fever of excess liberty. The editor of the Democratic *Pennsylvanian,* normally a defender of the city's Irish immigrants and native workingmen, wondered aloud if the nation's political institutions were "too far in advance of the general intelligence to work as they should." Addressing the county grand jury, Judge Anson V. Parsons asked from the bench "whether some fault did not exist in the vital organisms of the social system, the workings of which displayed such terrifying irregularities." The *Spirit of the Times* tried to imagine how William Penn would feel if he rose from his grave in the second week of May 1844 to see the "bristling bayonets" and the "pomp and panoply of war" parading in his streets. Doubtless he would have pronounced his "Holy Experiment," "founded as an asylum of the persecuted for opinion's sake, and . . . particularly consecrated to religious freedom," a failure. The city's abolitionist weekly, *Pennsylvania Freeman,* recalling the burning of Pennsylvania Hall as well as Kensington, bluntly charged that "Philadelphia is ruled by the mob, and it is farcical to pretend that civil law protects, in the least degree, the property or person of our citizens."[13]

The *Freeman*'s disgust was echoed widely throughout the upper-class ranks. The *Ledger,* for example, asked rhetorically, "Who generally constitutes mobs?" and supplied its own answer: "The least informed portion of the community; those who understand no other mode of resistance or disapprobation than yielding to the dictates of mere animal nature." Judge Joel B. Jones told the county grand jury in July 1844 that "when the tumult is gathered, the mass of excited men, the mob, however virtuous as individuals, cannot reason, and is the sport of every casual impulse." With characteristic contempt for his social "inferiors" as well as a sincere foreboding about the future of aristocracy in America, Sidney George Fisher intoned his judgment that "the present civilization of the world, Europe and America, is destined to be destroyed by the eruption of the dark masses of ignorance and brutality which lie beneath it, like the fires of a volcano."[14]

The *Public Ledger* suggested a method for handling the "mob," one perfected by Napoleon, who had the intelligence, claimed the *Ledger,* to greet crowds with a "whiff of grapeshot" rather than a lecture or a round of blanks fired over their heads. Weak measures, the paper was certain, only enraged crowds rather than dispersed them, making it nec-

essary to expend many more bullets and lives to subdue them later. The
first round of live ammunition sobered the crowd; the second dispelled
it. Thus a mailed fist was really "humanity, mercy; it saved bloodshed."[15]

The *Ledger* compared neither Sheriff McMichael, Mayor Scott, nor
General Cadwalader favorably with Napoleon because of their handling
of the Kensington riots. McMichael received the lion's share of the blame,
and the May grand jury even suggested that his failure to control the
rioters and prevent the rally in the state house yard on Tuesday, May 7,
might warrant an investigation. Some persons spread rumors that the
militia refused to serve in Kensington because they had not been promised sufficient pay. While such speculation was idle, the open and implied criticism of the sheriff and military clearly influenced their behavior when violence erupted two months later in Southwark. General Cadwalader especially seemed determined during that second riot to live down
his reputation as a sluggard in facing the Kensington crowd, and his rash
actions attempting to restore his image in Southwark led directly to an
unnecessary loss of several lives.[16]

While the jeremiads poured forth from the pens and tongues of leading
Philadelphians, a variety of public-minded citizens set to work to find some
long-range solutions for the problem of popular disorder. Some ideas were
serious and thoughtful, such as the suggestion that Philadelphia organize
a police force along the lines of London's "bobbies." The force would be
composed of professionals assigned permanently to a district, who would
get to know its inhabitants and help prevent small gatherings from growing
into large crowds. Officers would patrol around the clock, wear identifying uniforms, and earn as much respect from Philadelphians as their counterparts had won from Londoners. Second, civic leaders circulated a petition to introduce a riot law in the state legislature that would establish
the militia's right to fire on a crowd after sufficient warning had been
given. Sponsors of the bill wanted to free the soldiers from fear that they
might be held liable for any damage or injury that they inflicted in the
line of duty. The law eventually carried. Third, some Philadelphians insisted that the sheriff's powers needed clarification and strengthening.
McMichael himself had been uncertain whether he could ask for military
assistance without express authorization from the governor. The attorney general's ruling on the May 9 actions, however, seems to have cleared
up that question satisfactorily; no further legislation regarding the sheriff's rights and responsiblities was enacted. Other suggestions seem less

well grounded in logic: one man quite seriously suggested that the state legislature could effectively "prevent" riots by doubly indemnifying anyone who lost property during a riot, "even before the ruins had stopped smoking, if possible." That way, crowds would benefit those they sought to injure and would thus think twice about giving such a boon to their victims.[17]

One reform had been broached long before the Kensington riots and would be offered frequently in the decade that followed, when it was finally adopted. Led by the *Public Ledger,* a group of citizens launched a campaign to consolidate the city's many districts under a single government with a unified police force, one mayor, and one set of city councillors. In May 1844, Philadelphia was tasting its first sample of consolidated rule, unfortunately under martial, rather than civil, law. The lessons of strong centralized authority were not lost on consolidation advocates, however, even if the 1844 experiment was a highly unusual one. Given sufficient power and jurisdiction, they argued, a strong civil government could equally well bring peace and harmony to Philadelphia. Yet this solution was not tried for another decade. It was not until 1854 that the constitutional and political objections of traditionalists, bondholders, and office-seekers could be overcome and consolidation effected. Looking back over the decade of struggle to achieve consolidation, one of its strongest proponents recalled that memories of the Kensington riots proved the most potent force in securing legislative and popular approval for the measure.[18]

In the decade or so after 1844, Philadelphia's leaders placed increasing emphasis on the need to suppress collective disorder. Their efforts in this direction ran parallel to, and have distinct resemblances to, the evangelical, temperance, public education, and other reform movements, moral uplift crusades, and civic improvement campaigns that surfaced in the 1840s. As noted in Chapter 4, social historians recently have been trying to define more clearly the relationships between efforts at moral and religious uplift on the one hand and the desire for greater "social control" over the lower orders on the other. In a similar vein, they have been trying to fully understand the tie between what Allen Silver has called "the demand for order in civil society" and the needs of the emerging industrial sector of the antebellum economy. Both the agitation for evangelical moral reform and the imposition of a stricter public order are thought to be in some way or ways related to the transition from a preindustrial to an industrial society. The leaders of both the moral cru-

sades and civic peacekeeping, it is argued, were the elite upper classes who stood to gain from the continuation of the moral and cultural status quo, industrialization, an increased subordination and subservience on the part of the working classes, or some combination of the three.[19]

Recently, a few historians have challenged this interpretation and have attempted to salvage the tarnished reputations of the antebellum moral reformers. Lois Banner, for example, points out that these dedicated men and women were not simply trying to save the souls of urban working people by denying them the pleasures of drink and sex. They also tried to improve the condition of the working classes through free public education, the fight for women's rights, and abolition of imprisonment for debt. These reformers could be both liberal and intolerant, depending on the issue, but this is not to say that they were at all times manipulative or self-serving. After all, saving an individual from alcohol dependence by persuading him to abandon the bottle can hardly be thought of as other than a positive good.[20]

A defense along this same line can also be erected to protect the elite property owners who inveighed against the "democratic excesses" of popular crowds in Philadelphia. After all, it was the working classes themselves who were the victims as well as the perpetrators of the vast majority of acts of collective violence. To defend the majority's right to indulge in collective disorder on democratic grounds assumes that the rights of unpopular minorities are subordinate to the moods of their numerical superiors. One must distinguish between the demand for order as a defense for individual rights and the demand for order as an end in itself so that the status quo, for better or worse, can be preserved. In the aftermath of the Kensington riots, the ruling elite advanced arguments on both grounds for the suppression of collective disorder.

The demand for order united conservatives and liberals alike. Temperance advocate Peter A. Browne, later an American Republican, insisted that the riots simply confirmed the fact that youth was no longer taught "subordination of the passions." He claimed that the only hope for society was the reassertion of authority by parents, teachers, and clergymen.[21] Others took the view that the riots posed an indirect threat to personal liberty in that their continuation would lead some to cry for a strong man, a Napoleonic figure, to impose order on society. The need to find a method for peacekeeping that remained within the city's republican traditions became a pressing preoccupation of Philadelphians for the next decade.

Preoccupied with establishing order in the city, elite leaders were less concerned about ascribing blame for the events in Kensington to one or the other group of rioters. As a result, the two contending parties took it on themselves to assign the burden of guilt to each other, apparently in an attempt to woo support from the order-conscious upper classes as well as from their own dedicated supporters. The Irish could make the strongest claim to the role of victims with one of their neighborhoods laid waste and two of their churches in ashes. Catholic leaders took to the public press with assertions that their coreligionists had been forced to use their guns in defense of their lives and churches. They pinned the label of "church burners" on the American Republicans, sensing that the title would raise antinativist sentiments in elite circles. While they admitted that the Third Ward Irish had attacked the meeting in Nanny Goat Market, Catholic leaders were able to interpret even that excess as an act of self-defense. They contended that the American Republicans were dedicated to depriving the Irish of their rights on the ground of their religious faith, thus making the hostility felt by the immigrants perfectly understandable. It was the nativists who had raised the first aggressive cries, and the Irish were only responding, however unwisely, to that original provocation.

The Catholic response was based on more than cynical opportunism, however, or an effort to win sympathy from the mass of nonnativist Philadelphians. Bishop Kenrick sincerely urged his flock to moderation and did all in his power to see that no further confrontations occurred. Through the pages of his diocesan newspaper, the *Catholic Herald,* he dispensed a line of tolerance and forgiveness to his readers, while assuming, of course, that his words would reach beyond his Irish Catholic audience.

On May 16 the *Herald* reprinted Kenrick's 1842 sermon entitled "Charity toward Enemies," which preached that revenge belonged to God, not man, and closed with the refrain: "Father forgive them, they know not what they do." Considering that Philadelphia's Catholics comprised only 10 percent of the population, it is not surprising that the bishop urged no stronger action for his followers than prayer. Issues of the *Herald* throughout May and June asked readers to prove "peaceable and good citizens" despite any provocation. Speaking for the community, Kenrick pledged that "Catholics as a body desire to live in friendship with their fellow-citizens and utterly abhor violence."[22]

When the city's secular press revealed in subsequent weeks the horror that many Philadelphians felt toward the church burnings, the *Herald* began to trade a bit on this subject. While still offering nativists the olive branch, it published articles reminding Philadelphians that "the smoldering ruins of St. Augustine's and St. Michael's tell a doleful tale to the traveller who passes from the hall whence 'liberty was proclaimed throughout the land' to visit the far-famed spot where justice and liberty seem to have chosen a dwelling place that was said to be eternal."[23] St. Michael's provided especially melodramatic imagery: the only wall still standing bore the inscription, "The Lord Seeth," and the *Herald* did not let its readers miss the point.[24] The destroyed churches became a favorite theme for aspiring Catholic poets. One bard, referring to the overturned headstones in St. Augustine's churchyard, suffered

> To see them smash the silent tombs with great rapidity
> To destroy the silent moldering bones of Bishop Hurley.

Even the remains of the "father of the American Navy," Commodore James Barry, buried at St. Mary's Roman Catholic Church, were not immune from nativist hostility. The natives

> Threatened to destroy the church which his mouldering bones does shelter
> From the scorching sun in summer and the stormy blasts in winter.[25]

Finally, the Catholic side scored heavily when a fictitious "Charles Schiffler," supposedly the nativist martyr's brother but in fact an unidentified prankster, sent a death threat to New York's Bishop John Hughes. While the *Herald* admitted there was no such person as Charles Schiffler, it asserted that the threat was serious nonetheless. Such incidents scored points for the Catholic side.[26]

By the end of May, when the reaction of the elite against the "church burners" was at a peak, Kenrick focused the *Herald*'s editorial campaign on the errors of nativism and the American Republican program. Challenging the argument that naturalization should come only after a residence of twenty-one years, Kenrick retorted that "America ought to be an asylum for our fellow men who are driven from the Old World by op-

pression or by the disproportion of the population to the means of subsistence." After all, he noted, "God has given us a new world, ample in
extent, in resources . . . It is a gift we have no more right to monopolize
than the few savages who centuries since were the sole proprietors of the
soil." Speedy naturalization, the editorial argued, would make the immigrant feel that he had a stake in society and integrate him into wider community patterns. Admitting that the new arrivals were occasionally victims of demagogy, the *Herald* suggested that the best prevention against
permanent corruption was a useful education and a secure place in the
political system. The possibility of real power would convince immigrants to choose their leadership more carefully.[27]

While Kenrick spoke out as the official voice of the diocese, lay Catholic leaders, especially those who were not Irish, launched a simultaneous
campaign of verbal protest and propaganda in the secular press. The
bishop had probably encouraged his lay congregants to raise their own
united voices to dispel the nativist argument that Kenrick alone was concerned with the question of the Bible in the public schools and had
forced his personal stand on his disinterested followers. Prominent Catholic attorneys and physicians like Charles Repplier, William A. Stokes,
and Frederick Eckard defended the church and their fellow Catholics
from attacks in the nativist press. One development especially aroused
an anguished protest. In mid-June, a nativist-sympathizing county grand
jury published the findings of its investigation into the Kensington riots.
The jury condemned the Irish *as Catholics* for causing the violence. Of
the sixteen jurors who signed the report, none appears to have had an
Irish name, and at least two were members of the American Republican
party. One juror, Edwin Greble, was the father of a young nativist
wounded in the riot. The jury certainly perceived the issues from the
nativist point of view. It concluded that the riots resulted from the "efforts of a portion of the community to exclude the Bible from the Public Schools," thereby endorsing the false accusations against Bishop Kenrick and Hugh Clark that nativist propagandists had been circulating despite all evidence to the contrary. These alleged Catholic efforts, the
jury explained, "in some measure gave rise to the formation of a new
[American Republican] party which called and held . . . meetings in the
district of Kensington." The jury considered the American Republican
meetings no more than "the peaceful exercise of the sacred rights and
privileges guaranteed to every citizen by the constitution and laws of
our state and country" and concluded that they were disrupted "by

bands of irresponsible men, some of whom resided in this country only a short period."[28] Thus they laid all the blame on the Irish Catholic side.

While these findings pleased self-righteous nativists, the leading Catholics took umbrage at the jury's one-sided judgments. On June 18, a blue-ribbon Catholic committee (including Judge Archibald Randall, attorneys William Stokes and Charles Repplier, and physicians J. G. Nancrede, Frederick Eckard, and William A. Horner) replied to the jury's accusations. In their "Address of the Catholic Laity," the committee protested that the Catholic community had been condemned by *ex parte* evidence. "They [the jury] seem to have assumed that one party [the Irish] were the rioters and the other the assailed," dismissing the fact that Irish churches and houses were burned and Irishmen were injured. The address strongly denied that the bishop's position on the school Bible issue had led to the emergence of political nativism. Rather, it claimed that it was simple anti-Catholic prejudice that created "a new political party . . . hostile to liberty of conscience." To prove that Catholics had not started the Bible controversy, the committee appended depositions from seven county school controllers affirming that no Catholic had ever requested that the King James Bible be removed from any Philadelphia school. As for the supposedly "wanton" attack on the American Republican rally that the jury attributed to "bands of irresponsible men, some of whom resided in this country only a short time," the committee averred that "it would be most unjust on the presumption, or *prima facie* evidence, of the guilt of a small group of men, to visit their offenses on the entire community, from the mere accidental circumstances that most of them are said to hold the religious faith that we profess."[29]

While the address was endorsed by several hundred Catholics at a public rally on June 20, there is no record that the Irish or Catholic communities held any other meetings. Bishop Kenrick suggested to his followers after the rally that it be their last for a while as the public mood was not hospitable to large Catholic gatherings. His supporters accepted this judgment and chose to argue their case only in public print. There was one group of Irish Catholic activists, however, who pursued a course that the bishop would have frowned upon had he known about it. William Dunn, a leader of the Repeal Association and brother of Thomas Dunn, the pastor of St. Philip de Neri Catholic Church in Southwark, quietly asked Governor David Porter for permission to form a militia company to guard his brother's church. Without making a public

announcement, Porter granted Dunn a captaincy and the right to draw twenty muskets from the Frankford armory. In July, these muskets would set off new riots in Southwark, but when Porter granted Dunn his commission in June the incident went unnoticed.[30]

Other than the near-secret formation of William Dunn's volunteer company, there is little to show that the city's Catholic community, upper-class or working-class, took militant steps to counteract any further threats posed by organized nativism, real or imagined. The most cohesive and combative Irish community, that of Third Ward, Kensington, was in no condition to launch an antinativist campaign. The destruction of the neighborhood had so demoralized the handloom weavers that their strike, lingering on against some employers since winter 1842, was finally broken, and their employers, most of them fellow countrymen, lowered wages to a bare subsistence.[31] Sheer survival, rather than political nativism, became the weavers' first preoccupation. Physically, the Third Ward was slowly rebuilt, but St. Michael's and the Nanny Goat Market, the two social centers of the community, would take years to replace. Some families moved from Kensington permanently because their homes were gutted. Others left Philadelphia entirely. Contemporaries observed that the rate of Irish immigration to the city fell off in the months following the Kensington riots. Throughout June and July, neighborhood men would disappear in the hands of the constables for appearance at hearings or trials. Third Ward residents would need time to pull themselves back together.

Like their Catholic counterparts, leaders of the American Republican party tried to establish their own and the party's innocence in the events that had transpired in Kensington. The first order of business was countering the galling epithet of "church burners" that Catholic elements had attached to the movement. There was truth to the American Republican assertion that not they, but the rowdy Irish Catholics, young boys, and turbulent native partisans outside the party itself were responsible for the fighting. Of all those persons whose names were later connected with the rioting, only four—Peter Albright, Wright Ardis, Augustin R. Peale, and Charles J. Jack—were definitely party members. It is not even clear that Albright and Jack were actively involved in the fighting.[32] Still, the party had to bear the blame for the passions it had loosed through its verbal attacks on Catholics and foreigners. Even if no American Republicans were implicated in the actual incendiarism, their organization was still identified as the church burners' choice.

Like the Irish, the American Republican case rested on self-defense. The uncouth foreigners had disrupted the perfectly legitimate exercise of free speech and right of assembly on May 3 and 6. Such abuses could be borne, but the slaughter of innocent Americans for merely trying to exercise these rights was more than patriotic souls could tolerate. According to the party's offical address on the subject, "with the burning of churches which followed this foreign massacre the American Republicans had nothing to do." However, the sheer horror of the deed provoked retaliation from "an infuriated mob, who looked upon the Roman Catholic Churches as armed fortresses of the ferocious beings who were reeking with the blood of their murdered fellow citizens." However justified such behavior might have been, American Republicans were not involved in the fighting. The *North American* blamed the fighting on teenagers and "well-known outlaws" on both sides, while the *Native American* described them as "ragamuffins" and "the residue and very scum of the population." Like some upper-class elements, the nativist press also blamed the sheriff for not acting sooner to break up the fighting. But even if the actors were an "infuriated mob" of criminals and ragamuffins who had broken the laws of God and man by burning churches, the American Republicans held the Irish in even greater contempt for their role in the riots. "Disgraceful as is the burning of churches, fearful and appalling as is the act by which buildings dedicated to the worship of God are given to the flames, is it an outrage of greater character," they asked, "than that which sends the souls of men without a moment's time for preparation to the bar of God's judgment?"[33]

The party denied that it had created the unrest that had brought on the riots because it had never agitated the immigrant question in anything but a peaceful political campaign. Lewis Levin declared that he had always admonished his paper's readers to "reserve your energies to be concentrated in a legal and constitutional manner and never let provocation, however galling, tempt you into commission of a wrong in retribution for an injury." Levin's injunction was probably sincere. Native-born Americans represented a vast majority of the Philadelphia population, and according to the rules of democratic politics, their views would always prevail by majority vote. Indeed, American Republicans often spoke of the ballot box as a panacea for the social ills of the nation. It was their majoritarian logic that caused them to demand so strongly that the "purity" of the electoral process be maintained.[34]

As moderate as Lewis Levin's position might have been in advocating a political solution to the immigrant-native conflict, he had a way of appending incendiary additions to almost all his statements. In the very next breath after calling for a resolution of the conflict at the ballot box, he blamed the Kensington riots on the Repeal Association, which had "turned traitors to American principles, and prostituted the American press against American institutions," thereby "fomenting the passions of the Irish to madness." He was certain, in fact, that the Repeal Association, composed of the more prosperous Irish elements in Philadelphia, was at the bottom of a serious plot. Levin observed that

> splendid rifles and warlike munitions not appropriate to their condition have been found in the possession of Irish Catholics of the *lowest grade* of poverty, clearly showing that the chief actors or instigators in this bloody assault on peaceable Americans are yet behind the scenes, and that they are persons of wealth, thus clearly indicating the deep-laid schemes of conspirators by heads as clear as their hearts were black.

He concluded with a self-righteous flourish: "We do assert before the most Holy Father of mercies that we are the wronged party, and we stand like persecuted martyrs defending our lives and liberties."[35]

The mixture of self-righteousness and apology that marked the early American Republican response to Kensington also characterized the response of Philadelphia's evangelical churches. Like American Republicanism, the Protestant crusade had loosed forces of collective emotion that it could not control. Yet the *Presbyterian* disingenuously denied that "any . . . members of this denomination . . . might be found guilty of aiding or abetting in the burning of churches or private dwellings," despite the fact that a portion of the crowd played the "Boyne Water" and cheered as the burning steeple toppled from St. Michael's. The paper denied that the riots were the "fruits of the spirit of intolerance," as the Catholics had been claiming; rather, they stemmed from the reflex actions of a mob infuriated by seeing its fellows shot to death. But even if the crowd had good grounds for its rage, the *Presbyterian* concluded, "There is not a Protestant church in our country which would not promptly exclude from its communion any of its members who might be found guilty" of church burning.[36]

Organized nativism was so preoccupied with living down its reputation for incendiary agitation that it was almost a month before the American Republicans dared resume their program of rallies and meetings.
When they did test the waters of public opinion, they were pleasantly
surprised to find that the riots had actually redounded to their favor, at
least in the short run. Thousands of previously uncommitted Philadelphians were won over to their cause by the aggressive behavior of the
Irish in Kensington. Perhaps it was merely that having to choose between
the Irish or native version of things, the majority of Americans in Philadelphia chose to side with their countrymen rather than the immigrants.
In any event, the first American Republican foray into the streets after
the riots proved a remarkable success. They organized a funeral procession for Joseph Cox, who had finally succumbed to wounds inflicted on
him May 6 during the fighting around the seminary. While several hundred persons walked behind the casket, another three thousand watched
along the line of march from Northern Liberties to Moyamensing ceme-
tery. Encouraged by this large turnout, the party set about to measure
its strength in the various portions of the city. On June 7, a substantial
crowd turned out to hear Peter Sken Smith attack the House Judiciary
Committee for tabling the party's petition urging Congress to change the
naturalization laws. He proclaimed war on those Pennsylvania congressmen who voted to impose the "gag rule" on nativist petitions. On June
17, more than eight hundred persons boarded the steamboat *Robert
Morris* for an outing to Burlington, New Jersey, where a branch association of the party was formed.[37] Such attendance indicated that the party
had gained numerous accessions to its ranks, probably even more than
its leadership had expected. By mid-June, American Republicanism went
off the defensive and aggressively set about to capture control of the public imagination and public office.

When the nativist grand jury's report appeared on June 17, placing
the blame for the Kensington riots on the Irish and the sheriff, the American Republicans were given a boost in prestige and morale. Technically
exonerated from blame, the party moved into upper-class neighborhoods,
hoping to organize branches of the movement. Thousands attended rallies in Dock Ward and the Exchange Building at the end of June. Speakers there applauded the jury's "forthright" findings and reiterated that
the party desired nothing more than the preservation of America for Americans through strictly peaceable political measures. To loud cheers,

Peter Sken Smith demanded that foreign governments keep their "but-termilk and potato gentry" at home.[38] At a rally in Southwark on June 25, American Republican physician George C. Chambers called for the resignations of Irishmen Hugh O'Donnell as district school board con-troller, Judge James Campbell (later a member of President Polk's cabi-net) from the Southwark municipal bench, and John McCoy from the district board of commissioners on the ground that "Americans are cap-able of making and administering their own laws."[39] McCoy, in fact, resigned. The movement was registering small but steady gains.

Bolstered by accessions to their ranks, the party was emboldened to declare that Independence Day, July Fourth, would be celebrated with the largest parade and rally that the city had ever seen. If the ward ral-lies gave the nativist rank and file an opportunity to cheer speeches and applaud their favorite politicians, the giant parade offered them a chance to participate in a truly gala fete to American Republican principles. His-torian Eric Hobsbawm has argued that modern political and social move-ments have lost the ability to communicate solidarity through festivals, parades, and symbolic collective ritual.[40] The July Fourth parade of 1844, however, showed that the preindustrial ritualism that Hobsbawm found among the "primitive rebels" of Europe still survived in the arti-san ranks of Philadelphia. The parade deserves note for other reasons as well: if the reports are accurate, a very large proportion of the city's populace either marched in or cheered the parade; and the response of William Dunn and Southwark's Irish to the July Fourth celebration led directly to another round of rioting.

The parade was by all accounts the most impressive Philadelphia had ever seen.[41] Upward of five thousand persons marched in its columns, and the estimates of the size of its audience ran as high as a hundred thou-sand, or a quarter of the city's population. The line of march ran from Southwark to Kensington, back to Northern Liberties and out the Wis-sahickon to Snyder's Woods on the Schuylkill. Thomas Grover, mounted on a white horse, served as chief marshal. A trumpeter led the proces-sion. The order of march behind Grover and the committee of arrange-ments indicated the traditional deference that Jacksonian society paid to agriculture, even though Philadelphia itself was dependent on com-merce and the crafts for its livelihood. The first men in line were farm-ers marching behind a plough and horses decorated with ripe grain. The customary homage thus paid to the tillers of the soil, the city's own la-

bor hierarchy came next. The butchers, dressed in clean white coats with blue silk scarves and sashes, were given first place. Then came twenty infirm native citizens, mounted, "in citizens' dress." The bereaved families of the Kensington victims followed in black carriages and elicited great sympathy from the spectators. After this maudlin show, a number of mechanical and seafaring trades marched delegations in the display. Sailors seemed the most popular, as many boys appeared in seaman's dress. To honor Philadelphia's shipbuilding crafts, no fewer than seven model boats were drawn on wheels through the streets. The largest, the twenty-eight-foot sloop *Native American,* was actually seaworthy and completed several voyages to New York City. (It later sunk with the loss of two lives.)[42] The city's fishermen brought one of their boats and marched in a place of honor in the parade.

After the trades and occupations were honored, each American Republican ward association was represented by a delegation bearing symbolic banners or pulling a float. The marchers' iconography helps communicate to us the imaginative hold that the nativist movement exerted on its followers. Several dozen associations in all sent contingents, most of them with roughly similar displays. One typical group, from Second Ward, Southwark, was composed of a band, followed by men with a banner depicting the goddess of liberty, an American flag draped around her as a mantle and an open Bible in her hand. Above Miss Liberty soared an eagle grasping a laurel-wreathed picture of Washington in one claw and a liberty pole in the other. From behind the eagle floated a flag bearing the motto, "Beware of Foreign Influence" (Washington's enduring legacy to American nativism). At her feet lay a bundle of rods tied together with another flag, this one with the motto, "United, who can break us." A serpent, symbolizing Rome, lay dead at her feet, while Fame flew aloft proclaiming the end of papal influence. In the background on one side appeared a temple of liberty, on the other a schoolhouse. Sixty men followed the honor guard, and then came an equal number of boys in liberty caps with flags and a banner reading, "young hearts but true."

From the accounts, it appears that the parade's iconography did not strongly emphasize the religious aspect of American Republicanism.. Except for the representations of the Bible in the ward association banners (always used in conjunction with the image of a schoolhouse) and an occasional dead serpent, most of the imagery was secular. Symbols of national unity and republican purity were the paraders' chief emblems.

Traditional religious formulations did, however, manage to creep in despite the parade's secular, patriotic theme, most notably in the display of the Walnut and Chestnut Ward Association. Their banner seems particularly incongruous in a parade extolling the death of papal influence: beneath a bust of George Washington's mother, replete with flags, oak leaves, and an eagle flying overhead, the artist inscribed the words "To Mary, Mother of Washington." The most impressive float was that presented by the central party organization itself. Several grooms, black and white, the first two dressed as Indians, led sixteen grey horses pulling a twenty-two-foot high temple of liberty. The structure, raised four steps on a pediment, had a domed roof and thirteen columns representing the original states. Stars, coats of arms, and names of the capitals of the states decorated the tops of the columns. The temple was as big as the average Philadelphia house and far more impressive.

July Fourth passed peacefully, much to the surprise of law-enforcement officials and the city's Irish Catholics. Only a scuffle on the evening of July 3, when several young rowdies attacked a group of native American picknickers along the Wissahickon, disturbed the quiet. A false rumor spread that the attackers were Irish but there was no native retaliation.[43] Had there been trouble, however, all three sides—Irish, native, and upper-class—were prepared for it.

Responding to the criticism that he was inadequately prepared for the Kensington riots, Sheriff McMichael took elaborate measures in anticipation of the Fourth. As early as June 13, he requested that the army arsenal at Frankford suspend its usual practice of selling surplus weapons to private citizens. The arsenal's commander rejected the request as illegal, thus deflecting one of the earliest recorded attempts at gun control in America. That same day, McMichael had discovered a shipment of muskets in Kensington whose owners claimed that they had bought it from the Bridesburg arsenal to equip themselves as a new militia company. The sheriff confiscated the guns, knowing that legally constituted militia companies received their weapons gratis from the state. On June 16, the sheriff asked General Patterson to detail some men to the predominantly nativist Weccacoe Engine Company on Queen Street, Southwark, near St. Philip's Catholic Church. The company's rival, the Democratic Weccacoe Hose, had threatened to destroy the engine company's house after a scuffle had drawn some blood. The troops remained on duty until June 19, and trouble was prevented.[44]

The July Fourth parade called for additional special preparation. On June 28, McMichael asked several prominent citizens and all county aldermen to recruit reliable friends to assist in keeping the peace on the Fourth. McMichael intended to deputize these volunteers at the first sign of trouble. He kept the plans secret for fear of exciting undue anxiety. Quarter Sessions Judge Joel Jones also took steps to preserve order. He requested every alderman to assign three new special policemen in each ward for the holiday. Jones ordered them paid from the county treasury. General Patterson, also sensitive to criticism that the militia had been unprepared for Kensington, placed his troops on alert July 3. Civil and military police forces stood in readiness on the eve of the great parade and festival.[45]

The Irish in Southwark also took defensive precautions. July Fourth seemed a likely time for anti-immigrant passions to run high, and the threat seemed more real than ever when a woman Sunday school teacher told William Dunn of a threat against St. Philip's that she had overheard a few days earlier.[46] Dunn, who had received permission from the governor earlier in the month to form a company of soldiers, busily drilled more than one hundred men in the church's aisles on July 3. Most of the volunteers carried broomsticks rather than weapons since parts were missing or broken in the arms that Dunn had been issued at the Frankford arsenal. Fortunately the Fourth passed without incident, but the very next morning a wagon loaded with the repaired muskets returned to St. Philip's from the arsenal. As Dunn's Irish volunteers unloaded the wagon, word spread through nativist sections of Southwark that the Catholics were arming the church. By midday, word had carried through the city. Nativists, buoyed by the successful parade and numerous accessions to their ranks, were not likely to let this turning of a Catholic church into an "armed fortress" pass unnoticed. The possibility that the anticipated trouble of the Fourth might yet occur on the fifth rose sharply.[47]

Perhaps no fighting would have occurred if generals Cadwalader and Patterson had not been so sensitive to the criticism of their failures in Kensington. Southwark's Catholics could not have hoped to resist the overwhelming numbers of nativists who wanted the church disarmed. As later events showed, Dunn proved willing to disarm the church in exchange for guarantees of its safety, and the American Republican leadership, conscious of the need to prevent a repetition of St. Michael's or St.

Augustine's, offered those guarantees. But General Cadwalader in particular seemed determined to apply the elite's new resolve against private
usurpations of public authority even if he caused worse chaos. His resolve led inexorably to bloody clashes between the military and the
strong-willed, self-righteous nativists who came to remove the arms from
St. Philip's.

NOTES

1. For a description of conservative popular riots of this nature, see
George Rudé, *The Crowd in History* (New York: Wiley, 1964), chaps.
3, 9.

2. See, for example, William T. Parsons, "The Bloody Election of
1742," *Pennsylvania History* 36 (July 1969): 290-306.

3. *Public Ledger,* May 15, 18, 22, 1844.

4. The ward patrol list is preserved in Cadwalader Papers, Historical
Society of Pennsylvania, Philadelphia.

5. To his diary, Sidney George Fisher confided his pleasure at serving on riot duty as part of the Bar Association contingent. He found it
an exhilarating break in his daily routine. *A Philadelphia Perspective:*
ed. N. B. Wainwright (Philadelphia: Historical Society of Pennsylvania,
1967), 167.

6. *Public Ledger*, May 14, 16, 1844.

7. For a more complete portrait of the elite in this period, see the
opening chapters of E. Digby Baltzell's *Philadelphia Gentlemen* (Glencoe:
Free Press, 1958).

8. Without reopening the already overworked question of whether
the workingmen of Philadelphia voted for the Whigs or the Jacksonians,
it seems clear that most of the city's upper classes voted Whig and it was
from this group that the Whig party's leadership was drawn.

9. For the career of Richard Vaux, see Sam Bass Warner, Jr., *Private
City* (Philadelphia: University of Pennsylvania Press, 1964), 91-98. For
Ingersoll, see Fisher, *Philadelphia Perspective,* 20.

10. Fisher, *Philadelphia Perspective*, 174.

11. Baltzell, *Philadelphia Gentlemen,* chap. 15.

12. For the county ordinance, see John Thomas Scharf and Thompson
Westcott, *History of Philadelphia* (Philadelphia: L. H. Everts, 1884), I, 6.
For concern about investments, see *Public Ledger,* May 13, 1844. For
quotation, *Catholic Herald,* May 10, 1844.

13. *Pennsylvanian,* May 9, 1844; *Public Ledger,* September 3, 1844; *Spirit of the Times* quoted in *Catholic Herald,* May 10, 1844; *Pennsylvania Freeman,* May 9, 1844.

14. *Public Ledger,* March 3, 1840, July 2, 1844; Fisher, *Philadelphia Perspective,* 169.

15. *Public Ledger,* May 13, 1844.

16. Ibid., June 10, 17, 1844; *Germantown Telegraph,* May 22, 1844.

17. *Public Ledger,* May 18, 1844; *Pennsylvanian,* May 17, 1844; *Public Ledger,* May 18-22, July 16, 1844.

18. *Public Ledger,* July 24-26, 1844. For the consolidation of 1854, see Eli Kirk Price, *The History of Consolidation in the City of Philadelphia* (Philadelphia: Lippincott, 1873).

19. Allen Silver, "The Demand for Order in Civil Society," in *The Police: Six Sociological Essays,* ed. David J. Bordua (New York: Wiley, 1967), 1-24. This argument also appears in David Montgomery, "The Shuttle and the Cross: Weavers and Artisans in the Kensington Riots of 1844," *Journal of Social History* 5 (September 1972), 411.

20. Lois W. Banner, "Religious Benevolence and Social Control: A Critique of an Interpretation," *Journal of American History* 60 (June 1973): 23-41.

21. *Public Ledger,* May 14, 1844.

22. *Catholic Herald,* May 16, 1844.

23. Ibid., May 23, 1844.

24. Ibid.

25. "Reflections on the Late Riots by Candid Writers in Poetry and Prose (Philadelphia, 1844)," *American Catholic Historical Society Researches* 28 (1911): 234.

26. *Catholic Herald,* June 6, 24, 1844.

27. Ibid., May 30, 1844.

28. Vincent P. Lannie and Bernard C. Diethorn, "For the Honor and Glory of God: The Philadelphia Bible Riots of 1844," *History of Education Quarterly* 8 (Spring 1968): 80; *Public Ledger,* June 17, 1844.

29. *Catholic Herald,* June 27, 1844.

30. *Public Ledger,* July 6, 1844.

31. *Spirit of the Times,* September 13, 1848.

32. A jury later cleared Albright of any wrongdoing in Kensington, and Jack led the march from the state house yard on May 7 but then apparently backed out of the action. *Public Ledger,* May 8, 1844, February 1, 1845.

33. Ibid., May 15, 1844; *Native American* and *North American* quoted in John Hancock Lee, *Origin and Progress of the American Party in Politics* (Philadelphia: Elliot and Gihon, 1855), 103, 129.

34. *Sun,* May 11, 1844.

35. Ibid., May 13, 1844.

36. *Presbyterian,* May 18, 1844.

37. *Germantown Telegraph,* May 29, 1844; *Public Ledger,* June 8, 18, 1844.

38. *Public Ledger,* June 28, 29, 1844.

39. Ibid., June 26, 1844.

40. Eric J. Hobsbawm, *Primitive Rebels* (Glencoe: Free Press, 1959), 150-153.

41. For an account of the parade, see Lee, *Origin and Progress of the American Party,* 136-161, and *Public Ledger,* July 6, 1844.

42. For the sinking of the sloop *Native American,* see *Public Ledger,* December 20, 1844.

43. Ibid., July 6, 1844.

44. McMichael Papers, American Catholic Historical Society, letter of June 13, 1844; *Public Ledger,* June 14, 1844.

45. McMichael Papers, June 26, 29; *Public Ledger,* July 2; Cadwalader Papers, Historical Society of Pennsylvania, July 3, 1844.

46. *Public Ledger,* July 6, 1844.

47. Ibid.

7
The Southwark Riots

As word of the delivery of the guns at St. Philip's spread through the city's grapevine, four parties acted to remove them. A nativist crowd, a delegation of American Republicans, Sheriff McMichael, and General Cadwalader each had plans for preventing the Catholic arms from threatening the peace. Understandably, each conceived the threat differently, and each proposed to remedy it by a different method. The four set to work at cross-purposes and two of them—the nativist crowd and the general's troops—ended up shooting at each other. Two legitimacies had come into conflict: on the one side, a community-supported crowd was deeply troubled by the imprudent actions of the Catholic defenders of St. Philip's and wanted to see it disarmed; on the other, a military officer and his men were intent on carrying out a mandate from the leaders of the city to maintain order at any cost.

Southwark's rank-and-file nativists responded spontaneously to the arming of the church. In early evening, a crowd swelling to more than a thousand gathered on Queen Street to demand the removal of the guns. Frightened by the size of the crowd, Third Ward alderman Charles Hortz dispatched a call for the sheriff. McMichael responded immediately, stopping on his way to Southwark at General Patterson's home in the city for consultation. Patterson then informed McMichael for the first time that Governor Porter had authorized William Dunn in mid-June to arm the church as a defensive measure.[1] McMichael thus had to find a means of quieting the crowd without infringing on Dunn's right to bear arms. Arriving at the church, he explained the dilemma to alderman Hortz and two other Southwark aldermen, Robert Palmer and Nathan McKinley, the latter an employing cobbler and charter member of the American Republican party. With McKinley's help, McMichael collected

a few volunteer citizens to stand watch outside the building. Leaving
McKinley in charge, McMichael, Palmer, and Hortz went inside and spoke
to William Dunn and his brother, Father Peter Dunn. The former confirmed
that the governor had authorized him to obtain the muskets from Frankford arsenal: he showed the group the warning sent by the Sunday school
teacher. Dunn also informed McMichael privately that additional arms
were stored in the church.[2]

McMichael began to steer a middle course between Dunn's right to
defend the church and the angry sentiments displayed in the street. He
decided to confiscate the newly arrived muskets and bayonets but to
say nothing about the other arms stored inside. Dunn agreed to this
measure. Making a show that he hoped would quiet the crowd's fear
and hostility, McMichael turned the twenty muskets over to his deputies guarding the entrances and ordered them to try the barrels with
ramrods to prove that they were unloaded. After this demonstration,
McMichael told the crowd: "I have, in company with Alderman Hortz
and Palmer, been in the church, and taken possession of all the arms we
were able to find." He reminded them that "a number of your own citizens, selected by your own aldermen, are here to prevent any more arms
from being taken in, as well as to protect the church from injury. I therefore beg of you, as good citizens, to disperse and return to your homes."[3]

The incident might have closed with that if a part of the crowd had
not suspected Dunn and the Catholics of bad intentions. While a portion
of those gathered accompanied the posse down Queen Street to Commissioners' Hall, where the guns were deposited with the district watchmen for safekeeping, and many others drifted home, several hundred persons chose to remain at the church and demand the right to search for
additional arms. Perhaps one of the aldermen leaked word that other
guns were inside. Perhaps the crowd simply distrusted the Catholics.
Wright Ardis, a wounded victim of the Kensington shooting, was especially insistent.[4] Yielding to this pressure, McMichael asked Alderman
McKinley to appoint a posse of trustworthy men to search the building.

"Trustworthy," to McKinley, meant nativist, and all seventeen chosen
were hostile to the Catholics. At least three had helped found the American Republican party and another three were relatives of founders. A
seventh searcher, John W. Smith, would be arrested on a charge of firing
a cannon at the militia during the subsequent riot. The search committee's
composition reflected, once again, nativism's characteristically artisan
roots: fourteen of the seventeen were skilled craftsmen such as carpen-

ters, cordwainers, and coachmakers. The other three were a grocer, a brewer, and a merchant. This delegation entered the church around midnight, accompanied by McKinley, the sheriff, and Alderman Palmer. William Dunn greeted them, a pair of pistols hanging from his waist. Poking around in closets and back rooms, the committee uncovered fifty-three muskets and light fowling pieces, twenty-three of which were so deeply (and ineptly) loaded that they could not have been fired without exploding in the users' faces. Two armed Irishmen, posted by Dunn as sentries, were discovered and disarmed by McMichael.[5] The sheriff, however, advised the aldermen not to try removing the newly discovered arms before morning because such actions might excite the crowd. Despite their vexation at discovering the cache of arms, the posse agreed to McMichael's strategy. Above all, the American Republicans among them wanted to avoid another church burning. The sheriff then returned to General Patterson to ask for aid in guarding the church. Patterson dispatched Captain Hill's Company of City Guards, and the troops cleared the street with no resistance. While the search committee, now deputized by the sheriff, remained inside the church, Hill's soldiers stood guard outside. Friday night, which began so inauspiciously, thus ended quietly.

By inviting the militia to the scene, McMichael increased the possibilities of violent conflict, if only because the soldiers were armed. Patterson and Cadwalader were still smarting from public accusations that their men had been ill prepared and reluctant during the Kensington riots. This time, the generals had determined, if there was to be any trouble, there would be no ground for civilian criticism. At the same time, nativist ardor had been increasing steadily since the Kensington fight, and the anti-immigrant movement encompassed an ever larger percentage of the population. It seems fair to say that the overwhelming majority of Philadelphia's native-born lower classes, reinforced by at least a portion of the middle and upper classes, resented the Irish "ambush" at the Nanny Goat Market and sympathized with those dedicated to fighting the "papal menace." As noted earlier, nativism's rank-and-file adherents were accustomed to enforcing their will by direct action. Thus the sides were drawn: nativists resolved not to tolerate any more armed Irish Catholics, even within the sanctuary of a church; catholics determined to defend their churches; and upper-class Philadelphians, for their part, pledged to suppress private collective violence even if it represented an overwhelmingly popular will. The American Republicans

were caught in the midst of these three competing pulls. While they
were mortified by their identification as "church burners" and "ruffians,"
they could not stand by while their own followers resisted militant Catholic attempts to arm a church. Party leaders were obliged to search for
a position somewhere between further anti-Catholic violence and a recognition of the Catholic right to bear arms in defense of church property.
To propitiate their respectable critics, the party wished to uphold the
peace, but it also had to support its own rank and file. The assignment
proved difficult.

By mid-morning on Saturday, a crowd had gathered again in Queen
Street, and by noon perhaps a thousand persons had congregated in the
narrow streets around the church, gawking at the soldiers and peering

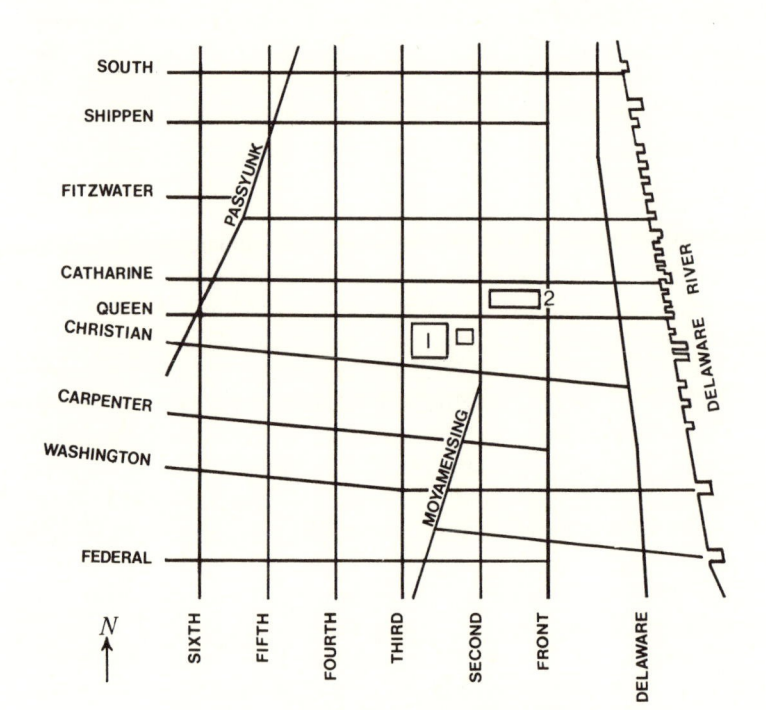

Map 3   Third Ward, Southwark, in 1844

1. St. Philip de Neri Church   2. Commissioner's Hall

at the occupied church. Around two-thirty, General Cadwalader arrived to survey the situation first hand. He found the City Guard's position precarious. Even by Philadelphia standards, Queen Street was narrow, built up on both sides with three-story brick row houses crowded close to the street. There would be little room for maneuver if more troops were needed or if the street had to be cleared. St. Philip's itself was a sturdy brick structure, set back a few feet from the narrow sidewalk and surrounded by a waist-high brick wall topped with a fence. Because of its brick exterior, incendiaries would have to get inside to threaten it. Cadwalader moved to relieve the pressure on Hill's men and the posse who were, in reality, prisoners within as much as guardians of the church. Unavailingly, he requested that the crowd disperse. In reply a voice from the throng asked by what authority the church had been armed. Cadwalader replied that the governor had legally granted William Dunn permission to obtain twenty muskets for the building's defense. Neither he nor General Patterson, Cadwalader went on, were informed of this decision and therefore could not have prevented it. Once more, he asked the crowd to go home. Alderman Sanders reassured the crowd that all weapons had been removed from the church and that the sheriff's posse and City Guards occupied the building. He saw no reason for the people to remain in the area. No one left. Fuming at the crowd's intransigence, Cadwalader rode off to make further preparations for clearing the street. Residents of Queen Street worried too at Cadwalader's failure and resulting anger. Sensing his mood, some evacuated with their possessions and others displayed American flags in their windows, as had been done in Kensington.[6]

Soon after Cadwalader left Southwark, Sheriff McMichael appeared. He had spent the day gathering 150 friends and supporters to act as his official posse. He had asked for 600 but the others failed to appear. Armed with clubs and batons, the usual weapons of civilian posses, his supporters carried no guns. At McMichael's orders, they marched up Queen Street from Second, driving the crowd from in front of the church. The posse met no physical resistance. McMichael then ordered the street closed to everyone but residents and dismissed the original search committee still on duty in the church. Acting at the sheriff's request, Patterson sent four more companies to relieve the City Guard and help McMichael keep order.[7] The combined forces of posse and military, without using bayonets, had little trouble keeping the streets clear, and it appeared that the church would once again be safe for the night.

Acting on his own, and at cross-purposes with McMichael, General Cadwalader now forcibly intruded himself into this stable situation. He went beyond McMichael's tactic of simply closing off Queen Street in front of the church. The general decided not to let persons congregate in nearby areas and took aggressive measures to enforce this decision. Around 11 P.M., when darkness made the task more difficult, he brought a company to St. Philip's with three small cannons. He ordered these troops to clear the corners of Second and Third streets with fixed bayonets and turn all resisters over to the posse. His men first charged into a group at Second and Queen. The surprised gathering backed down Second toward Christian. There was little room to dodge the soldiers' rush in narrow Queen Street. Cadwalader then wheeled his men and had them repeat the tactic up Second Street. Finally, he chased the remaining onlookers up Queen toward Fourth Street. While the troops herded the crowd, the posse—acting in response to Cadwalader's initiative—arrested nearly twenty persons who hurled paving stones, rocks, and insults at the soldiers.[8] Some of the missiles struck the military officers in the front ranks. Provoked by this resistance, Cadwalader announced his intention to open fire if the brickbatting continued. Equally aroused, persons in the crowd dared him to fire. Word passed through the crowd to keep out of the center of the street in case Cadwalader carried out his threat. After hesitating a moment, the general gave the order to fire by platoons. Cadwalader later testified that he especially ordered firing by platoons so that there would be a minimum of shooting and so that it could be stopped as soon as possible. He hesitated, he claimed, long enough for all the bystanders to disassociate themselves from the rock throwers. Those remaining in the streets, he believed, had ample warning and knew of his intentions.[9] The consequences were on their own heads. Before the troops could fire, however, Whig ex-Congressman Charles Naylor, serving with the posse, stepped in front of the guns, raised his arms, and frantically yelled something like, "My God, don't shoot! Don't shoot!"[10]

Naylor's act no doubt saved several lives. Cadwalader, later events demonstrated, fully intended to carry out his command. Some persons, such as the editors of the *Catholic Herald,* later argued that Naylor risked the military's wrath and muskets in order to regain the political influence he had once exercised in Southwark.[11] Naylor, an attorney, held a congressional seat from 1838 through 1842, running as a "workingmen's friend." He proudly claimed shoemaking as his past profession and cap-

italized on this background in his campaigns. Whatever his motive, Naylor's intervention prevented the soldiers from firing. Outraged, Cadwalader ordered Naylor arrested for attempting to incite mutiny among the military and posse. When informed that Naylor himself was a posseman and McMichael's friend, Cadwalader replied, "All the more important to make an example of him." Cadwalader later reflected that had the posse mutinied after Naylor's intervention, "it was my intention to have wheeled a platoon and fired on them."[12] Cadwalader was so intent on maintaining discipline in his own and the posse's ranks that he paid no attention to the crowd. While the troops arrested Naylor, the throng, detecting Cadwalader's seriousness, dispersed.

While the general's action did little to endear him to the nativists, his order to fire did clear the streets. Naylor and the others taken prisoner were placed in St. Philip's under military guard. Quiet was thus brought to the district. Before dawn on Sunday morning, most of the soldiers and the posse were dismissed, and Cadwalader assigned two companies, the Markle Rifles and Hibernia Greens, to guard the church. The latter, an Irish company dressed in their distinctive Kelly green uniforms, proved a fateful choice. Cadwalader probably chose them as a company likely to take an active interest in guarding the church, but their presence proved provocative to nativists. Their captain, wealthy broker and Repeal Association member John B. Colahan, was placed in command of both companies. Colahan later complained that his thirty men had no provisions and little ammunition when placed on duty.[13] At dawn, he dismissed the Markle Rifles' twelve men to get breakfast and supplies, ordering them to return by nine. They did not return until noon, and in their absence a series of events transpired that brought the Hibernia Greens and Southwark's nativists to the brink of tragedy.

The trouble began when a group of nativists appeared on Sunday morning to demand the militia's prisoners. Aldermen McKinley and Hortz led the delegation. Colahan had been ordered to release all the prisoners except for Naylor under the condition that a civil magistrate take responsibility for them, and so he released them to Hortz. Supporters waiting outside cheered when the prisoners emerged, and the alderman immediately released them on their good behavior. When the crowd realized that Naylor was not among those freed, they began demanding his release. Although Naylor was later to reject American Republicanism and remain a loyal Whig, at this moment he became a nativist darling. His confinement by an Irish company in a popish church

was a direct affront to "American" spirits. They sent word to Colahan that if Naylor was not released immediately, they would storm the church and liberate the prisoner. To back this threat persuasively, a group of boys and young men, led by Naylor's good friend, Andrew McClain,[14] a grain merchant, brought a four-pound cannon up from a ship at the docks. One witness claimed that, as they marched, the group pounded a tin kettle as a drum. Colahan had strict orders to hold Naylor for treason hearings, but the show of force outside the church convinced him that adherence to duty might cost him and his men their lives. He dispatched an appeal to Cadwalader for immediate reinforcement.[15]

Awaiting the return of the Markle Rifles or additional help from Cadwalader, Colahan tried to stall for time. He ordered his eighteen men to load their guns and make a public show of preparation in hopes that this might slow any nativist plan to attack the church immediately. By this time, the crowd had grown to more than two thousand persons. Around noon, the Markle Rifles returned to St. Philip's, and on their arrival the crowd cheered their commander, Captain Thomas L. Saunders, and begged him not to enter the church unless Naylor was released. Assessing the crowd's mood, Saunders agreed to talk to Colahan on their behalf. The company entered the church and informed Colahan they could not agree to defend it if Naylor was detained. Unfortunately, no muster role of the Markle Rifles still exists, but Saunders himself was an active nativist. Colahan could not hope to defend the building without his assistance, and he agreed to release Naylor to an alderman if Cadwalader failed to send reinforcements in a short time. Saunders accepted this decision but would wait only ten minutes before marching his men out of the church. When no help appeared, Colahan capitulated and turned Naylor over to Alderman Hortz.[16] Admirers cheered as Naylor appeared on the church steps. Acknowledging the crowd's acclamations, he begged them, "as they loved him, to do as he intended to do, to retire to their homes."[17] Andrew McClain and several hundred others accompanied Naylor home.

Naylor's release did not end the Hibernia Green's ordeal, however; the siege, in fact, was growing more serious. More than half the crowd remained at St. Philip's after Naylor's departure. A few young people in the crowd brought the cannon to the back of the church and set it in a vacant lot across the back street. Lacking heavier ammunition, they filled it with scrap iron and old nuts and bolts. The boys took aim at the church's rear windows and fired, but the fusillade only broke a few bricks on the building's edge. The cannon then had to be rolled back

to the wharf, where it was loaded with more scrap and returned for a second volley. This time, while there was no damage to the church, shrapnel showered a hundred yards in all directions.[18]

While Generals Cadwalader and Patterson inexplicably sent no aid to the Hibernia Greens, leaders of the American Republican party came to their aid. After the cannoneers' second shot, Lewis Levin and Thomas Grover arrived at St. Philip's. Both men, desperately trying to avoid any further unfavorable publicity for their movement, took steps to prevent a repetition of the Kensington holocaust. The two consulted rapidly and Levin, the more popular orator, mounted the cannon and asked the crowd to desist. Most of the spectators stopped to listen, but a few of the more recalcitrant continued pelting the church with stones. Grover then mounted a second cannon (brought up from the wharf after the second shot) and proposed that the crowd stop attacking the church in exchange for the Hibernia Green's withdrawal. The crowd gave its general assent, and Levin entered the church to negotiate with Colahan and Saunders. The youths agreed to remove the first cannon if Grover would ride it back to the docks at the head of a procession. Alderman McKinley supervised the return of the second gun.[19]

While Levin parleyed and pledged to Colahan that his fellow American Republicans would protect the church after the troops' departure, several persons smashed in one of the building's side doors. Colahan ordered the Markle Rifles stationed near the door to fire on the invaders. The soldiers balked, one of them yelling, "Don't shoot, you'll hit Alderman McKinley!"[20] Hearing the order to fire, the crowd did not enter the breach. Some American Republicans, such as Grover, who had returned from the docks, Cephas G. Childs, and others, quickly moved to block the door from the outside, separating the crowd from the soldiers. Convinced that he could no longer delay as the Markle Rifles refused to follow his commands, Colahan agreed to Levin's offer and ordered Saunders and his men to stay with the American Republicans to help guard St. Philip's. Saunders replied instead that the crowd requested, for its own safety, that the Markle Rifles convey the Greens out of the area and that the Irish company open its flashpans and discard its musket primings. Colahan agreed to comply with these conditions but never ordered his men to discard their primings.

Turning the church over to Levin and approximately forty other American Republicans, the Greens marched out two by two; the Markle Rifles marched on each side to insulate them from the crowd. Jeering

nativists followed the Greens up Third Street, hurling taunts and insults until the unit turned into German Street. At this point, residents hurled bricks and stones from alleyways along the street, and the Greens broke into a trot. Colahan unwisely ordered the Greens, who were being pelted heavily by their pursuers, to turn and fire. After the volley (which wounded no one and from which the Markle Rifles abstained), the crowd took off after the Irishmen with a vengeance. One unfortunate soldier, Robert Gallagher, was beaten by the crowd when they caught him and left for dead. Captain Colahan was pursued into the city where he took refuge at a Pine Street home until some "gentlemen of the neighborhood" persuaded his antagonists to desist.[21] Acknowledging the power of the city's traditional deference patterns, the crowd returned peacefully to Southwark where it rejoined several hundred persons at St. Philip's.

The American Republicans experienced difficulty in fulfilling their pledge to guard the church. Grover, Levin, and company managed to keep anyone from passing through the gate, but the milling crowd, curious to enter what was for most a place of mystery, threatened to overwhelm them at any moment. At four o'clock, Charles J. Jack, leader of the May march from the state house yard that had culminated in the second day of Kensington rioting, arrived at St. Philip's. He appealed to the crowd from the second floor window of a nearby house, but the crowd, in his own words "ruffians and sailors,"[22] threw stones at the house and hooted him down. Soon after Jack abandoned his efforts, a few in the crowd, using a log, battered a hole in the concrete fence fronting the church. As hundreds of persons squeezed through the breach and pressed their way in through the broken side and basement doors, more American Republicans, including Colonel Jack, entered with them to help their fellow party members guard the church. Hundreds of men and boys circulated through the building in a holiday mood but did no harm on the scale of the Kensington church invasions. A group of boys removed a painting, "The Scourge of Christ," stripped it from its frame, and presented it for the approval of the curiosity seekers in the chapel. The crowd responded with cheers and spicy remarks. Some American Republicans, however, grabbed the painting and unceremoniously escorted the boys from the building. A few minutes later, smoke was discovered pouring from the basement, and Grover and some friends hurriedly extinguished the flames. A while later, incendiarism was tried once more in a closet on the main floor, but again the American Repub-

licans redeemed their pledge to protect the church. They slowly weeded out the troublemakers, and by six o'clock probably no more than eighty persons, most of them American Republicans, remained inside. Now in control of the situation, the party convened a meeting in a vacant lot across Queen Street to attract those persons milling about outside the church. Edward M. Spencer asked the crowd to go home as the Irish no longer threatened the neighborhood. As the crowd started leaving, according to the *Ledger,* "the excitement seemed to be gradually disappearing."[23]

Once again, however, General Cadwalader prevented a quiet resolution to a dangerous confrontation. This time his interference cost several lives. Soon after the meeting ended and persons began trickling out of the area, militia headed personally by General Cadwalader arrived in the area in "great force,"[24] probably in belated answer to Colahan's plea for help. By coincidence, the soldiers had joined with a number of armed sheriff's deputies whom McMichael was marching to St. Philip's because he heard mistakenly that it was aflame. The two groups arrived in Southwark together, accompanied by many curiosity seekers attracted by the roll of military drums. The soldiers were formally under McMichael's command, but Cadwalader moved first to gain control of the church and streets. As they had on Saturday, the civil forces took a back seat to military authority.

Cadwalader's initives could not have been better calculated to embarrass the American Republicans and provoke the nativist crowd to resistance. Despite Grover's protestations that they were doing an excellent job, Cadwalader ordered the American Republicans to turn the church over to him. Reluctantly, the volunteer guardians filed out and joined the gathering crowd in the street. Having secured the church, Cadwalader ordered his men to clear Queen Street. Some in the crowd still remembered with anger the previous evening's confrontation, in which citizen-soldiers would have fired on fellow citizens but for Charles Naylor's intervention. Some tried to undermine the soldiers' discipline with personal appeals to their community spirit; others threw paving stones. Captain Hill, who led the first charge into the crowd, later testified: "I told them I had received my orders and I would certainly obey them; the reply was 'obey and be damned!'"[25] Hill had reason for complaint. As he tried making arrests, a large man, a Northern Liberties butcher named Washington Conrad, grabbed Hill's sword and wrestled him to the ground.

From the rear, Cadwalader ordered his troops to prime their muskets. Alderman McKinley pleaded with Cadwalader to arrest only the actual offenders and not fire indiscriminately into the crowd. Cadwalader— livid with rage by all accounts—rejected the appeal.[26] The crowd knew of his intentions, he argued, and if they continued to break the law then they must pay the price.[27] With irony, McKinley suggested that the general raise a red flag of anarchy before shooting into the crowd. Hill's men did not need advice from their commanding general. Two of his men drove Conrad and his friends from Hill with their bayonets. Hill rose and struck an assailant with the flat side of his sword before a brick hit him in the back of his head and again felled him. Hill's lieutenant, Thomas Dougherty, ordered the City Guards to open fire. Simultaneously, Cadwalader gave the same command from the rear. This time no guardian angel appeared to intervene on the crowd's behalf. The militia's volley cut down two Southwark residents, Isaac Freed, an elderly bystander, and William Crozier, a lame carpet weaver. His jaw shot away, Crozier was carried by angry nativists to Commissioners' Hall, where he died. Freed also died soon after. Four others were wounded, none seriously. Subsequent testimony revealed that some soldiers had fired high or low intentionally (two of the wounded men were shot in the heel).[28] But some of the citizen-soldiers had shot to kill. The crowd's appeals to community spirit had been in vain. For the first time in Philadelphia history, the militia had killed citizens while upholding civil order.

The crowd and its supporters did not take this treatment passively. Shortly after the military "whiff of grapeshot," native partisans living on Queen and Second streets began a desultory gunfire from their houses. An occasional shot also came from Commissioners' Hall below Second Street, where the confiscated Irish guns had been stored at dawn on Saturday. Cadwalader sent search units to disarm the houses, and Mc-Michael sent his posse to take Commissioners' Hall from the nativists.[29] These measures temporarily quieted the shooting, but the native populace had just begun to fight. Around 8:30 P.M., an hour or so after the militia's volley, a large group met in the Wharton Street Market to protest the military's shooting. The meeting's leadership has never been established but Andrew McClain was later charged with "treason" for allegedly calling it. All that is known is that Bennett Lowe, otherwise unidentified urged that General Cadwalader be hung and that the crowd warmly cheered him. Some young men did more than simply cheer and

went again to the docks for cannons. This time they rolled the guns on muffled wheels so as to surprise the military. Not more than forty or fifty persons gathered around the two guns, but the number was large enough to turn the Queen Street vicinity into a theater of war. The citizens rolled the guns into place at the corners of Second and Third on Christian Street. Someone blew out the district street lamps so that the lights from the city silhouetted the soldiers from the rear while the military faced the disadvantage of searching for their enemies in the dark.[30]

The first blast from the insurgents' cannon took the lives of two Germantown Blues. Three other company members fell wounded from the flying iron scraps. The Blues manned a field piece of their own and fired at the spot where they had seen the cannon flash. Three nativists were wounded by the shot. After the volunteers' first blast, according to Lieutenant Dougherty of the City Guards, Andrew McClain approached him excitedly and asked him to persuade the Blues to hold their fire. Rejected, McClain then told Dougherty's soldiers that they had "no Yankee blood in their veins" and would "go to hell before long."[31]

The nativist cannoneers worked hard to make McClain's prediction come true. The muffled wheels allowed the cannons to be rolled silently from one position to another after each shot, making it difficult for the military to locate the guns. If the natives had had grapeshot and ball instead of scrap for ammunition, military casualties surely would have been much higher. Musket shots from neighborhood houses regularly supplemented the cannon fire, and the military found itself in a highly vulnerable position. Shooting persisted for over two hours. At eleven, the *Ledger* reporter noted: "There is a continued discharge of cannon to be heard, followed by the regular roll and rattle of the [militia's] muskets."[32] By then, more than a dozen militiamen as well as a large but unknown number of rioters had been wounded. During these exchanges journeyman weaver David Kithcart and a thirty-five-year-old laborer, Elisha Jester, were killed on the native side.

Cadwalader called for additional help. When the nativists' tactical plan became apparent, he asked General Patterson for a cavalry unit to silence the guns. Patterson responded more quickly than Cadwalader himself had to Colahan. By midnight, the horsemen of the First City Troop, commanded by General Alexander L. Roumfort, a city attorney, arrived in Southwark. Cadwalader advised Roumfort to wait until a piece was fired and then charge at the position of its flash. Moments

later, the cannon at Third and Queen spouted fire. The horsemen charged up Third but were tripped by a rope that the natives had stretched across the street. Perhaps the insurgents had friends in the military lines who warned them of Cadwalader's plan or perhaps the clatter of hooves alerted them to the cavalry's arrival. While Roumfort and his men lay sprawled in the street, the nativists reloaded the cannon, aimed point-blank, and lit the charge. But the cannon had been improperly loaded and the fuse fizzled. Regaining their horses and cutting the rope, the fortunate soldiers then captured the gun and dispersed its operators with little mercy. They killed two men, a Southwark oysterman, John Cook, and Enos Waters, a carpenter visiting the city from New York.

Soon after the shooting ended, Alderman McKinley carried Waters' remains to Commissioners' Hall. The building was now occupied by Captain Drayton and his company of soldiers. A witness later recalled the dramatic scene between McKinley and Drayton that reflected not only nativist rage at the soldiers but the military's own nervous guilt about its role in the shootings. When McKinley announced that he was bringing Waters' remains into the hall, the captain told him to keep out. "Have you no place for a dead man?" McKinley countered, and asserted his right as alderman to enter the building. Drayton responded, "I'll let you know that my authority is a little more than yours, and if you come in here I'll fire on you!" The crowd behind McKinley exploded, "You've murdered enough citizens already." One man tapped McKinley on the back and urged, "Go on, Alderman, I'll back you, by God!" The soldiers defensively denied any role in the shooting and warned, "If you come in *we will* fire." The crowd retired, frustrated but wary that Drayton would keep his word.[33]

The capture of the Third Street cannon marked the turning point in the night's fighting. While the cavalry never found the second cannon (it was later said that they rode right past it once in the dark), the nativists were afraid to fire for fear of revealing their position. The only continued resistance took the form of occasional gunfire from neighborhood houses. By 2:00 A.M. this, too, ended. The military suffered two dead and twenty-three wounded. The figures are less exact for the nativists and bystanders, but the *Ledger* reports suggest that ten persons were killed and at least twenty more wounded.

Viewing the scene Monday morning, a *Ledger* reporter captured the neighborhood's mood:

The greatest excitement prevails throughout our whole community.
Terror has seized upon all, and there is none who knows what an
hour will bring forth. People are busily engaged moving from the
neighborhood of the church and the streets are crowded in every direction—business is at a complete standstill, and the mind of every
person being absorbed by the terrific scenes being enacted around us.[34]

Hundreds of soldiers from throughout the state patrolled the streets around
the church. Bullets and grapeshot scarred every house on Queen Street.
From all over Philadelphia, sightseers wandered through the area, shouting,
hurling epithets at the militia, creating an air of uneasiness. Soldiers quickly arrested those who uttered inflammatory remarks, but this only increased the friction between military and citizens. General Cadwalader
later described the difficulties that his men experienced that Monday.
"The houses of the people were closed against us," he recalled. Despite
the intense heat, neighborhood women refused to give the soldiers the
water they asked for. Instead, they hurled insults and buckets of dirty
water from upper windows. Cadwalader recalled, "Some of our men fell
at their guns from heat and exhaustion, and sickness and privation."[35]

   More than buckets of water and shrewish obscenities greeted the militia that Monday morning. Before noon, citizens convened at Wharton
Market to hear Andrew McClain, Peter Sken Smith, and others demand
that the troops be removed from the neighborhood. Some breathed
veiled threats. Meeting simultaneously at their hall, the Southwark commissioners discerned that "the continuance of the militia . . . has the tendency to keep in existence the present excitement." "If the troops now
occupying the public streets . . . are not withdrawn," the commissioners
concluded, "there will probably be an additional shedding of blood."[36]
American Republican commissioner Lemuel Paynter and two others
went to General Patterson to press for withdrawal. Sheriff McMichael
had reached the same conclusion, and even before the commissioners
arrived he urged Patterson to remove the troops. Patterson's visitors convinced him, but before withdrawing his men he demanded that the Southwark commissioners publicly announce their intention to keep order.
The commissioners agreed to establish a citizens' police force. In mid-
afternoon, they asked Colonel Jack to read an announcement of the
troops' withdrawal and their replacement by district police and civilian
volunteers. Quarter Sessions Judge Joel Jones came to Southwark at

the commissioners' request to prosecute immediately any offender they might arrest. The tone of events in Commissioners' Hall thus underwent a complete change in less than twenty-four hours: the night before, nativists were shooting at soldiers from its windows. Now the judge "exhorted to peace and decorum," noted the *Ledger*, "and he was received with cheers."[37]

Which Southwark residents cheered is unclear, but more than edicts and speeches were needed to placate the outraged nativists outside the hall. Queen Street remained crowded with disquieted citizens. Tempers flared when friends came to take Robert Gallagher, the beaten Hibernia Green, from the hall to Pennsylvania Hospital for treatment. The police and others interested in maintaining order worked hard to protect Gallagher from the threatening crowd. Later an Irishman, James O'Neill, was knocked down, kicked, and had his jaw broken for making what the *Ledger* called "imprudent remarks."[38] A few minutes later, Doctor William Bunting, a militia surgeon, arrived at the hall to aid the injured there. Someone in the crowd mistook him for the general and yelled out "Cadwalader!" Pounced on, Bunting was punched in the face by several men until Colonel Jack and Andrew McClain, among others, intervened in his behalf.

With the troops gone by Monday night, Southwark quieted completely. Trouble, however, threatened in Moyamensing. Around nine o'clock, that district's police intercepted a group of young men rolling a cannon on dray wheels toward the Catholic church on Christian Street between Ninth and Tenth. An alderman persuaded the would-be attackers to leave, but as the police turned to go a few of the boys started throwing stones at Catholics' houses on Ninth Street. The police drove them away with batons.[39]

The Moyamensing incident brought the Philadelphia riots of 1844 to a close. Tuesday morning found the city occupied by two thousand troops, many of them from adjacent counties to minimize possible conflicts of loyalty. At least an equal number of private citizens with clubs and pistols helped patrol the city. The next day, July 10, Bishop Kenrick, sure that the police could maintain order, asked the commissioners to return St. Philip de Neri to the parishioners. They consented. That Wednesday afternoon, General Patterson began withdrawing troops from the rest of the city, and Philadelphia returned to business as usual. As a final reminder of events, Southwark residents, when they passed in front of

St. Philip's, would now find their way lighted by six street lamps instead of the usual two.

In retrospect, the Southwark riots, much more than the Kensington disturbances, were probably avoidable. Twice, General Cadwalader had disturbed a stabilized situation by turning his troops loose on crowds that threatened no harm. On Saturday night he chose to contravene the sheriff's decision to clear only that part of Queen Street directly in front of St. Philip's. If not for Charles Naylor's intervention, Cadwalader's orders to clear the surrounding streets would have led to civilian deaths. On Sunday, his troops began herding the crowd just as the American Republicans had convinced it to disperse voluntarily. The two incidents point out how differently the crowd and the general viewed the situation. In 1844, the use of troops to control a civilian population was still an innovation. To an extent forgotten today, the militia prided itself on being known as "citizen soldiery." Many citizens, and especially the nativists, in this instance, viewed the use of their fellow citizens against them as a radical innovation in violation of their liberties.[40] They bitterly resented not only Cadwalader's attitudes and actions but the disregard for popular rights that his orders implied. On the other side, the general himself was mandated by his respectable peers to institute a new era of order in Philadelphia. After Kensington, Cadwalader had been criticized for hesitating to act outside the traditionally restricted role that practice had assigned the military in domestic peacekeeping. The new demand for order superseded old limitations and traditions, at least in the minds of the middle and upper classes. Changes in the next decade clearly illustrated the desire and ability of Philadelphians to end the city's violent traditions.

NOTES

1. *Public Ledger,* July 6, 1844.
2. Ibid., July 15, 1844.
3. Ibid., July 6, 1844.
4. Ibid., July 15, 1844.
5. Ibid., July 8, 1844.
6. Ibid.
7. Legally, Patterson, his subordinate officers, and the troops were serving under McMichael's civilian command. In practice, however, the

military had great autonomy. McMichael's demands on Patterson were likely put in the form of requests rather than orders.

8. *Public Ledger,* July 8, 1844. Eighteen names of those resisting arrest have survived. Nine were listed in the *City Directory,* and this sample conforms to the usual pattern among nativists. Eight were skilled artisans or workmen: two printers, two in the shipbuilding trades, a bonnetmaker, a coppersmith, a shoemaker, and a grain measurer. One was listed as a laborer, a designation reserved for the unskilled. None was listed elsewhere as an active member of the American Republican party.

9. *Public Ledger,* July 8, 27, 1844.

10. Ibid., July 27, 1844.

11. See Hugh F. Nolan, *The Most Reverend Francis Patrick Kenrick, Third Bishop of Philadelphia* (Philadelphia: American Catholic Historical Society, 1948), 320.

12. *Public Ledger,* July 20, 1844.

13. Ibid., July 15, 1844.

14. A jury later acquitted McClain but on-the-spot accounts place him at the head of the crowd. *Public Ledger,* July 8, 1844.

15. Ibid., November 14, 1844.

16. Ibid., July 15, 1844.

17. Ibid., July 8, 1844.

18. Alderman McKinley, perhaps with an interest in dissociating the gunners from American Republicanism, claimed that they were all youths between fourteen and twenty years of age, none of them from the neighborhood. The only rioter positively identified in this incident was Eaton Harwood, who already had a reputation as a leader in many of the Weccacoe Engine's fire fights. *Public Ledger,* July 8, 1844.

19. Ibid., July 24, 1844.

20. Ibid., July 22, 1844.

21. Ibid.

22. *Native American,* August 2, 1844.

23. *Public Ledger,* July 8, 1844.

24. Ibid.

25. Ibid., July 19, 1844.

26. Ibid., July 15, 1844.

27. Ibid., July 17, 1844.

28. Ibid., July 8, 1844.

29. Ibid., July 20, 1844.

30. Ibid.

31. Ibid., July 16, 1844.

32. Ibid., July 8, 1844.

33. Ibid., July 15, 1844.

34. Ibid., July 9, 1844.

35. Ibid., July 20, 1844.

36. Ibid., July 9, 1844.

37. Ibid.

38. Ibid.

39. Ibid.

40. See, for example, *Street Talk about an Ordinance . . . [of] July Eleventh* (Philadelphia: n.p., 1844), discussed below in chap. 9.

8
Aftermath

The Southwark riots had been police riots; in a sense, then, they are only a footnote to the main story of ethnic conflict between Irish and native Philadelphians. The Kensington riots, by contrast, had directly pitted nativists and Irish Catholic immigrants in pitched battle, while in Southwark only the brief confrontation between the crowd and the Hibernia Greens in German Street on Sunday morning brought these two sides face to face. Certainly, the battles between native soldiers and their heavily armed native opponents on Sunday night far overshadowed the short German Street clash between Irish and Americans. Yet, from the long-term historical viewpoint, the Southwark riots take on a significance equal to that of the Kensington affair. Southwark marked the first time in the history of Philadelphia that officers of the law proved willing to take human life in large numbers to guarantee the public peace. The Southwark struggle posed constituted authority against a disaffected group taking its version of the law into its own hands; conflict between the state and its citizens had been relatively uncommon in American history up to that time, at least in comparison to Europe. Kensington conformed to the more common pattern of American preindustrial rioting: two private groups confronting each other rather than a single group attacking officials. In the twentieth century, however, the form of collective disorder that Kensington typified has increasingly diminished, replaced instead by Southwark-style uprisings against authority by insurgents. The term "race riots," for example, used to refer to white citizens' attacking black neighborhoods, such as those in New York in 1863 or East St. Louis in 1917. Today, the term applies to confrontations between blacks and the police in which the private white community plays little or no active role. In short, Southwark was one of the first entries on a new page of national history, one that is still being writ-

ten. Southwark signaled a new resolve on the part of Philadelphia's leaders and elected officials to keep order between private groups, even if it meant fighting those groups themselves at the cost of human life.

In the short run, nonetheless, the military's attack on the Southwark crowd served to strengthen nativism rather than intimidate it. American Republican spokesmen embraced the military's Southwark victims as martyrs and pointed with outrage to the seemingly needless character of the bloodletting. Substantial evidence did point to the conclusion that Thomas Grover and his associates had the church in safe hands before Cadwalader's troops arrived. Charles Naylor bluntly testified that if anyone was responsible for rioting and disorder, it was the troops themselves: "In the district of Southwark . . . there was no riot, no disturbance, no intention manifested even to do an illegal act until a few men in the name of the law set themselves above the law, became themselves utterly lawless, trampled on the rights of the people and created a riot." Cadwalader's orders to open fire on both Saturday and Sunday, the former of which Naylor himself undermined, were an "outrage against humanity without parallel in our land" and the loss of life on Sunday was "wanton and inexcusable murder."[1] In February 1845, a special committee of the Southwark Board of Commissioners, now controlled by the districts' American Republican machine, investigated the riot's causes and concluded that Cadwalader's actions had been "cruel, unnecessary and . . . a wanton sacrifice of human life" because "immediately before the arrival of the soldiers, order, peace, and quiet had been perfectly restored."[2]

The American Republicans turned the riots into a partisan issue by pursuing a politics of moral indignation. John Perry detected a conspiracy by the Whigs and Democrats, claiming they had callously staged the incident at St. Philip's hoping to "bring odium and reproach upon our party in order to disunite and dismember it." Perry wondered why the church was armed on July 5 if the Fourth had already passed quietly. Clearly, the Whigs and Democrats had concocted the scheme to provoke the natives into an embarrassing outburst. The plot failed, Perry boasted, because "the American Republican party are friends of law and order" who stood "ready and willing at all times to assist the *civil* power in maintaining the same."[3] Heavily attended American Republican political rallies protested the slaughter of innocent citizens by "Rome's besotted slaves" and bloodthirsty soldiers. The "torn flag of Kensington"

(there were several in circulation) appeared at all official occasions. Sixty-year-old Isaac Freed, killed in the first round of military fire in Southwark, was mourned as a helpless and unoffending old cripple, and the Weccacoe Engine Company gave company member Enos Waters, who died while firing the cannon at the Germantown Blues, a funeral with honors. Rallies, newspaper advertisements, and broadsides were the main vehicles of political propaganda in the Jackson period, and no form of the written word was left untried in an attempt to mobilize party support. One poet, in an epic memorial entitled "Six Months Ago," tried to rekindle rage and hatred on the half-year anniversary of the Kensington riot. The anonymous author enshrined George Schiffler above the immortals by pronouncing that

> Bright Fame has stricken from her scroll
> The names of him of Corsica, and all
> Of Rome's Proud Caesars, and enrolled
> Thine [Schiffler's], sheathed with fadeless laurels, boldly there.

He recalled a scene in which

> The slot-hounds of the Pope, rushing on their prey,
> Scattering the advocates of Native Rights
> And tearing from its staff our blood-bought flag,
> Trample and rend each brilliant star and stripe
> And mar its texture with their rabid slime

while leaving

> Our own soil crimsoned with a brother's blood,
> Shed by a hireling cur! Revenge! Revenge![4]

Whether such disturbed verses won converts to American Republicanism we will never know, but the party did create a political machine effective enough by October 1844 to capture two of Philadelphia's four congressional seats, the county's state senatorship, and several important county offices. Their vote distribution confirms our class and occupational analysis of nativism's strength. In the old city, where Philadelphia's wealthiest wards were located, the party did least well. It managed to

win only 20 percent of the vote in the three wealthiest wards, Chestnut, South, and Walnut, while North Mulberry and Lower Delaware wards on the city's northern edge, two of the poorest and most heavily populated with artisans, produced the party's best showing.[5] North Mulberry, in fact, provided the only American Republican majority in the city proper. Thanks to their good showing in the working-class wards, the American Republicans finished the races for mayor and the city councils with five hundred more votes than the Democrats, although they ran an average of fourteen hundred votes behind the Whig ticket, except for the mayoral race, in which they did somewhat better. In the mayoralty contest, the vote was: Peter McCall (Whig), 5506; Elhanan Keyser (American Republican), 5065; Samuel Badger (Democrat), 4032. In this race, Keyser ran approximately five hundred votes ahead of the city American Republican ticket, while McCall ran four hundred votes behind the Whig council tickets.

While the party made a strong showing in the city, the industrial suburbs rewarded American Republican efforts with nearly a clean sweep. Nativists Lewis C. Levin and John H. Campbell took two of the four contested congressional seats. Levin's First Congressional District, composed of industrial suburban Southwark, Passyunk, and Moyamensing, plus two working-class wards (Cedar and New Market), was perfectly constructed for a strong nativist showing. Southwark in particular had long been a strong native Democratic ward. The home of Philadelphia's shipbuilding and ironworking industries, it had previously produced such dauntless Jacksonians as Joel Sutherland (who used Locofoco radical rhetoric but supported high tariffs to protect the district's iron industry) and Lemuel Paynter, ex-Democratic successor of Sutherland who had turned to American Republicanism before the 1844 elections. In the previous year, Democrat George F. Lehman had nosed out Whig E. Joy Morris by 1,155 votes to 1,075. A nativist candidate running on an "Independent" ticket had polled only 661. As a result of the riots and the fact that 1844 was a presidential year, voter turnout in Southwark was 50 percent higher than in 1843. Levin, the American Republican, seems to have picked up almost all of the voter increase. He inherited the 661 independent votes and added another 1,700 nativists to that total. Fifty Democrats deserted Lehman (doubtless the true number of native desertions must have been higher since the Irish most likely turned out for Lehman in greater strength than previously). Morris's Whig vote dropped

from 1,075 to 561. Most of his supporters likely switched to Levin. While the latter did not carry Moyamensing, heavily populated in two of its four wards with Irish weavers, Levin improved on the 1843 "independent" vote there, raising it from 121 to 562. Morris, the Whig, lost 154 votes, while Democrat Lehman gained only 92. Passyunk, a rural district with few voters, went safely for nativism, while the two city wards remained loyal to Whiggery. But neither Lehman's margin in Moyamensing nor Morris's in the two city wards was enough to overcome Levin's wide margin in Southwark. He defeated Lehman, his closest rival, by more than one thousand votes. Morris, the Whig incumbent, was a badly beaten third.[6]

While Levin was sweeping the First District, John H. Campbell, an attorney from Northern Liberties, was winning in the Third, a constituency very much like Levin's. The Third was composed of two working-class sections on the northern border of the city, Spring Garden and Northern Liberties. Immigrants were concentrated in only two of the seven wards in Northern Liberties; the remainder of both districts was heavily artisan and native. Campbell put together his margin over Democrat John S. Smith by drawing off 2,500 votes from Whig Thomas C. Steel and producing an additional 2,800 votes on his own. In 1843, the district had gone Democratic, Northern Liberties supporting the Democrats by a margin of more than 400 votes over the Whigs, while Spring Garden provided a three-hundred-and-fifty-vote Democratic majority. In 1844, the Democrat turnout inched up by 50 votes in each district, while the Whig vote plummeted from approximatley 3,200 to 700. Total voter turnout increased dramatically, and Campbell won easily, carrying eight of the eleven wards in the two communities. A year later, Northern Liberties slipped back into the Democratic camp, but Spring Garden, like Southwark and Kensington, remained safely American Republican through 1848.[7]

The native party came close to winning the Fourth District Congressional seat as well. Its candidate, Jacob Shearer, ran well in Kensington, Germantown, and Penn Township, three of the nearer industrial suburbs, with only Third Ward, Kensington—home of the Irish weaving community—going for Democrat Charles Jared Ingersoll. In Kensington, 800 voters deserted Ingersoll for the American Republicans, but small exurban districts like Byberry, Moreland, and Kingsessing townships, areas too far from the center city or industrial areas to have an "immigrant problem," continued their support. Two of the remoter districts, Blockley and Oxford townships, supported the Whig candidate, Thomas W. Duf-

field, rather than bolt to the American Republican ticket. Duffield's combined margin over Shearer in these two districts was 481 votes, while Shearer lost the entire Fourth to Ingersoll by a small margin of 79 votes.[8] Duffield's Whig candidacy thus acted as a spoiler. This and similar occurrences in subsequent elections paved the way for an alliance between the Whigs and natives in 1848, when they formed a united front against the "Irish party."

The heavy American Republican pluralities in the industrial suburbs carried the party to victory in the county. The 1844 turnout was the heaviest in Philadelphia's history. Thomas Grover led all nativist candidates in his race for county commissioner, polling 16,605 votes to his Democratic opponent's 14,583 and the Whig's 9,785. Augustin R. Peale, the dentist who lost an arm in Kensington, won his race for county auditor with 50 votes fewer than Grover received. Oliver P. Cornman, a Spring Garden butcher who would later be active in the post-Civil War movement to exclude Oriental immigration, defeated workingmen's Democrat Edward A. Penniman and Whig Henry S. Mallory for the privilege of representing the county in the state senate. In the county-wide state assembly race, the native ticket ran 1,700 votes ahead of its Democratic competition and almost 10,000 better than the Whigs. In short, except for the old city, which stayed loyal to Whiggery, and the northern exurbs that Charles Jared Ingersoll and the Democratic machine kept under their control, Philadelphia County went solidly for American Republicanism.

Contemporaries explained the nativist party's sudden success by suggesting that the natives and Whigs had made a secret deal: in exchange for American Republican votes for their state gubernatorial candidate, Joseph Markle, the Whigs promised to vote for native candidates in the Philadelphia county and congressional races. The large number of abandoned Whig candidates lends some credence to this claim. Since many American Republicans previously were Democrats, the deal proved a boon to Markle, who carried the county by 4,000 votes. Where the alliance held up in local races, as it did Southwark and Spring Garden, it also helped elect American Republicans Levin and Campbell to Congress; where it failed to take hold, such as in Oxford and Blockley townships, the American Republicans and Whigs split the anti-Democratic vote and the Jacksonian Charles Jared Ingersoll managed to slip in with a plurality. Since Markle was ultimately defeated for the governorship by Democrat Francis Shunk in the statewide count and the Democrats still won two of four congressional seats in the county, the deal was less than a com-

plete success. The returns for 1845 show that the alliance had already broken down in the course of the year between elections. Campbell's congressional seat returned to the Democrats, and the American Republicans also lost their seats on the county board of commissioners; with the exception of Lewis Levin's congressional district and some portions of Kensington and Spring Garden, the American Republican wave of 1844 had already begun to ebb.[9]

Still, the party was able to exercise considerable influence over the day-to-day lives of citizens in the districts that remained under their control. The various boards of district commissioners appointed school controllers (and through them, public school teachers), policemen, and other municipal workers, and theirs was the last word on municipal appropriations. Equally important in the context of the cultural politics of the period, the district commissioners licensed the taverns and hotels in each community, thus controlling the sales of alcoholic beverages. Since they maintained their grip on the administrative machinery in Southwark, Kensington, and Spring Garden for several years after 1844, the American Republicans were in a position to enact many of the "reforms" their followers considered paramount even though they had lost control of the county offices they held in 1844.

The party's exercise of power in Southwark typified the way in which American Republicanism employed its authority at the local level. Applying the party maxim that "Americans are competent to make and administer their own laws," the nine American Republicans who formed a majority of the board of commissioners from 1844 through 1846 (including Thomas Grover and Lemuel Paynter) requested and received resignations from John McCoy, Irish police magistrate, and Southwark district auditor Hugh O'Donnell, both Democrats. Loyal nativists such as John H. Scott, Archibald Cozzens, and Albert Collins were appointed to the police force in place of Irish incumbents. In June 1845, when the terms of two Democratic school controllers expired, the American Republican majority on the board replaced them with loyal party members Joseph Maull and William Colcord. The following March Lemuel Paynter assumed one of the school posts, and two American Republicans were named to the county board of health to defend Southwark's interests in that body.[10]

American Republicanism succeeded above all through intensive organizational efforts on a district-by-district level. The party generated a variety of nativist clubs, ward political associations, burial societies, insurance

plans, and reading rooms that helped keep the rank and file tied to the organization. Volunteers were recruited for the newly formed "Native" and "Schiffler" hose companies. Captain Matthew Berriman, a cabinet-maker by trade, formed the Native American Rifles, a new volunteer militia unit. A special effort was aimed at winning the city's youth for American Republicanism through the Young Native, Schiffler, and Rhinedollar associations. Youth, in fact, had been a special concern of the American Republicans from their stumbling beginnings in 1837, when their founding statement proclaimed that they were asking for changes in the naturalization laws "not so much for ourselves as for future generations." The goal of the youth clubs was strictly political; the Schiffler Association's motto read: "We pledge to avenge the death of Schiffler at the ballot box." Soon after its founding, the Young Natives claimed a membership of three hundred and met almost weekly to hear lectures by leading American Republicans. Young men also appropriated nativist names for their street gangs, doubtless without official party sanction. Moyamensing was plagued by fights between Irish youths and the "Schifflers," a band of native teenagers. As mentioned earlier, one of the most effective American Republican organizations was the United Order of American Mechanics, founded by John Botsford and others to provide welfare services and employment information as well as social recreation for native-born workingmen.[11]

Despite their special efforts to woo artisans and young voters, the American Republicans were simply unable to maintain the strength they had shown in 1844. While they retained local control in Kensington, Southwark, and Spring Garden through 1848, their margin of victory slipped in each election, with one or two exceptions in isolated wards or districts. In 1846, a Democratic hopeful defeated Henry A. Salter, the man designated by the natives to succeed Oliver P. Cornman in the state legislature. John H. Campbell did not stand for reelection to Congress, and his successor designate failed by four hundred votes to keep the Third District in the American Republican column. Even the overwhelmingly popular Lewis Levin saw his margin of victory in the First Congressional District trimmed to four hundred votes. A year earlier, in 1845, the nativists lost the eight seats they held in the county assembly when they fell victims to an accusation that they had opposed a public school appropriation earlier in that session. The county delegation was also hurt by its stand against the construction of a street railroad through the city much like one that Kensington's residents had

fought against from 1840 to 1842. Commercially oriented city residents did not applaud the party's antirailroad position as the voters of Kensington might have done, and the decline of American Republican votes in the city proper was enough to spell the downfall of the party as a force in the county. Control of county government lapsed back into the hands of the Democrats. Unallied with the Whigs, the American Republicans consistently lagged one to two thousand votes behind the Democratic machine in county-wide races.[12]

The one break in this pattern of decline came in 1846, when the party's nominee for county sheriff, Henry Lelar, defeated his two rivals. Lelar was a highly respected ship captain who as a youth had guided an East Indian trading vessel safely back to Philadelphia after its officers fell ill. His reputation for strength of character, based on this incident, carried him into office. Once there, he immediately broke his pledge to the party binding him to appoint no one but American Republicans to the lucrative offices under his patronage. By appointing Whig John L. Woolf to be his first deputy, Lelar chose to repay debts to that party first. The American Republicans denounced Lelar, and County Prosecutor Peter A. Browne, one of the more elite American Republicans and a Lelar appointee, resigned in indignation.[13] American Republicanism's one apparent major victory after 1844 had slipped from its grasp.

After 1846, it became clear the American Republicans were not going to develop a statewide following. Instead, they turned their efforts toward forcing the Whigs to adopt their naturalization program. In 1847, the nativists nominated Emanuel Reigart of Lancaster for governor, apparently in hopes of stealing enough Whig votes to guarantee victory for the Democratic nominee. The strategem worked: Reigart polled approximately ten thousand votes, the same number by which Francis Shunk, the Democrat, defeated Whig James Irwin.[14] While an alliance in the 1848 election seemed obvious, the American Republicans took no chances and forced themselves directly on the Whigs. Almost two months before the Whigs offered the presidential nomination to Zachary Taylor, the American Republican "national" convention (two-thirds of the delegates were from Pennsylvania and New York) met in Harrisburg and designated Taylor electors to appear on their presidential ballot. The *Sun* had called for Taylor's nomination a full year earlier. A minority of American Republicans warned against swallowing Taylor whole, fearing that the Whigs would swallow the American Republican organization in turn and simply

merge it with their own, but a majority of delegates at a second national convention agreed to adopt Whig nominee Millard Fillmore for Vice-President as well and drop their own, General Henry Dearborne of Boston.[15]

Amalgamation worked beautifully for the Whigs. With American Republican cooperation, they were able to elect a full slate of county officials for the first time since the Jacksonian wave broke over them in the late 1820s. The American Republican ticket received fewer than a hundred votes in the city. By contrast, in 1846, American Republican mayoral candidate Peter A. Browne had polled better than three thousand votes. The Whigs and the nativists had agreed to split the nominations for county commissioners, canal commissioner, sheriff, and prothonotary, but only the Whig aspirants were actually elected. Lewis Levin and the district commissioners of Southwark, Kensington, and Spring Garden proved the only survivors of these years of decline. Levin's loyal constituents continued to return him to Congress despite accusations by both major parties that he was remiss in his efforts to win a new drydock for the federal navy yard in Southwark. Finally, in 1850, for reasons not entirely clear, Levin's string ran out, and he was defeated by twelve hundred votes. The last independent American Republican above the district level had thus been defeated.[16]

Several factors contributed to the decline of American Republicanism after 1844. One was internal schism. An "ultra" wing split the Pennsylvania and national conventions in 1847 by rejecting the official party plank on naturalization. The renegades, led by Peter Sken Smith and William J. A. Birkey, denounced the notion of a twenty-one-year apprenticeship before naturalized citizens were given the vote and advocated in its place the "birthright principle" under which only those persons actually born on American soil would be enfranchised. Evidence on what distinguished the birthright advocates from the more moderate twenty-one-year majority can no longer be found, but Smith and Birkey caused a bitter floor fight at the national convention in Pittsburgh before going down to defeat.[17]

External factors also militated against the spread of a united American Republican party. The movement never flourished outside port cities like Philadelphia, New York, and Boston, where most of the immigrants disembarked. For most other Americans, the "wild Irish" were just a stereotype rather than a reality. In the 1847 gubernatorial campaign, Emanuel Reigart polled fewer than a thousand of his ten thousand votes

in Allegheny and Lancaster counties, the two most populous in the state after Philadelphia. By 1845, in addition, the state and national Whig parties began adopting mild nativist rhetoric and vague anti-immigrant postures, stealing some of American Republicanism's thunder.[18]

Paradoxically, the failure of the party to grow after 1844 probably resulted in part from its very success. So long as the nativists ran the schools, licensed the bars, policed the streets, and filled municipal patronage positions, there was no need for the rank and file to waste its gubernatorial and congressional votes on American Republican candidates who would either not be elected or whose voices would be lost in the great halls of state and national government. On the pressing national political question of 1845 and 1846, the relationship of Texas to the United States, the Whigs and American Republicans were more or less in perfect accord anyway, although Lewis Levin based his opposition to Texas annexation on the grounds that such a move would incorporate millions of Mexican Catholics into the United States, an argument not made publicly in official Whig statements. On questions of tariff policy, especially the Democratic Walker tariff of 1846, which lowered rates on manufactured imports, the Whigs and American Republicans were in perfect agreement in their opposition.[19]

The party declined in direct proportion to the amount of time that passed after the riotous summer of 1844. Memories of the Kensington riots grew vaguer. Each annual American Republican memorial service and rally held in Kensington on May 6 was more sparsely attended than the year before. There is no record of an observance to mark the anniversary in 1848.[20] Passions were further cooled by the Irish Catholic decision to lower their profile in Philadelphia politics after the 1844 riots. Bishop Kenrick abandoned his fight for the Catholic Bible in the public schools and turned instead to constructing a parochial school system. This was part of that broad effort, mentioned in Chapter 2, to create a complete set of separate but equal parallel institutions designed to insulate the Irish Catholic population from dependence on or contact with native Protestant institutions, such as the public schools or the Protestant charity hospitals, in which sectarian proselytizing was the rule. While the attempt at economic separatism was never fully successful, the Irish were able to establish their cultural and political independence by the time of the Civil War.

The low profile the Irish Catholic community adopted as a whole con-

tributed to the declining sense of urgency impelling native-born Americans to back the nativist movement, but the decline of one Irish community in particular demonstrated above all that the immigrants were not nearly as serious a threat to the stability of society as they had appeared earlier. The weavers of Kensington and Moyamensing, once so turbulent and defiant, were humbled by the 1844 riots, and the Kensington weavers' community in particular was badly disrupted by the destruction of their neighborhood. When the next general walkout occurred in 1846 to restore the postriot wage cuts of 1844, the weavers were far more peaceable than they had been in recent memory. Ironically, the weavers were so well behaved that several temperance leaders felt sympathetic enough toward them to help them face the hard winter of 1846 through appeals for public charity and the construction of a "House of Industry" for unemployed weavers in Moyamensing. The strike was settled in favor of the employers, a result that the weavers did not resist with open force.[21] Within a generation, the Irish handloom weavers of Philadelphia would no longer exist as an identifiable group as the power loom and competition from New England would destroy their place in the economy.

The pressures of market competition and technological change the Irish weavers experienced also had their effect on workmen in other trades, notably tailoring and shoemaking. Thus it is not surprising that when the organized power of political nativism declined by the late 1840s, native artisans in these trades turned to a degree of cooperation with the immigrant hands in the industry to defend themselves from mutual economic extinction. While they would not join the same organizations as the Irish or the Germans in the trade, the native American craft unions in tailoring and shoemaking extended invitations to immigrant leaders to organize their fellow workers and form an alliance to resist their employers. Some strikes were attempted to cut hours or restore wages, and a few even maintained sufficient solidarity to succeed. But these coalitions never gained stability because of the ambivalent feelings nativists and immigrants had toward each other. When organized nativism resurfaced in the Know-Nothing movement of the early 1850s, these ethnic federations in tailoring and shoemaking broke down completely. Ethnic harmony in the name of class solidarity was not resuscitated until after the Civil War, when a new set of factors had transformed Philadelphia's preindustrial artisans into industrial workers and the issues of the 1840s had lost much of their relevance.[22]

If mutual class interest was not enough to reduce ethnic tensions completely in Philadelphia during the late 1840s, nationalistic fervor had a greater effect. When war broke out with Mexico over the annexation of Texas in 1846, thousands of Irishmen volunteered for service, and most citizens were sincerely grateful for the brave manner in which they fought for the nation's honor. The question of Irish loyalty to their adopted homeland was, for a few years at least, laid to rest.[23] The war also served to remove from the city's streets many of the young native and Irish toughs who had spent their spare time fighting in gangs and harrassing unoffending citizens.

The same factors leading to a decline in the strength of the nativist movement in Philadelphia by the end of the 1840s also led to a reduction in the amount of collective violence between natives and immigrants. While the violence between the Irish and their enemies did not disappear, it was channeled into clearly limited areas. Much of it was disguised in the form of fire company and gang fights, which were not strictly ethnic battles but which often coincided with ethnic divisions. While the fire and gang fights were brutal and sometimes marked by heavy gunplay, they did not grow into general riots attracting hundreds of participants and thousands of bystanders. For five years after 1844, the city was spared any major battles, and when one finally erupted it was between blacks and whites rather than between Irish and natives. In 1849, a Moyamensing gang, the Killers, attacked a pub called the California House and burned it to the ground, allegedly because the black proprietor was cohabiting there with his white wife. The gang was heavily Irish and controlled by Democratic boss William McMullin. The fighting took approximately seventeen lives on both sides as it spread through the black ghetto. Sam Bass Warner, Jr., has observed that despite the wide scale of the fighting at the California House, great crowds did not gather to observe it. He surmises that they were afraid to go to the scene for fear that the soldiers would be called out to fire on the rioters, much as had been done in Southwark five years previously.[24]

Ultimately, it was this new respect for the willingness of Philadelphia's public authorities to keep order at any cost that ended the reign of private collective violence in Philadelphia. The local districts' efforts to control the fire fights were barely successful, as we shall see in the next chapter, but aside from the California House riot the city remained peaceful

until the Civil War. To insure that tranquility would be preserved, the leaders in Philadelphia society began a process of government reorganization and the creation of a professional police force that resulted in a new political structure for Philadelphia. After the riots, Philadelphia put itself on the road to becoming a modern, centralized metropolis.

NOTES

1. *Public Ledger,* October 4, 1845.

2. Ibid., February 1, 1845.

3. Ibid., July 31, 1844.

4. Ibid., July 9, 1844, October 4, 1845. *Six Months Ago* (Philadelphia: n.p., 1844), 6-8.

5. For an analysis of Philadelphia's wealth distribution by wards, see Stuart Blumin, "Mobility in a Nineteenth-Century City: Philadelphia, 1820-1860" (Ph.D. diss., University of Pennsylvania, 1968), 129.

6. Compared Returns, 1843 and 1844, First Congressional District *Public Ledger,* October 9, 1844.

| | 1844 | | | 1843 | | |
	Lehman(D)	Morris(W)	Levin(AR)	D	W	Ind.
Southwark	1206	561	2367	1155	1075	661
Moyamensing	806	466	562	714	620	121
Passyunk	117	21	172	73	46	79
Cedar	467	1083	512	260	769	73
New Market	289	305	253	174	355	98
Total	2885	2436	3866	2376	2865	1032

7. Compared Returns, 1843 and 1844, Third Congressional District *Public Ledger,* October 9, 1844.

| | 1844 | | | 1843 | |
	Smith(D)	Steel(W)	Campbell(AR)	D	W
Spring Garden	1865	463	2938	2199	1771
Northern Liberties	2240	258	2343	1796	1431
Total	4105	721	5281	3995	3202

8. Fourth Congressional District Returns, 1844.

	Ingersoll(D)	Duffield(W)	Shearer(AR)
Kensington	1437	193	2042
Kingsessing	121	12	81
West Philadelphia	141	36	132
Blockley	252	225	78
Roxborough	439	17	430
Lower Dublin	260	165	180
Oxford	309	413	79
Bristol	132	51	123
Unincorporated North Liberties	321	134	148
Germantown	360	147	468
North and South Penn Township	278	53	268
Byberry	69	66	67
Moreland	65	23	9
Total	**4184**	**1535**	**4105**

9. *Public Ledger,* October 9, 1844, October 16, 1845.

10. Ibid., August 10, 16, 1844, June 4, 1845, March 10, 1846.

11. For the proliferation of nativistic voluntary associations, see *Public Ledger,* January 14, May 15, June 27, July 7, 1845, and the *Sun,* January 27, 29, 1845, February 9, 1847; John Hancock Lee, *Origin and Progress of the American Party in Politics* (Philadelphia: Elliot and Gihon, 1855), 15.

12. *Public Ledger,* October 20, 16, 1845, October 17, 1847.

13. *Sun,* November 25, 1846.

14. Sister M. Theophane Geary, *Third Parties in Pennsylvania, 1840-1860* (Washington, D.C.: Catholic University of America Press, 1934), 125.

15. *Sun,* April 3, 1847, April 4, June 10, 1848; *Public Ledger,* October 11, 14, 1845.

16. *Public Ledger,* October 17, 1848, October 18, 1850.

17. *Sun,* March 15, May 5, 15, 1847.

18. Geary, *Third Parties in Pennsylvania,* 125.

19. For the tariff issue in 1846, see the *Sun,* passim.

20. For the anniversary celebrations, see the *Public Ledger,* May 7 editions, for the years 1845 to 1847.

21. Bruce Laurie, "The Working People of Philadelphia, 1827-1854" (Ph.D. diss., University of Pittsburgh, 1971), 214-218; *Public Ledger,* February 4, 11, 17, March 7, 1846.

22. Laurie, "Working People of Philadelphia," chap. 8, passim. For a beginning discussion of the attempts of urban working people to reunite against the rise of industrial capitalism after the Civil War, see David Montgomery, *Beyond Equality: Labor and the Radical Republicans, 1862-1872* (New York: Knopf, 1967).

23. In December 1846, Lewis Levin tried to introduce a bill calling for the twenty-one-year naturalization period, but he was soundly rebuffed on the floor of the House and the bill died in committee. Ray Allen Billington, *The Protestant Crusade, 1800-1860: A Study of the Origins of American Nativism* (Chicago: Quadrangle Books, 1964), 208.

24. For the California House riot, see Sam Bass Warner, Jr., *The Private City: Philadelphia in Three Periods of Its Growth* (Philadelphia: University of Pennsylvania Press, 1968), 158; for the judgment on crowd behavior, ibid., 151.

9
Conclusion

The relative decline in private collective violence in Philadelphia after 1844 depended only in part on the confinement of Irish-native hostility. More important in the long run was the creation of a municipal government and police force capable of preventing major breaches of the peace. While American Republicanism faded in the late 1840s, the movement to police Philadelphia effectively transformed the city permanently. Pointing to the fighting in Southwark, those who had argued for consolidation and a professional police force in the aftermath of the Kensington efforts now redoubled their efforts. Although the process of governmental consolidation was not completed for a decade, their efforts to police the city more effectively bore fruit more quickly. The various local police forces throughout the county were merged and professionalized in stages between 1844 and 1850. Finally, in 1854, the state legislature mandated a unified government for metropolitan Philadelphia county. At its head they placed a mayor and bicameral city council, eliminating the many district and township jurisdictions. The elected sheriff was replaced by an appointed police chief whose legal powers and resources far exceeded those of his predecessor. Philadelphia thus assumed its modern form on the eve of the Civil War.

Rationalized administration, an orderly supply of civic services, and a professional force for the maintenance of order and authority are now the hallmarks of the modern city. The transition from the basically eighteenth-century town form of social and political organization to the modern metropolis of the late nineteenth century occurred in Philadelphia in the decades of the 1840s and 1850s. This change paralleled the transformation of the city's economy from a preindustrial to an industrial base, and, as Allen Silver has pointed out, the two forms of change are intimately related to each other.[1] Yet

like industrialization, the change to a well-ordered, law-abiding modern city did not occur in a smooth flow. Consolidation and police professionalization had to overcome stiff opposition from elite conservatives and a portion of the working classes, just as the newer forms of industrial capitalism had to overcome resistance from the commercially based wealthy elite and the artisans and immigrants whose lives were disrupted by the introduction of machines and factories. Still, consolidation, like industrialization, won out, and in doing so it brought major transformations in the consciousness of those it touched. The changes in the form of Philadelphia's municipal structure during the 1840s and 1850s reflect alterations in the consciousness and chosen roles of the elite governing classes in the city.

In the week after the Southwark riot, Philadelphia resembled an armed camp even more than it did after the bloody May days in Kensington. The last out-of-town troops were kept on duty until July 17, almost two weeks after the fighting ended. General Patterson served notice on the populace that he would brook no further resistance to military authority by regularly marching his heavily armed men up and down the streets of the city. When Patterson's drama was played out, several of the armed volunteer citizens' patrols continued to muster for a few weeks longer. Civil government took its own steps to maintain the peace and punish those who broke it. The Philadelphia county commissioners offered a five hundred dollar reward for information leading to the arrest and conviction of anyone bearing arms against the militia in Southwark.[2] Judge Joel Jones of the Quarter Sessions court ruled that any person possessing firearms in a private home without express government authorization was liable to criminal charges.[3] County Recorder Richard Vaux, a staunch Democrat, ordered editors Lewis Levin and Samuel Kramer arrested for "inciting to treason" in the pages of their newspapers. Since these charges were vague at best and unconstitutional at worst, Vaux released the two men on low bail and later dropped all charges against them. His primary purpose was probably to harrass and intimidate rather than convict them. Vaux also arrested former sheriff John Watmough for using "inflammatory language" against the militia. Watmough had allegedly cursed the soldiers for firing on native citizens and suggested that the cavalry tripped up by the rope stretched across Third Street should have been shot in cold blood. Vaux sternly lectured Watmough on conduct becoming a gentleman—the ex-sheriff was a man of wealth

who later became president of the Pennsylvania Railroad—and released him on his own recognizance.[4]

While public officials were taking these measures to prevent further disorder or its incitement, private citizens were taking symbolic political steps of their own to reinforce the consensus against violence. A group of Philadelphia notables led by Horace Binney announced a public campaign to "sustain the laws" and give "CONFIDENCE . . . TO THE SERVANTS OF THE LAW, UNTIL ITS ENEMIES ARE SUPPRESSED." With this as their rallying call, the group convened a demonstration in the state house yard on July 11. Those present overwhelmingly endorsed resolutions justifying the behavior of the military in Southwark. The rally applauded Generals Patterson and Cadwalader for upholding the law in such a fearless manner (the resolutions actually referred to the need to maintain "law and order"). The common soldiers especially were commended for "performing the highest service that a citizen can be called upon to perform, the duty of perilling their lives in defense of the laws and the constitution." All those who were killed, "even innocent bystanders," had no complaint, such was their reward for not "retiring from the presence of the lawless as persons whom it is the bounden duty of every good citizen to denounce and forsake."[5]

Perhaps it is too much to place great stress on one sentence when trying to understand the evolving consciousness of a whole class of persons such as Philadelphia's elite. But the principle contained in the final phrase was a new one in the lexicon of the governing class. Only two months before, self-conscious upper-class critics were calling on their fellow citizens to take a more active role in intervening to support law-enforcement officials as part of the tradition of voluntarism by which the order of the city had always been maintained. Now, however, after the second major disturbance in three months, the futility of relying on citizen support for the maintenance of the peace became overwhelmingly apparent. Abandoning the doctrine of voluntarism, the rally replaced it with the modern doctrine of police professionalism, raising it to a first principle of good citizenship. After July 11, 1844, when Philadelphians found themselves at the scene of a public disorder, they agreed, "It is the duty of all to retire but those to whom the law has confided the defense of property and life."[6]

More than two thousand persons of all classes, ethnic origins, and political parties eventually signed the resolutions adopted at the July 11 rally. Significantly, the first name at the top of the list belonged to Horace Binney, followed immediately by those of Whig Congressman Joseph R. Ingersoll, John Sergeant, Samuel Norris, George M. Wharton, two members of the Biddle family, a Morris, and two Tilghmans, easily the most respected names in Philadelphia since the time of the Revolution. In an earlier day, the forefathers of these same civic leaders had given active physical assistance as well as moral support in maintaining order in the city. Now, this latest generation, given its turn to provide a model for good citizenship, resolved that personal involvement in the actual mechanics of peacekeeping no longer had a place in an urbanizing Philadelphia.[7]

In place of the old system, the elite—led once again by Horace Binney—proposed a new system for maintaining order. On July 11, the same day as the mass rally to "sustain the laws," Binney and two other attorneys, John M. Read and John K. Kane, petitioned the select and common councils of the city, asking for the creation of a military regiment whose commander would be under the direct authority of the mayor and the councils. Events had convinced Binney that the "civil force [constabulary and watch] is inadequate to the occasion" and that "something more is required . . . which, impressing the minds of evilly-disposed persons with the certainty of peril in evil deeds, may prevent calamity and obviate the necessity and cause of punishment, by deterring them from crime." While Philadelphia had fortunately been aided in the late riots by troops from outisde the city, Binney observed, such help by its very nature "must be temporary and occasional." If the city had its own troops, he concluded, a permanent deterrent to collective violence would be perpetually at hand.[8]

Binney's plan for troops was simple: the councils would retain the services of General Cadwalader's First City Brigade of the state militia for its own purposes. Since the law was silent on the question of dual service, Binney saw no impediment to recruiting the state's volunteers for simultaneous duty as a paid city force. Accepting the force of Binney's logic, the councils appropriated ten thousand dollars for the general to use at his discretion to buy uniforms and sup-

plies for his men. Using these funds liberally, Cadwalader soon collected pledges of loyalty to the city of Philadelphia from a full regiment of infantry, a battalion of artillery, and two troops of cavalry. Even though these volunteers retained their membership in the state militia, no state official ever challenged their dual enrollment as a conflict of interest. The government of Philadelphia thus retained its own loyal militia ready to serve local authority in any emergency.[9]

Support for the new city militia poured in from all sides. Even the semiofficial American Republican press agreed that strong measures were needed to keep order and that the new militia company was necessary for the defense of life and property. After all, a party groping for respectability and trying to live down a violent reputation could not defend even its own following when that following attacked the forces of legal authority. Yet there were some dissenting voices raised in opposition to the "mercenary army" created by the city councils' decree of July 11. While their identity is no longer available because of their use of pseudonyms, the level of their written discourse indicates that they were men of education and standing in the community. The dissenters were strict constitutional constructionists who were not opposed to keeping order as such and gave no support to the right of the nativist crowd to resist General Cadwalader's authority. Rather, they simply objected to Philadelphia's hiring a band of soldiers to perform a job that traditionally had been reserved to civilian officials.

Opposition to the creation of the city's own army did not prevent the recruitment of the troops; the nature of the conservative challenge to the city councils' step seems important at this remove only because of the way in which it illuminated the assumptions on which the elite had based its approval of the idea of a municipal military force. At bottom, the conservatives were asking the citizens of Philadelphia to choose between their respect for older values and the need to respond to more recently perceived imperatives. The new militia company, created specifically to enforce order in Philadelphia as an adjunct to the civil authorities, symbolized the abandonment by Philadelphians of the traditional limitations placed on the power of government in exchange for order as an end in itself. The opposition movement coalesced around an anonymous pamphlet entitled *Street Talk about an Ordinance of Councils, Passed July Eleventh, 1844, Organizing a Military Force for the Government of Philadelphia.*[10] While the pamphlet did not succeed in causing the councils to rescind

their ordinance or withdraw support from the militia, the pamphlet's recommendations for an alternative system of law enforcement were ultimately adopted in the course of the next decade.

Street Talk began by arguing that the streets of Philadelphia were no longer "free" but rather controlled by an instrument of "British despotism." The pamphlet asserted that the councils' ordinance provided for nothing less than the unconstitutional ascendancy of the military over civilian authority in the city. While conceding that at the present moment the mayor and the constabulary could not quell disturbances alone, the author argued that the remedy for this failing did not lie in turning to armed soldiers, most of whom were simply "high-spirited young men" ready to use their firearms at the first provocation. The only sure protection against escalating civil disturbances, argued *Street Talk,* was a "preventive" police. A volunteer militia, regardless of whom it was responsible to, could never head off a disturbance because it could not be brought to the scene until hours after trouble was well under way. The movement of a large force of soldiers, experience had proved, always attracted large numbers of spectators. Professional, full-time policemen, on the other hand, men who would be constantly on patrol and experienced in dealing with neighborhood citizens, would be able to disperse crowds in their early stages. According to *Street Talk,* the savings in life, property, money, and civic harmony would be well worth the cost and effort of organizing and supporting a well-run, civilian-controlled professional force similar to the London "bobbies."

While the cry for a professional police force had been raised before, *Street Talk* invoked a constitutional as well as practical argument in its behalf. The founding fathers, the pamphlet's author noted, had made no provision in their fundamental laws for the use of soldiers against civilians. Martial law was, in this sense, "revolutionary," without foundation in the Constitution; it invoked not the law of the land but the law of the jungle, not the social contract but the war of all against all. The July 11 ordinance, properly understood, provided the mayor with a force of mercenaries to turn loose on the populace at his will. Should any sign of popular disturbance appear, *Street Talk* hyperbolized, "We, the people of the city of Penn . . . will be saddled and bridled and ready to be ridden after the fashion of St. Petersburg."[11]

As far as *Street Talk* was concerned, the main cause of the violence in Southwark had nothing to do with the nativist principles of

the rioters. Rather, it was popular opposition to the military's intrusion into a civilian matter that created the hostility toward General Cadwalader and his men. "Who does not believe," the author asked, "that the crowds in Southwark and Kensington were made more angry and fierce by seeing armed soldiers instead of officers of the peace sent against them, and that a much smaller body of active policemen than we had troops could have effectually put down the mob without resort to deadly weapons?"[12] The populace resented the soldiers' pretensions to be better than their fellow citizens: "We have actually seen that the main topic of obloquy heaped by the late mob on the soldiers was what they called their 'pretty coats.' "[13] Provoked by insults to their source of dignity, the soldiers retaliated with the only means they had at hand—their guns. By contrast, a policeman would wield only a baton or club. The author argued that such instruments were not only more humane but more effective. Since they do not take life, their use would not further inflame an already excited multitude.

The *Public Ledger* led the battle in favor of the new city militia and against the charges contained in *Street Talk.* The paper's editorials argued that the pamphlet was based on a false premise: that in the United States there was a meaningful distinction between a soldier and a policeman, or a soldier and a private citizen, as there was in despotic nations with standing armies. Under the American political system, argued the *Ledger,* both the volunteer militia and the elected constabulary were mandated to carry out the public desire for order through law. To portray the soldiers as different from other citizens or as enemies of the public will was nothing less than a malicious slander. As the paper saw it, the citizen-soldiers embodied the general will itself when they performed their peacekeeping functions. The law was made by all the people, lectured the editors, and the military was simply an instrument for carrying out that law. Turning to less abstract arguments, the *Ledger* pointed out that the mere existence of a city militia did not preclude prior efforts by a civilian police. Doubtless, the willingness of elected officials to use military troops if necessary rendered the civil police (if it were to be created) or the constabulary more effective in preventing disorder. The *Ledger* explained that when crowds believed that soldiers were sure to come if the police failed to control them, they would be more responsive to police commands. The implicit threat of fatal force prevented its having to be used.[14]

Contrary to *Street Talk*'s assertion, the *Ledger*'s editorialists insisted, the issue was not one between the will of the people and usurping military despotism. Rather, the struggle was one of "the civil power and its [subordinate] military force" against completely illegal "insurgents." Law, the *Ledger* asserted, was above the interests of class or community. The paper explained that the law cannot "make [*sic*] account of public excitement arising from every stimulant which may be applied to the public mind." Whatever is legal, even the arming of St. Philip's church, no matter how obnoxious to a portion of the citizenry, must be tolerated by them; what is illegal, such as the Irish rowdies' attack on the American Republican rally at the Nanny Goat Market, must be punished by the proper authorities only. A crowd could not take such matters into its own hands.

> If in the future we regain lost dignity, security, liberty and law, we must purge the administration of justice of all deference to popular violence, and renovate public virtue by insisting on this truth: that popular violence, approved and unpunished, always contains within it the seeds of future and greater crimes which if not arrested by the most terrible powers of the law, must result in anarchy, ultimately ending in military despotism.[15]

The *Ledger* and *Street Talk* did agree on one fundamental point: a preventive civilian police force would be preferable to a volunteer regiment for the prevention of future collective outbreaks. But action toward the creation of such a force was relatively slow in coming. In the interim, the city, several of the districts, and the county board of commissioners took steps to cope with the immediate problems of peacekeeping that they faced. Various efforts were made to strengthen the elected constabulary and the appointed night watch. The city even experimented with a paid day watch for a few weeks, but taxpayer reluctance to support it marked its end. In May 1845, the first anniversary of the great riots, the Kensington board of commissioners appropriated funds to install gaslights in the district. In August, a group of Southwark civic leaders, many of them American Republicans, formed a committee of public safety, composed of five volunteer citizens from each ward who were to meet at least once each month to conduct public investigations into personal injuries, property damage, and the quality of law enforcement in the district. Its founders hoped

that through public revelation by the district's leading citizens, law enforcement officials would be prodded to crack down on the rowdy but politically powerful street gangs and fire companies that made Southwark their home. The committee even promised to take an active personal role in peacekeeping should the constabulary prove remiss, but there is no record that its members ever did so. Still, the creation of a body combining both an investigatory and vigilante function showed that the tradition of voluntarism was not completely dead. That many of the members of the committee were American Republicans reminds us of the desire of the leaders of that party to live down the violent image that had attached itself to the organization.[16]

Southwark was not the only district that groped for a way to control the violent gangs and fire companies that were the shock troops in an ongoing ethnic warfare. The county commissioners tried to supply some leadership in this area in June 1844 when they divided greater Philadelphia into three zones—northern districts, southern districts, and the city—and forbade any fire company to leave its own zone. Going one step further, the city councils barred any company guilty of misconduct from drawing Schuylkill water, and one company, the Hope Hose, was actually banned from plugging into city hydrants during September. In February 1845, the Moyamensing commissioners refused to grant the district's annual appropriation for the Franklin and Native hose companies, two groups that had a particulary bad record of feuding. Three years later, the Kensington commissioners decreed that any company convicted of fighting twice in one year had to disband. Yet none of these measures had any great effect. An experiment by the Southwark commissioners in fall 1845 made this point most clearly. Taking the most thoroughgoing step yet tried to control fire company violence, the commissioners appropriated $9,000 to outfit four of their own municipal fire companies, hoping to demonstrate that the volunteer companies were unnecessary. But the plan to phase out the volunteers failed miserably. When the district's uniformed fire companies appeared to answer an alarm, irate volunteer firemen attacked them and destroyed their equipment. Rather than risk the hazard of a serious fire loss, the commissioners abandoned their experiment with paid professional fire fighters and reinstated their appropriations to the volunteers.[17]

While local efforts to bring a modicum of order to the troubled city yielded meager results, a movement to place municipal peacekeep-

ing on a metropolitan level was finally launched in earnest during the winter of 1844-1845. The obvious first step in this direction was consolidation of the many districts and jurisdictions in the city, and this became the pet project of an important faction of the elite. Former mayor of Philadelphia John Swift, merchants Edward P. Cope and Francis Wharton, and numerous politicians and attorneys favored the merger. Whigs, Democrats, American Republicans, Irishmen, and native-born citizens all spoke up for the measure at a large meeting in the county courthouse in December 1844, and those present even forwarded a resolution to the state legislature proposing a bill to consolidate the city into one administrative unit.[18]

The proconsolidation forces won overwhelming approval for their resolutions at the rally but had a more difficult time on the floor of the legislature itself. An equally distinguished and powerful group of businessmen and attorneys opposed consolidation and continued to do so until the 1850s. At their head was none other than Horace Binney. He and his followers feared that by merging the city with less affluent districts the value of city municipal bonds (of which Binney, for one, was a major holder) would decline.[19] Furthermore, as Whigs, many city leaders feared that merger with the Democratic suburbs would weaken their control over their political domain. Finally, both city and district patronage appointees stood to lose their sinecures if local governments were reduced in size or made to function more efficiently. Consequently, Binney, his son-in-law Sidney George Fisher, Josiah Randall, and William Stokes (ex-president of the Repeal Association) offered a compromise counterproposal to consolidation. In their plan, the districts would remain separate political entities but would establish standardized and somewhat coordinated police systems. On April 12, 1845, the state legislature adopted an amended version of Binney's plan, specifying that several districts had to create new police forces to supplement the old elected constabulary. Under the state plan, the voters in the city, Spring Garden, Northern Liberties, and Moyamensing were each required to elect a police commissioner who would then appoint a force of "not less than one able-bodied man for each of one hundred and fifty taxable inhabitants." Kensington and Southwark voluntarily complied with this act as well. Each of the new police commissioners—and the sheriff—was empowered by the legislature to command crowds to disperse under threat of immediate arrest. The sheriff was given overall command of these new dis-

trict forces and could call on them in any emergency. He was thus freed
from dependence on a volunteer posse or the cooperation of the militia.
Should he need the troops, however, he was now armed with a riot act.
As part of the police reorganization effort, the legislature specified that
the militia might act at the sheriff's request (that is, without prior assent
from the governor) to "proceed in suppression of . . . riot, tumult, and
unlawful assembly . . . in like manner as in the case of war or public insurrection." The soldiers could no longer be held liable for any loss of
life that they inflicted in the line of duty.[20]

The new district forces were not necessarily full time or professional.
To keep down expenses, most districts used their "one to one hundred
and fifty" policemen only during the daylight hours, relying on the traditional night watch after dark. Furthermore, the new force was less
than a single, unified police force with jurisdiction throughout the county. While the policemen could be brought from district to district by
the sheriff, in normal times each district's force operated only within
its own boundaries. Nothing demonstrated the inadequacy of the system
more clearly than the California House riot of 1849 in which several
blacks and whites were killed and fighting raged on for two days. After
that outbreak, the consolidation faction regrouped for another round
of agitation. The campaign was led by attorney and temperance advocate Eli Kirk Price, industrialist Matthias Baldwin, and Judge John Cadwalader, cousin to the general. John Naglee, former president of the
Philadelphia and Trenton Railroad, whose tavern had been burned in
the Kensington antirailroad riots of 1840, was but one of those who
sponsored a town meeting in favor of consolidation.[21]

The story of consolidation remains unexamined by modern historians,
and at the present time little is known about the processes by which
the pro- and anticonsolidation forces managed their respective campaigns.
The result shows, however, that the coalition of fiscal and political conservatives such as Horace Binney, district officials fearing unemployment,
and political leaders reluctant to dilute their local power continued to
stave off consolidation for five years after the California House affair.
In its place, they engineered yet another centralization of police forces.
In May 1850, at Binney's suggestion, the state legislature approved a
full-time, well-paid, county-wide professional police force to supplement the existing district and city forces. The citizenry was empowered
to elect a police marshal for the county who replaced the sheriff and inherited all of his powers, such as the right to convene a posse, but also

had control over the use of the new police force. Under the first elected marshal, Peter Keyser, the "marshal's police" proved a willing if somewhat strong-armed force prepared to slug it out with the fire gangs and young toughs who had been terrorizing the city for a decade. For the first time in the history of Philadelphia, the streets were patrolled by a coordinated, professional force whose movements were unrestrained by artificial political boundaries.[22]

For reasons not perfectly clear, the "marshal's police" were unable to perform satisfactorily. Although their range was not confined to any single district, the new force was apparently undermanned, and the citizens of the city's many districts did not completely accept it. The elected constabulary still continued to function, and Marshal Keyser, a Whig, did not generate unanimous enthusiasm among those who lived outside the city proper. It was not until the legislature finally gave its consent to consolidation that a fully effective police force was established in Philadelphia. On February 2, 1854, the city charter of Philadelphia was amended to annex all of Philadelphia County and place it under the jurisdiction of the mayor and councils of the city proper. All previous district boundaries were thus abolished. The mayor assumed the duties of police magistrate, and the marshal's office and his police were disbanded. The councils assumed the functions of the county legislature and commissioners. Philadelphia thus took its contemporary political and administrative form: a strong executive, a bicameral council, a centralized professional police force, and a single set of boundaries.[23]

The chief motive for consolidating the city and professionalizing its police had been to curb the disorder between the Irish and nativist gangs and fire companies. What was not anticipated was that the creation of the police would solve that problem by converting the rowdies themselves into the policemen. The first consolidation mayor, Robert T. Conrad, ran as a coalition candidate of the Whigs and Know-Nothings. When he created a nine-hundred-man police force, he recruited "none but native Americans" for the job, thus legitimizing their use of violence against the disorderly Irish of the city. When Conrad was defeated for reelection in 1856 and his place was taken by Democrat Richard Vaux, the new incumbent expanded the force to a thousand men and filled any vacancies with loyal party men, many of them Irish. One notorious leader of the violent Columbia Hose Company, Samuel Ruggles, served as chief of police under both Conrad and Vaux, while William McMullin parlayed his leadership in a street gang and fire company into a prom-

inent role in the Democrat party under Vaux. Six members of McMullin's
Moyamensing Hose were named to "Dick Vaux's police" in 1856. The
creation of ethnically oriented police forces did more than simply define
away violence by calling it a police action; in an important way the creation of a nativist police under Conrad and an increasingly Irish police
force under Vaux helps explain the decline in open hostility between the
Irish and the nativists that was explored in the previous chapter. By controlling the police forces in their turn, each side had an opportunity to
exercise a kind of dominance over the other that eliminated the need
for open collective conflict outside of the regular and peaceful political
channels. The reward for victory in the ethnic electoral process of the
1850s was the legal right to crack the heads of hated enemies without
having to resort to open warfare as in the Kensington conflict. Sam
Bass Warner, Jr., has suggested that the institutionalization of ethnic
politics after the consolidation of 1854 helped to divert ethnic aggressions into more peaceful channels;[24] one might extend that insight to
conclude that riots declined in Philadelphia after 1854 because one
group of potential rioters was usually wearing the uniform of a policeman.

The anticonsolidationists did not abandon their opposition to the
unification of Philadelphia until 1853 when Horace Binney, their leading spokesman, finally admitted that many of his allies were in fact pet-
ty district officeholders fearful of losing their sinecures. He permitted
himself to be swayed by the argument that consolidation would save
Philadelphia County one hundred thousand dollars annually in administrative costs and increase the efficiency of tax collections.[25] Eli Kirk
Price, who was elected to the state senate in order to argue the case for
consolidation in that body, later revealed that at least some consolida-
tionists saw their movement as a moral as well as political reform. Price
argued that a centralized city government with jurisdiction over the suburbs would be able to control the granting of tavern licenses in the less
well-to-do reaches of the county. He claimed that the temperance movement was being undermined by the permissiveness with which venal district commissioners were granting tavern licenses to all comers. Price
was not a nativist; by the 1850s, temperance had spread to wide portions
of the community, not just its more fervent evangelicals.[26]

It is no coincidence that Price discerned an interest in consolidation
among the advocates of temperance. Both movements showed a primary
concern for the maintenance of public order and morals; both similarly reflected the changing consciousness of a society evolving from a preindustrial

to an industrial form. Modernization involves not merely technological and organizational innovations but transformations of values as well. Price and Binney could advocate temperance and consolidation because both were intended to moderate the customarily disruptive behavior of Philadelphia's working-class elements; either through externally imposed measures such as the creation of an effective police or through internally generated acceptance of temperate limits to their personal indulgences. It would be too much to say that either of these men was self-consciously attempting to recondition the lower orders to render them more pliant and passive victims of industrial discipline; neither man ever expressed such ideas. Binney, in fact, was a leading member of the old commercial elite whose personal wealth stemmed from the preindustrial "free" profession of the law.[27] The categories of pro- and anticonsolidation would be neater if all the proconsolidation advocates were factory owners like Matthias Baldwin, with his eyes set squarely on the industrial future, and all the opponents of a professional police force old-line merchants, Irish politicians, and riotous weavers with their values drawn from the preindustrial past. But such distinctions are never so clear. In fact, nothing is known directly of what the great mass of working people in Philadelphia, Irish or native, thought of consolidation, since a referendum on the question was never conducted. Still, when Eli Price, Baldwin, and their nonpartisan running mates were elected to the state legislature to argue for consolidation, they could not have won their seats if the artisan classes had uniformly rejected their cause. It seems safe to conclude that the appeal of civic stability through a reorganization and strengthening of government reached into all levels of Philadelphia's class structure.

While consolidation and centralization reflected a growing consensus on the need for order, the older traditions of localism and "popular sovereignty" did not expire overnight. In 1844, when a newly created district police force took to the streets in Moyamensing, a "bacchanalian" crowd, in the words of the *Public Ledger,* attacked the officers, dispersed them, and destroyed a watch house. The rioters considered the new police a violation of their "liberty" to elect their own peace officers. Many constables organized to protest the 1845 "one to one hundred and fifty" law establishing an appointed police in the city and some districts. In a similar vein, when the marshal's police force was created in 1850, most of the newly appointed officers refused to wear standard uniforms. They claimed that such regalia was a blatant effort to "imitate the English" and constituted a "glaring violation of our republican institutions." His-

torian Ellis Paxson Oberholtzer suggests that the policemen likely feared that the volunteer firemen would resent the policemen's pretensions and attack them if they appeared in uniform. (Earlier, in 1844, the rank-and-file soldiers in the newly established city militia regiment won a battle with General Cadwalader and the city councils when they refused to wear a standard United States Army uniform rather than individual uniforms of their personal choice. The soldiers argued that even though the city was supplying their equipment and pay, they were still volunteers rather than regulars and would never abandon their traditional right as volunteers to identify themselves as they chose.) By 1851, however, the marshal's police abandoned their objections and adopted standard uniforms. The traditional consciousness was slowly bending before the imperatives of professionalization.[28]

Even today, opponents still protest the ever-increasing power of centralized governments and the expansion of the sphere of the police. In the streets, crowds still attempt to rescue suspects apprehended by police officers, and many communities resent the behavior and prerogatives of the men in blue. But the response on the part of the police themselves to these timeless objections has changed dramatically from what it was in Jacksonian Philadelphia. Confronted with challenges to their authority by a hostile crowd, the police no longer throw away their weapons and badges in an attempt to blend inobtrusively into the mass. The police have become professionals, uniformed, confident, well-armed, trained in crowd control, and in some cases well-disciplined. The residents of contemporary Philadelphia have long since accustomed themselves to the presence of armed and uniformed police professionals in their streets. Philadelphia is known, in fact, as one of the most policed, if not best policed, cities in America.[29] The federal government, through the use of the National Guard and the military reserve, has interjected itself in what were previously considered to be strictly local and state areas of jurisdiction in cases of civil disorder. As a result, historians generally agree that the cities and the nation as a whole are more peaceful now than they were in the nineteenth century. Certainly a great deal more of the collective violence occurring today involves direct clashes between protestors of one kind or another and the forces of authority rather than between two discontented groups. The consolidation and police professionalization growing out of the 1844 riots marked a beginning of Philadelphia's entry into the contemporary era.

NOTES

1. Allen Silver, "The Demand for Order in Civil Society," in *The Police: Six Sociological Essays,* ed. David J. Bordua (New York: Wiley, 1967), 3-21.

2. *Public Ledger,* July 18, 16, 1844.

3. Ibid., July 17, 1844.

4. Ibid., July 12, 1844.

5. Ibid.

6. Ibid.

7. E. Digby Baltzell, *Philadelphia Gentlemen: The Making of a National Upper Class* (Glencoe: Free Press, 1958), chap. 4; Sam Bass Warner, Jr., *The Private City: Philadelphia in Three Periods of Its Growth* (Philadelphia: University of Pennsylvania Press, 1968), chap. 1. Voluntarism was far from completely dead but was limited to certain less personally involving areas, such as the giving of charity. A collection in the month of July for the families of the dead and wounded soldiers, for example, garnered more than ten thousand dollars.

8. *Public Ledger,* July 12, 1844. Cf. *Journal of the Select Council of Philadelphia for 1844* (Philadelphia: n.p., 1845), 143.

9. *Street Talk about an Ordinance of Councils, Passed July Eleventh, 1844, Organizing a Military Force for the Government of Philadelphia* (Philadelphia: n.p., 1844).

10. Ibid., 7.

11. Ibid., 15.

12. Ibid.

13. Ibid.

14. *Public Ledger,* September 19-21, 1844.

15. Ibid., July 11, 18, 1844.

16. Ibid., May 18, August 25, 1845.

17. Ibid., August 11, September 2, 1845; *Sun,* January 22, 1847; *Public Ledger,* February 5, 1845; *Supplement-Digest of Kensington Ordinances for 1848* (act of March 7); *Public Ledger,* December 27, 1844, January 14, 28, August 5, Ocotber 20, 1845.

18. J. Thomas Scharf and Thompson Westcott, *History of Philadelphia, 1609-1884* (Philadelphia: L. H. Evarts, 1887), I: 694.

19. Sidney George Fisher, *A Philadelphia Perspective: The Diary of Sidney George Fisher,* ed. Nicholas B. Wainwright (Philadelphia: Historical Society of Pennsylvania, 1967), 179.

20. Scharf and Westcott, *History of Philadelphia,* I: 674-675.

21. Ibid., 693.

22. *Kensington Ordinances for 1845* (decree of May 5); *Sun,* June 6, 1845; Scharf and Westcott, *History of Philadelphia,* I: 674.

23. Russell F. Weigley, " 'A Peaceful City': Public Order in Philadelphia from Consolidation through the Civil War," in *The Peoples of Philadelphia: A History of Ethnic Groups and Lower-Class Life, 1790-1940,* ed. Allen F. Davis and Mark H. Haller (Philadelphia: Temple University Press, 1973), 157-159.

24. David R. Johnson, "Crime Patterns in Philadelphia, 1840-1870," in *Peoples of Philadelphia,* 101-107; Warner, *Private City,* 156.

25. Eli Kirk Price, *The History of the Consolidation of the City of Philadelphia* (Philadelphia: Lippincott, 1873), 18-19.

26. Ibid., 16-25.

27. This distinction between modernizers and conservatives within the ranks of the upper classes is suggested in Leonard L. Richards, *"Gentlemen of Property and Standing": Anti-Abolition Mobs in Jacksonian America* (New York: Oxford University Press, 1970), chap. 5.

28. *Public Ledger,* November 6, 1844; Ellis Paxson Oberholtzer, *Philadelphia: A History of the City and Its People* (Philadelphia: S. J. Clark, 1911), III: 298.

29 For a recent study of the contemporary police force in Philadelphia, see Jonathan Rubinstein, *City Police* (New York: Farrar, Straus and Giroux, 1973).

Bibliography

NEWSPAPERS, 1836-1848

Germantown *Telegraph.*
Philadelphia *Banner of the Cross.*
Philadelphia *Catholic Herald.*
Philadelphia *Daily Sun.*
Philadelphia *Native American.*
Philadelphia *North American.*
Philadelphia *Pennsylvania Freeman.*
Philadelphia *Presbyterian.*
Philadelphia *Public Ledger and Transcript.*
Philadelphia *Spirit of the Times.*
Philadelphia *Pennsylvanian.*

PRIMARY SOURCES

George Cadwalader. Papers. Historical Society of Pennsylvania, Philadelphia.

Colton, Walter. *The Bible in the Public Schools. A Reply to the Allegations and Complaints Contained in the Letter of Bishop Kenrick to the Board of School Controllers of the Public Schools.* Philadelphia: n.p., 1844.

Dickerson, William R. *The Letters of Junius, Exposing to the Public, for Their Benefit, the Mal-Practises in the Administration of the Law, the Corruption in the Offices in the State House Row, in the County of Philadelphia, the Extortions Practised by the Public Officers, etc.* Philadelphia: W. R. Dickerson, 1850.

Fisher, Sidney George. *A Philadelphia Perspective: The Diary of Sidney George Fisher, Covering the Years 1834-1871.* Edited by Nicholas B. Wainwright. Philadelphia: Historical Society of Pennsylvania, 1967.

Freedley, Edwin T. *Philadelphia and Its Manufactures: A Handbook of the Great Manufactories and Representative Mercantile Houses of Philadelphia in 1867.* Philadelphia: E. Young and Co., 1867.

A Full and Accurate Report of the Trial for Riot before the Mayor's Court of Philadelphia, on the Thirteenth of October, 1831, Arising out of a Protestant Procession on the Twelfth of July, and in Which the Concerned Parties Were Protestants and Catholics. Including the Indictments, Examination of Witnesses, Speeches of Counsel, Verdict and Sentences. Philadelphia: Jesper Harding, 1831.

Lee, John Hancock. *Origin and Progress of the American Party in Politics; Embracing a Complete History of the Philadelphia Riots in May and July of 1844 and a Refutation of the Arguments Founded on the Charges of Religious Proscription and Secret Combinations.* Philadelphia: Elliot and Gihon, 1855.

Pennsylvania. General Assembly. Senate. *Report of the Select Committee Appointed to Visit the Manufacturing Districts, for the Purpose of Investigating the Subject of the Employment of Children in Manufactories.* Harrisburg, 1838.

Pennsylvania Hall Association. *The History of Pennsylvania Hall, Which Was Destroyed by a Mob on May Eighteenth, 1838.* Philadelphia: Pennsylvania Hall Association, 1838.

Price, Eli Kirk. *The History of the Consolidation of the City of Philadelphia.* Philadelphia: J. B. Lippincott, 1873.

"Reflections on the Late Riots by Candid Writers in Poetry and Prose (Philadelphia, 1844)." Reprinted in *Researches of the American Catholic Historical Society of Philadelphia* 28 (1911): 234.

Six Months Later. Philadelphia: n.p., 1845.

Street Talk about an Ordinance of Councils, Passed July Eleventh, 1844, Organizing a Military Force for the Government of Philadelphia. Philadelphia: n.p., 1844.

SECONDARY SOURCES

Adams, William Forbes. *Ireland and the Irish Emigration to the New World from 1815 to the Famine.* New Haven: Yale University Press, 1932.

Alexander, John K. "The City of Brotherly Fear: The Poor in Eighteenth-Century Philadelphia." In *Cities in American History.* Edited by Kenneth T. Jackson and Stanley K. Schultz. New York: Alfred A. Knopf, 1972.

──── . "Poverty, Fear, and Continuity: An Analysis of the Poor in Late Eighteenth-Century Philadelphia." In *The Peoples of Philadelphia: A History of Ethnic Groups and Lower-Class Life, 1790-1940.* Edited by Allen F. Davis and Mark H. Haller. Philadelphia: Temple University Press, 1973.

Baltzell, E. Digby. *Philadelphia Gentlemen: The Making of a National Upper Class.* Glencoe: Free Press, 1958.

Banner, Lois W. "Religious Benevolence as Social Control: A Critique of an Interpretation." *Journal of American History* 60 (1973): 23-41.

Benson, Lee. *The Concept of Jacksonian Democracy: New York as a Test Case.* Princeton: Princeton University Press, 1961.

Berger, Max. "The Irish Emigrant and American Nativism as Seen by British Visitors, 1836-1860." *Pennsylvania Magazine of History and Biography* 7 (1946): 146-160.

Billington, Ray Allen. *The Protestant Crusade, 1800-1860: A Study of the Origins of American Nativism.* Chicago: Quadrangle Books, 1964.

Bordua, David J. *The Police: Six Sociological Essays.* New York: John Wiley & Sons, 1967.

Brown, Richard Maxwell. "The American Vigilante Tradition." In *Violence in America: Historical and Comparative Perspectives.* Edited by Hugh David Graham and Ted Robert Gurr. Washington, D.C.: U.S. Government Printing Office, 1969.

Brown, Thomas N. *Irish-American Nationalism, 1870-1890.* Philadelphia: J. B. Lippincott, 1966.

Burchard, John Ely, and Handlin, Oscar, eds. *The Historian and the City.* Cambridge: MIT Press, 1963.

Clark, Dennis. "Kellyville: An Immigrant Success Story." *Pennsylvania History* 39 (January 1972): 39-51.

Curry, Richard O., and Brown, Thomas More. *Conspiracy: The Fear of Subversion in American History.* New York: Holt, Rinehart and Winston, 1972.

Davis, Allen F., and Haller, Mark H. *The Peoples of Philadelphia: A History of Ethnic Groups and Lower-Class Life, 1790-1940.* Philadelphia: Temple University Press, 1973.

Davis, David Brion, ed. *The Fear of Conspiracy: Images of Un-American Subversion from the Revolution to the Present.* Ithaca: Cornell University Press, 1971.

──── . "Some Themes of Counter-Subversion: An Analysis of Anti-Masonic, Anti-Catholic, and Anti-Mormon Literature." *Mississippi*

Valley Historical Review 47 (1960): 205-224.

Ernst, Robert. "Economic Nativism in New York City during the 1840s." *New-York History* 29 (1948): 170-186.

Feldberg, Michael. "The Crowd in Philadelphia History: A Comparative Perspective." *Labor History* 15 (Summer 1974): 323-336.

———. "Urbanization as a Cause of Violence: Jacksonian Philadelphia as a Test Case." In *The Peoples of Philadelphia: A History of Ethnic Groups and Lower-Class Life, 1790-1940.* Edited by Allen F. Davis and Mark H. Haller. Philadelphia: Temple University Press, 1973.

Geary, Sister M. Theophane. *Third Parties in Pennsylvania, 1840-1860.* Washington, D.C.: Catholic University of America Press, 1938.

Geffen, Elizabeth M. "Violence in Philadelphia in the 1840s and 1850s." *Pennsylvania History* 36 (1969): 381-410.

Gordon, Milton M. "Assimilation in America: Theory and Reality." In *Minority Responses: Comparative Views of Reactions to Subordination.* Edited by Minako Kurokawa. New York: Random House, 1970.

Graham, Hugh Davis, and Gurr, Ted Robert. *Violence in America: Historical and Comparative Perspectives.* Washington, D.C.: U.S. Government Printing Office, 1969.

Gusfield, Joseph R. *Symbolic Crusade: Status Politics and the American Temperance Movement.* Urbana: University of Illinois Press, 1966.

Handlin, Oscar. *Boston's Immigrants, 1790-1880: A Study in Acculturation.* New York: Atheneum, 1970.

Hansen, Klaus. "The Millennium, The West, and Race in the Antebellum Mind." *Western Historical Quarterly* 3 (1972): 372-390.

Higham, John. "Another Look at Nativism." *Catholic Historical Review* 44 (1958): 147-158.

Hobsbawm, Eric. *Labouring Men: Studies in the History of Labour.* Garden City: Doubleday Books, 1967.

Hofstadter, Richard. *The American Political Tradition and the Men Who Made It.* New York: Random House, 1948.

———. *The Paranoid Style in American Politics and Other Essays.* New York: Alfred A. Knopf, 1966.

———, and Wallace, Michael, eds. *American Violence: A Documentary History.* New York: Alfred A. Knopf, 1970.

Holt, Michael Fitzgibbon. "The Politics of Impatience: The Origins of Know-Nothingism." *Journal of American History* 60 (1973): 309-331.

Jackson, Kenneth T., and Schultz, Stanley K., eds. *Cities in American History.* New York: Alfred A. Knopf, 1972.

Johnson, David R. "Crime Patterns in Philadelphia, 1840-1870." In *The Peoples of Philadelphia: A History of Ethnic Groups and Lower-Class Life, 1790-1940.* Edited by Allen F. Davis and Mark H. Haller. Philadelphia: Temple University Press, 1973.

Kurokawa, Minako, ed. *Minority Responses: Comparative Views of Reactions to Subordination.* New York: Random House, 1970.

Lannie, Vincent P., and Deithorn, Bernard C. "For the Honor and Glory of God: The Philadelphia Bible Riots of 1844." *History of Education Quarterly* 8 (1968): 44-106.

Laurie, Bruce Gordon. "Fire Companies and Gangs in Southwark: the 1840s." In *The Peoples of Philadelphia: A History of Ethnic Groups and Lower-Class Life, 1790-1940.* Edited by Allen F. Davis and Mark H. Haller. Philadelphia: Temple University Press, 1973.

———. "'Nothing on Compulsion': Life Styles of Philadelphia Artisans, 1820-1850." *Labor History* 15 (Summer 1974): 337-366.

Lipset, Seymour Martin, and Raab, Earl. *The Politics of Unreason: Right-Wing Extremism in America, 1790-1970.* New York, Harper & Row, 1970.

McAvoy, T. Thomas. "The Formation of the Catholic Minority in the United States, 1820-1860." *Review of Politics* 10(1948): 13-34.

Montgomery, David. *Beyond Equality: Labor and the Radical Republicans, 1862-1872.* New York: Alfred A. Knopf, 1967.

———. "The Working Classes of the Pre-Industrial City." *Labor History* 9 (1968): 3-22.

———. "The Shuttle and the Cross: Weavers and Artisans in the Kensington Riots of 1844." *Journal of Social History* 5 (1972): 411-446.

Nieburg, Harold L. *Political Violence: The Behavioral Process.* New York: St. Martin's Press, 1969.

Nolan, Hugh Joseph. *The Most Reverend Francis Patrick Kenrick, Third Bishop of Philadelphia, 1830-1851.* Philadelphia: American Catholic Historical Society of Philadelphia, 1948.

Oberholtzer, Ellis Paxson. *Philadelphia: A History of the City and Its People, A Record of 225 Years.* Philadelphia: S. J. Clarke, 1912.

Parsons, William T. "The Bloody Election of 1742." *Pennsylvania History* 36 (1969): 290-306.

Richards, Leonard L. *"Gentlemen of Property and Standing": Anti-Abolition Mobs in Jacksonian America.* New York: Oxford University Press, 1970.

Rogin, Michael Paul. *The Intellectuals and McCarthy: The Radical*

Specter. Cambridge: MIT Press, 1967.

Rudé, George F. E. *The Crowd in History: A Study of Popular Disturbances in France and England, 1730-1848.* New York: John Wiley & Sons, 1964.

Runcie, John. "'Hunting the Nigs' in Philadelphia: The Race Riot of 1834." *Pennsylvania History* 39 (1972): 187-218.

Scharf, John Thomas, and Westcott, Thompson. *History of Philadelphia, 1609-1884.* Philadelphia: L. H. Everts, 1884. 3 vols.

Shannon, William Vincent. *The American Irish.* New York: Macmillan, 1964.

Silver, Allen. "The Demand for Order in Civil Society." In *The Police: Six Sociological Essays.* Edited by David J. Bordua. New York: John Wiley & Sons, 1967.

Taylor, George Rogers. *The Transportation Revolution, 1815-1860.* New York: Holt, Rinehart and Winston, 1964.

Wallace, Michael. "The Uses of Violence in American History." *American Scholar* 40 (1970-1972): 81-102.

Warner, Sam Bass, Jr. "Innovation and the Industrialization of Philadelphia, 1800-1850." In *The Historian and the City.* Edited by John Ely Burchard and Oscar Handlin. Cambridge: MIT Press, 1963.

———. *The Private City: Philadelphia in Three Periods of Its Growth.* Philadelphia: University of Pennsylvania Press, 1968.

Weigley, Russell F. "'A Peaceful City': Public Order in Philadelphia from Consolidation through the Civil War." In *The Peoples of Philadelphia: A History of Ethnic Groups and Lower-Class Life, 1790-1940.* Edited by Allen F. Davis and Mark H. Haller. Philadelphia: Temple University Press, 1973.

DISSERTATIONS

Blumin, Stuart. "Mobility in a Nineteenth-Century City: Philadelphia, 1820-1860." University of Pennsylvania, 1968.

Clark, Dennis. "The Adjustment of Irish Immigrants to Urban Life: The Philadelphia Experience, 1840-1860." Temple University, 1970.

Kane, John J. "The Irish in Philadelphia, 1840-1880." University of Pennsylvania, 1950.

Laurie, Bruce Gordon. "The Working People of Philadelphia, 1827-1852." University of Pittsburgh, 1971.

Sheridan, Peter B. "The Immigrants in Philadelphia, 1827-1860: The Contemporary Published Report." Georgetown University, 1957.

Index

Abolitionism, 7, 14-15, 23, 75; and the Irish, 30, 34
Act of Union, 22, 27
"Address of the Catholic Laity," 131
Albright, Peter, 104, 109, 132
Alexander, John K., 13
Amalgamation, political ("secret deal"), 167, 170, 171
American Protestant Association (APA), 59-60, 87
American Republican Party: attitudes toward elections, 60-62, 65; attitudes toward immigration, 60; attitudes toward naturalization, 61, 62, 66; and consolidation, 182, 186, 187; control of local government, 168; and cultural politics, 81-82; decline of, 171-74; economic philosophy, 71; and election of 1844, 94-96, 164-73; former political affiliations, 54-55; and immigrant voters, 31; and Kensington riots, 100-103, 107, 110, 129, 130-31, 133-34; and majority rule, 133; organizing efforts, 132-36, 168-69; platform, 49, 64; and Protestant clergy, 59-60, 69; as reform movement, 60, 64-65; and Re-

peal Association, 31, 134; and school Bible controversy, 94-96; socioeconomic profile of, 51-55, 58; and Southwark riots, 143, 145-46, 151-53, 157; and United Order of American Mechanics, 71-72; voluntary associations, 168-69
American Revolution, 17, 68, 181
Antimasonic party, 44, 45, 81
Antirailroad riots, 4, 14-15, 37, 69, 170, 188
Ardis, Wright, 110, 132, 144
Artisans, 47-48, 55-58; as American Republican leaders, 55; and American Republican program, 71-72; and consolidation, 191; and evangelical Protestantism, 82-84; ideology of, 71-72; and Know-Nothingism, 173; as nativists, 67-72; and pluralism, 50-51; and temperance, 48; and violence, 38
"Authoritarian personality," 46

Baldwin, Matthias, 53, 188, 191
Bank War, 81
Banner, Lois, 127
Bar Association, 10, 121, 123
Barry, James, 129
Bedford, Louisa, 94-95

Beecher, Henry Ward, 86
Benson, Lee, 80-82, 84
Berg, Joseph F., 86-87
Bible. *See* School Bible controversy
Billington, Ray Allen, 39, 41, 42
Binney, Horace, 114, 120; and consolidation, 180-81, 187-88, 190-91
"Birthright" principle, 171
Blacks, in Philadelphia: 6, 7, 14; and the immigrant Irish, 23, 34, 84, 99
Blumin, Stuart, 13, 55
Botsford, 71, 169
Boyne, Battle of the, 21, 34
"Boyne Water" (song), 112, 114, 134
Brown, David Paul, 52, 75
Browne, Peter A., 52, 127, 170, 171
Burgin, George H., 87, 95

Cadwalader, George: 8, 163; and city militia company, 180-84, 192; in Kensington riots, 105-106, 110, 111, 113, 117, 125, 139-40; in Southwark riots, 143, 145-51, 153-58
California House riot, 5, 174, 188
Campbell, John H., 165-66, 168, 169
"Carroll Hall" slate, 191
Catholic Bible. *See* Douay Bible
Catholic Herald (newspaper), 90, 128-29, 130, 148
Catholics. *See* Roman Catholic Church
Chambers, John H., 60, 64, 69, 87
Citizens' patrols. *See* Voluntarism

City Guards, 145, 147
City militia company, 181-85, 191-92
Clark, Dennis, 25
Clark, Hugh, 31, 32, 36, 54, 88; and grand jury, 130; in Kensington riots, 112-13; and school Bible controversy, 93-95
Class consciousness, 13, 15, 18, 173, 174; and consensus historians, 80-82; and evangelical religion, 83-84; and the General Trades' Union, 47; and temperance, 45, 64, 97
Clergy, Catholic, 66, 83, 89. *See also* Priests, parish
Clergy, Protestant, 45, 59-60, 69, 83, 86-88. *See also* Evangelical Protestantism
Colahan, John B., 149-52
Colportage, 5, 96
Colton, Walter, 93
Commissioner's Hall, Southwark, 144, 154, 156, 158
Community, 12-13, 17; Irish Catholic, in Philadelphia, 24, 26, 32
Conrad, Robert, 189
Consensus historians, 79-84
Consolidation, 9, 126, 175, 178-79, 187-92
Conspiracy theories, 42-44, 63-64, 66, 134, 163
Constabulary, 6-8, 121, 181, 183-86
Cornman, Oliver P., 71, 167, 169
Cox, Joseph, 104, 135
Craftsmen. *See* Artisans
Craig, William R., 100-102
Cultural nativism, 59, 78, 85
Cultural pluralism, 66, 79, 94

Daley, John, 107, 109-10
Davis, David Brion, 42-45, 50, 73
Dearborne, Henry, 170
Democratic party (national), 63, 71, 81-82
Democratic party (New York City), 91
Democratic party (Philadelphia): and consolidation, 187; defections from, 54-55; in the districts, 9; and election fraud, 66; and elections of 1844, 163, 165-68; "Incorruptible" or "Independent" (reform), 54-55, 88-89, 95, 165-66; and the Irish, 25, 30-32; and nativism, 45
Depression of 1837, 36, 47-48, 83
Diocese, Roman Catholic (Philadelphia), 26-27
Donohoe, Michael, 111-12
Douay Bible, 78, 90, 92-94
Dougherty, Thomas, 154-55
Dunn, Thomas, 131, 144
Dunn, William, 131-32, 136, 139, 143-45, 147

Eckard, Frederick, 130, 131
Economic nativism, 58, 59, 64-65, 85
Elite (upper class): and consolidation, 9, 180-82, 186-88, 190-92; description of, in Philadelphia, 122-23; and industrialization, 127, 159; leadership traditions, 122, 128; pluralist theory of, 44, 46; and public service, 122; reaction to riots, 120-21, 128, 180-82, 186-88, 190-92; and social control, 126, 191-92
Ernst, Robert, 49

Ethnic conflict, 19, 29, 46, 79-86, 174
Ethnic consciousness, 12, 14, 18, 79, 81-82
Ethnic politics, 190
Eugenics, 62
Evangelical Protestanism: and American Republicanism, 59-60, 69; Benson interpretation of, 81-83; clergy, 59, 64, 92, 94; and Kensington riots, 134; and moral reforms, 85-87; and municipal reform, 126; and the school Bible controversy, 99; and temperance, 5, 24; and the working classes, 48-50

Fairlamb, Jonas, 111-13
Famine, Irish potato, 20, 39-40
Father Matthew, 24, 27
Festivity, 136
Fillmore, Millard, 171
Fire companies, 5, 12, 16-17, 25, 33, 51; professional, 186
Firemen's fights, 5, 16-17, 174
First City Brigade, 181-82
First City Troop, 119
Fisher, Patrick, 104, 118
Fisher, Sidney George, 122, 124, 187
Flags, American, 109, 112, 116, 117, 119, 147, 163-64
Frankford arsenal, 138, 139, 144
Freed, Isaac, 154, 164
Free Soil Movement, 81
Fundamentalism. See Evangelical Protestantism

"Gag rule," 135
Gallagher, Robert, 151, 158
Gangs, 12, 25, 33, 51, 174, 186

Gaslights, 159, 185
Gee, John, 96, 100
General Trades' Union (GTU), 13, 47-48, 49, 69, 71
Germantown Blues, 155
Gideon Society (1831 riot), 34, 52, 102
Gihon, John H., 60, 108
Grand Jury: May, 1844, 125; June, 1844, 130, 131, 135
Grover, Thomas, 53, 54, 71, 136; as political candidate, 613, 167, 168; in Southwark riots, 151-53
Gusfield, Joseph, 48, 55

Handlin, Oscar, 30
Handloom weavers, Irish: and American Republican party, 96; class consciousness of, 13; community life of, 35-38; decline of, 173; and Kensington riots, 107; strike of 1842-44, 32, 36-37; violent traditions, 4, 11, 35
Hansen, Klaus, 63
Hare, Isaac, 110, 117-18
Hibernia Greens, 149-52
Hibernia Hose House, 104, 109, 110
Higham, John, 46, 82
Hobsbawm, Eric J., 34, 136
Hofstadter, Richard, 42-43, 45, 46, 50, 71, 73, 79-80
Hortz, Charles, 143-44, 150
Hughes, John, 91, 94, 129

Illuminati, Society of the, 43
Immigrants: and Catholicism, 37; and consolidation, 179; and conspiracy theory, 63; and cultural conflict, 81-83; as day laborers, 47; in general strike of

1835, 45, 47; German, in Philadelphia, 3, 20; as factory workers, 49-50, 57; Irish, in American cities, 3, 21, 24; and nativism, 41-42, 45, 84-85; and prohibition, 88; and religion, 20-21; and temperance, 48
Industrialization: and American Republican party, 53-54; and consolidation, 178-79, 190-92; and evangelical Protestantism, 84-85; and nativist attitudes, 49-50; and pluralist theory, 74-75; and social control, 126-27; and technological change, 15, 46-47, 67; and urbanization, 12
Ingersoll, Charles Jared, 122, 166, 167
Ingersoll, Joseph R., 181
Internal Improvements, 56, 81
Irish. See Immigrants; Roman Catholic Church
Irish Protestants (Orangemen), 34, 64, 103, 112, 118-19
Isolation. See Separatism, Irish

Jack, Charles J., 52, 108, 132, 158
Jesuits, 63, 72, 91
Jones, Joel B., 124, 139, 157-58, 179
July Eleventh ordinance, 181-85
July Fourth parade, 136-39

Kane, John K., 25, 181
Kenrick, Francis Patrick, 27; and the Kensington riots, 99, 115, 118, 119, 128, 132; on naturalization, 129-30; and school Bible controversy, 89-93; and Southwark riots, 158, 172

Kensington, Third Ward: descrip-
   tion of, 96
Kensington riots: May 3, 100-102;
   May 6, 102-107; May 7, 107-11;
   May 8, 111-14
King James Bible, 78-79, 85, 89-
   95, 131
Know-Nothing party, 45, 173
Kramer, Samuel R., 100-103, 179

Lafferty, Patrick, 102, 104, 105,
   107, 111
Laurie, Bruce G., 46-48, 50, 72,
   97
Law enforcement. See Police
Lee, John Hancock, 103, 116
Lehman, George F., 165-66
Lelar, Henry, 170
Levin, Lewis C., 52, 53, 54, 64;
   and congressional elections,
   165-66, 168, 169, 171, 179; and
   Kensington riots, 99-100, 103,
   133, 134; on naturalization, 62;
   in school Bible controversy, 95;
   in Southwark riots, 151-52; and
   tariff policy, 71
Lipset, Seymour Martin, 42, 44-
   46, 50, 54, 71, 72-73

McAvoy, T. Thomas, 26
McCarthyism, 46
McClain, Andrew, 150, 155, 157,
   158
McCoy, John, 136, 168
McCully, Thomas, 89
McKinley, Nathan, 143-45, 151,
   154, 156, 160
McCall, Peter, 165
McElroy, James, 75
McMichael, Morton: and the Irish

vote, 31, 88; and July Fourth
   parade, 138, 139; in the Ken-
   sington riots, 105, 110, 113,
   115, 117, 125; in the Southwark
   riots, 11, 69, 143-45, 147-49,
   153, 154, 157, 159-60
McMullin, William, 174, 189-90
Manderfield, John, 99-100
Manifest Destiny, 44
Markle, Joseph, 167
Markle Rifles, 149-52
Marshal's police, 188-89, 191, 192
Martial law, 115, 126
Melting pot theory, 79
Merchant capitalism, 56-58
Merrick, Samuel V., 53, 121
Mexico, 66, 172; and Mexican
   War, 174
Militia, 8, 12, 180, 181-85, 188,
   192; and Kensington riot, 105,
   110-11, 118, 125, 145; and
   Southwark riot, 148-56, 159,
   163
Millerism, 5
Mobility, 13, 44, 55
"Mobs," 124
Monk, Maria, 87
Montgomery, David, 35, 46-50,
   54, 69, 72-73, 82-83, 84
Moore, Henry, 93-94
Morality (moral reform), 81, 85-
   88, 90, 122, 125-26, 190
Mormonism, 5, 43-44, 45
Morris, E. Joy, 165-66
Morse, Samuel F. B., 43
Municipal reform. See Consolida-
   tion

Nanny Goat Market, 35, 37, 100,
   103, 106, 109, 111, 128, 132,
   145

Napoleon, 124, 125, 127
Nationalism: and American identity, 44; American Republican
definition of, 62-63; Irish, 22,
25, 27-28, 32, 83
Native American (newspaper), 133
Nativism (as attitude): and
American nationalism, 63; and
American Republican ideology,
59-66; and anti-Catholicism,
44-45; and cultural conflict, 81,
84-85; and industrialization,
49-50, 75; and Irish violence,
33; and religious beliefs of
artisans, 69; and Repeal Association, 28; and social science
theory, 42-43; and working
classes, 46-47, 50, 67-68
Nativist movement (organized):
compared to anti-Masonry and
anti-Mormonism, 43-44; as elite
movement, 50-51; as guardians
of order, 33; and "good government," 23; and Irish violence,
38; and moral reform, 97; and
Repeal Association, 29, 32;
and Sabbatarianism, 97; and the
working classes, 49. *See also*
American Republican party
Nativist rank-and-file, 67-72, 143-
50, 152-58
Naturalization, 61, 65, 66, 130,
171
Naylor, Charles, 148-50, 159, 163
Negative reference theory, 81-82
New York: city, 7, 20, 91, 162;
state, 81
North American (newspaper), 133

O'Connell, Daniel, 27-30
O'Donnell, Hugh, 136, 168

"One to one hundred and fifty"
police, 187-88, 191
Orangemen, 34, 64, 103, 112,
118-19

Palmer, Robert, 143-45
Papacy (pope, popery, papal
menace), 23, 41, 63, 66, 72, 84,
89, 102, 108, 145, 164
"Paranoid style" rhetoric, 42-43,
58, 72, 82
Parliament, English, 23, 27
Parliament, Irish, 22-23, 27
Parochial schools, Roman Catholic
(in Philadelphia), 25, 27, 172
Patterson, Robert, 120, 138, 139;
and Kensington riots, 115, 119;
and Southwark riot, 143, 145,
147, 151, 155, 158, 159-60,
179, 180
Paynter, Lemuel, 54, 71, 95, 157,
165
Peale, Augustin R., 109, 132
Penal Code, Irish, 22
Penn, William, 124
Pennsylvania Freeman (newspaper), 124
Pennsylvania Hall, 4, 11, 14, 34,
69, 120, 124
Pennsylvanian (newspaper), 124
Perry, John, 60, 100-102, 108,
163
Pluralism, cultural, 46, 50, 66, 67
Pluralist historians, 42, 44, 46, 50,
58, 71-73, 74-75
Police: London "bobbies," 125,
175; "one to one hundred and
fifty," 187-88, 191; "preventive," 8, 12; professional, 7, 10,
178, 180, 183-85, 188, 190-92;
volunteer citizens', 179

Political nativism, 59
Political rights, restriction of immigrant, 49, 59, 61, 100
Political violence, 14-15, 22, 34, 120
Populism, 71-72
Porter, David, 132, 143-44, 147
Porter, William, 11, 100
Posse, 8, 10-11, 33-34, 147
Presbyterian (newspaper), 93, 134
Price, Eli Kirk, 188, 191
Priests, parish, 26, 28, 39, 66. See also, Clergy, Catholic
Prohibition (of liquor sales), 24, 70, 86, 88; Irish attitude toward, 23
Protestant Irish (Orangemen), 34, 52, 64, 103, 112, 118-19
Protestantism. *See* Evangelical Protestantism
Protestantism, English, 21
Protestants, Anglo-Irish, 21-22
Public Ledger (newspaper), 19, 28, 124, 126, 184-85
Public schools: and conspiracy theory, 64; and industrialists, 53; and municipal reform, 126; and nativism, 48; in Philadelphia, 89-95; Protestant control of, 23, 25, 49; as threat to Catholic youth, 23; and the working classes, 49
Public School Society of New York City, 91

Raab, Earl, 44-46, 50, 54, 72
Read, John M., 114, 181
Reductionism, 15
Reformers, moral, 23, 45, 126-27
Reigart, Emanuel, 170-71
Religious conflict, 41, 45, 85, 128

Religious consciousness, 12-14, 15
Religious nativism, 60, 65
Repeal Association, 27-30, 32, 131; divisions within, 29-30; "Loyal," 30; and Kensington riots, 111, 131, 134
Repplier, Charles, 130, 131
Republican party, 45
Restriction (of immigrant political rights), 49, 59, 61, 100
Rhinedollar, John Wesley, 109; Association, 169
Richards, Leonard L., 15, 75
Riot act (riot statute), 105-106, 123, 125-26
Riots. *See* Violence
Rogin, Michael Paul, 46, 73, 74-75
Roman Catholic Church, American: and cultural conflict, 186; and the Irish, 22-23; proselytizing efforts of, 72; and temperance, 24, 27
Roman Catholic Church, in Ireland, 21, 22, 37
Roman Catholic Church, in Philadelphia, 26-28, 128-32
Roumfort, Alexander L., 155-56
Rudé, George, 117
Ruggles, Samuel, 189

Sabbatarianism, 5, 81; and American Republican party, 58, 59; and industrialists, 53; and politics, 89; and Protestant clergy, 84, 87-88; as reform movement, 45, 53
Saint Augustine's Church, 113-14, 120, 122, 129, 139-40
Saint Mary's Church, 10, 121
Saint Michael's Church, 106, 111-12, 114, 129, 132, 134, 139

Saint Philip de Neri Church, 69, 115, 131, 139, 140; in Southwark riots, 143, 147-53, 158, 163

Saunders, Thomas L., 150, 151

Schiffler, Charles, 129

Schiffler, George, 104, 107, 116, 164; Association, 169

School Bible controversy, 32, 78, 96, 99; in American Republican parade, 137; and American Republican party, 58-59; and cultural conflict, 84-86; and grand jury, 130, 131; and Kensington riots, 89-95

School controversy, New York City, 91

Scott, John M., 113-14, 115, 125

"Secret deal" (amalgamation), 167, 170, 171

Separatism, Irish, 25-26, 28, 32, 35, 172

Sexual fantasy, nativist, 86-87

Shannon, William V., 21

Sheriffalty, 8-10, 33, 37, 69, 125, 178

Sherry, Edward (Barney), 107, 111

Shunk, Francis, 167, 170

"Sign of the Ball," 96

Silver, Allen, 126, 178

Sisters of Charity, 106, 112

"Six Months Ago" (poem), 164

Smith, Peter Sken, 95, 103, 135, 136, 157, 171

Social control, 126, 191-92

Sons of Temperance, 70

Southwark Commissioners, 157-58, 163, 186

Southwark Committee of Public Safety, 185

Southwark riots: July 5, 139, 143-45; July 6, 146-49; July 7, 149-56; July 8, 156-58

Spirit of the Times (newspaper), 123-24

State legislature, Pennsylvania, 89, 178, 187,

Status anxiety thesis, 46, 56, 72

Stokes, William A., 30, 31, 130, 131, 187

Street Talk about an Ordinance . . . of July Eleventh . . ., 182-85

Strikes: and the General Trades' Union, 13, 47-48; handloom weavers, 35-37; for ten-hour day, 47-48

Sutherland, Joel Barlow, 165

Swift, John, 69, 187

Tarr, A. DeKalb, 52

Tarr, Elihu D., 95

Tariffs, 65, 81, 172

Taylor, George Rogers, 56

Taylor, Zachary, 170

Technological change, 47, 67, 173. *See also* Industrialization

Temperance: 5, 58, 173; and American Republican leadership, 52; black, 33; and class consciousness, 45, 48-50; and consolidation, 190; and cultural conflict, 78; and elections, 54-55, 59, 88-89; and industrialists, 59; and Irish, 24, 27, 70; and Protestant clergy, 59, 87; as reform movement, 126; riots against, 33, 34; and United Order of American Mechanics, 71

Ten-hour day, 47-48

Terrorism, Irish, 22
Texas, 66, 172, 174
Transportation Revolution, 56-57
Tyler, Robert, 31

Uniforms, military, 191-92
United Order of American
  Mechanics (UOAM), 71, 169
Urbanization, 6, 12, 20, 24, 122

Values, cultural, 78-80; and conflict, 45, 81, 84-85, 191
Vaux, Richard, 122, 179, 189-90
Violence (riots): artisan tradition
  of, 67, 68; and consensus historians, 79-80; decline of, after
  1844, 174-75, 178-79; history
  of, in Philadelphia, 4-5; Irish,
  in Ireland, 22; Irish, in Philadelphia, 33-35; political, 14-15, 22,
  34, 120; racial, 33, 34, 162; and
  social control, 127, 190-92;
  strikes and, 36-37; temperance
  and, 33, 34. See also Kensington riots; Southwark riots
Voluntarism (citizen peacekeeping), 8-10; after Kensington
  riots, 114-16, 121-23, 139; after
  Southwark riot, 179-82
Voluntary associations, Irish,

25-27, 32; nativist, 168-69; in
  Philadelphia, 12

Warner, Sam Bass, Jr., 12, 33, 68,
  174
Washington, George, 137
Waters, Enos, 156, 164
Watmough, John, 11, 179-80
Weavers. See Handloom weavers
Weccacoe Engine company, 138,
  164
Weccacoe Hose company, 138
Welch, Robert, 43
Westcott, Thompson, 53
Wharton, Robert, 121
Whig party: and amalgamation,
  167, 170, 171; national, 63,
  81-82; and nativism, 45, 55,
  66, 88-89; in New York City,
  91; in Philadelphia, 9, 30-31,
  72, 163, 165-68
White, Philip S., 53, 62, 69
Working classes: and consolidation, 179; and Democratic
  party, 54; and ethnic conflict,
  47; Irish, 26, 31; and Mc-
  Carthyism, 46; and mobility, 13;
  and moral reform, 88, 127; and
  nativism, 45, 46-47, 49, 50,
  67-68; and pluralist historians,
  45-51; and temperance, 88; and
  violence, 14-16, 67, 68